My Next Life as a Villainess: All Routes Lead to Doom!

VOLUME 4

Character Design and Art by: Nami Hidaka
Story by: Satoru Yamaguchi

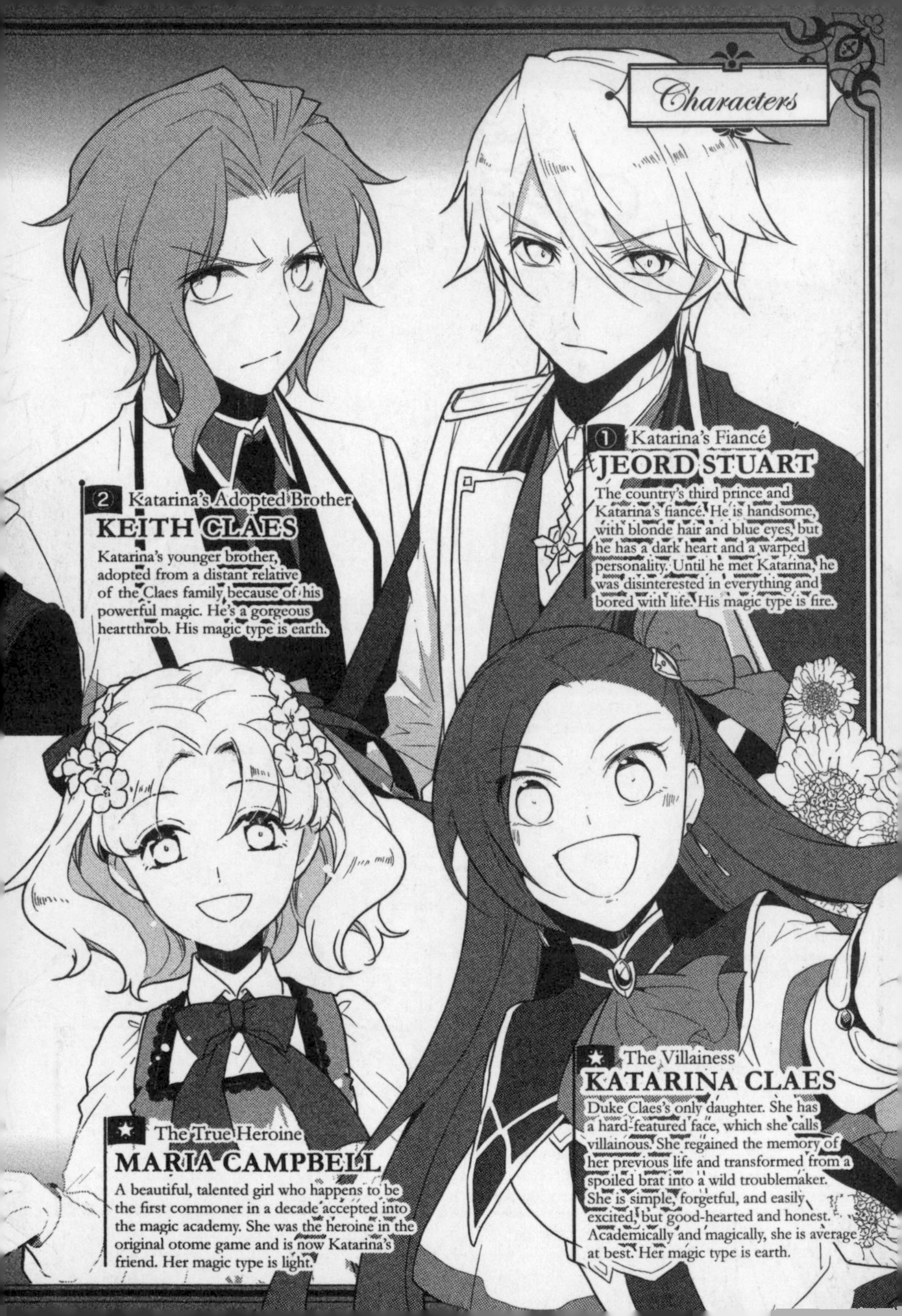
Characters
① Katarina's Fiancé
JEORD STUART
The country's third prince and Katarina's fiancé. He is handsome, with blonde hair and blue eyes, but he has a dark heart and a warped personality. Until he met Katarina, he was disinterested in everything and bored with life. His magic type is fire.
② Katarina's Adopted Brother
KEITH CLAES
Katarina's younger brother, adopted from a distant relative of the Claes family because of his powerful magic. He's a gorgeous heartthrob. His magic type is earth.
★ The Villainess
KATARINA CLAES
Duke Claes's only daughter. She has a hard-featured face, which she calls villainous. She regained the memory of her previous life and transformed from a spoiled brat into a wild troublemaker. She is simple, forgetful, and easily excited, but good-hearted and honest. Academically and magically, she is average at best. Her magic type is earth.
★ The True Heroine
MARIA CAMPBELL
A beautiful, talented girl who happens to be the first commoner in a decade accepted into the magic academy. She was the heroine in the original otome game and is now Katarina's friend. Her magic type is light.

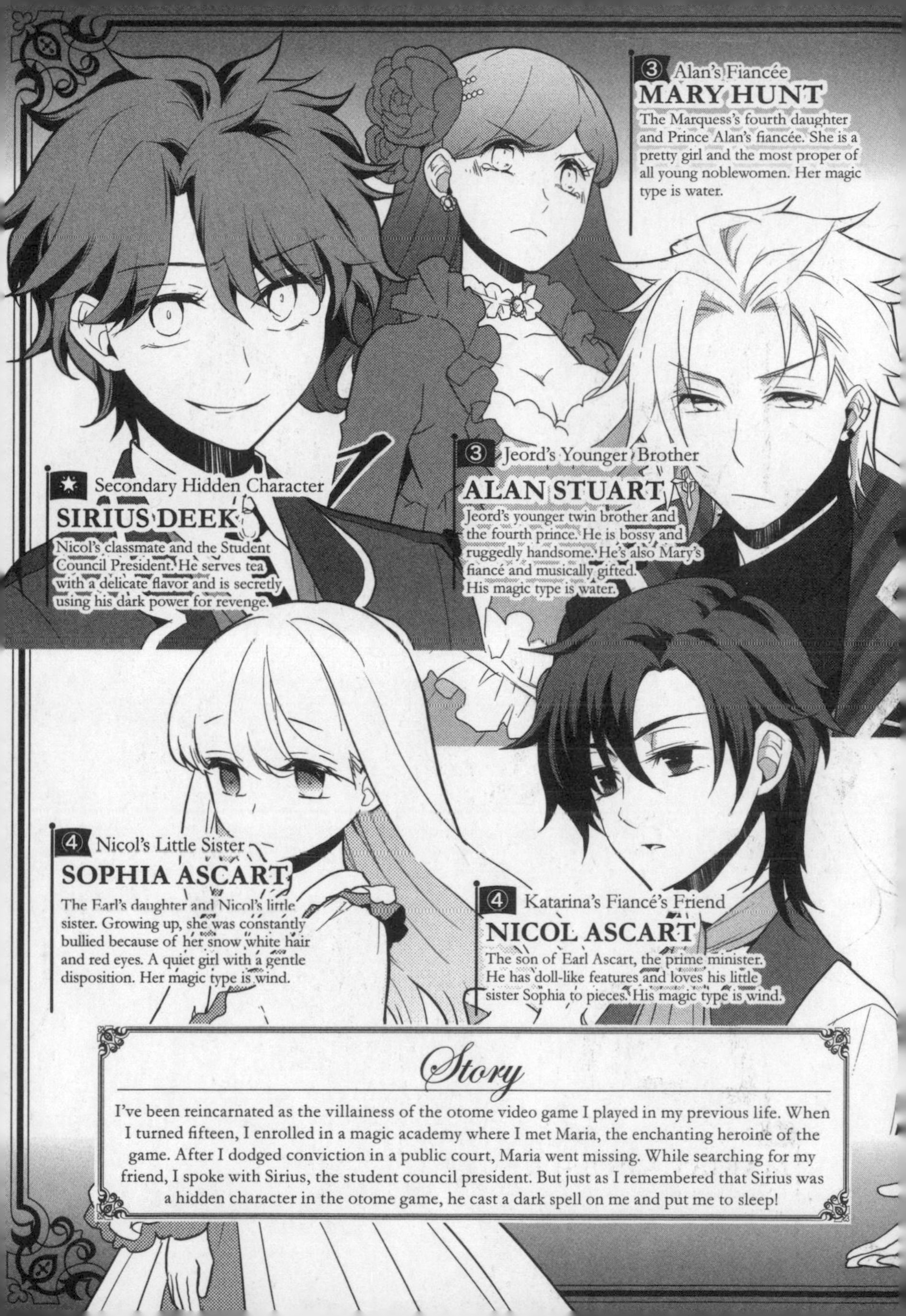
③ Alan's Fiancée
MARY HUNT
The Marquess's fourth daughter and Prince Alan's fiancée. She is a pretty girl and the most proper of all young noblewomen. Her magic type is water.
③ Jeord's Younger Brother
ALAN STUART
Jeord's younger twin brother and the fourth prince. He is bossy and ruggedly handsome. He's also Mary's fiancé and musically gifted. His magic type is water.
Secondary Hidden Character
SIRIUS DEEK
Nicol's classmate and the Student Council President. He serves tea with a delicate flavor and is secretly using his dark power for revenge.
④ Nicol's Little Sister
SOPHIA ASCART
The Earl's daughter and Nicol's little sister. Growing up, she was constantly bullied because of her snow white hair and red eyes. A quiet girl with a gentle disposition. Her magic type is wind.
④ Katarina's Fiancé's Friend
NICOL ASCART
The son of Earl Ascart, the prime minister. He has doll-like features and loves his little sister Sophia to pieces. His magic type is wind.

Story

I've been reincarnated as the villainess of the otome video game I played in my previous life. When I turned fifteen, I enrolled in a magic academy where I met Maria, the enchanting heroine of the game. After I dodged conviction in a public court, Maria went missing. While searching for my friend, I spoke with Sirius, the student council president. But just as I remembered that Sirius was a hidden character in the otome game, he cast a dark spell on me and put me to sleep!

My Next Life
as a VILLAINESS:
ALL ROUTES
LEAD TO DOOM!

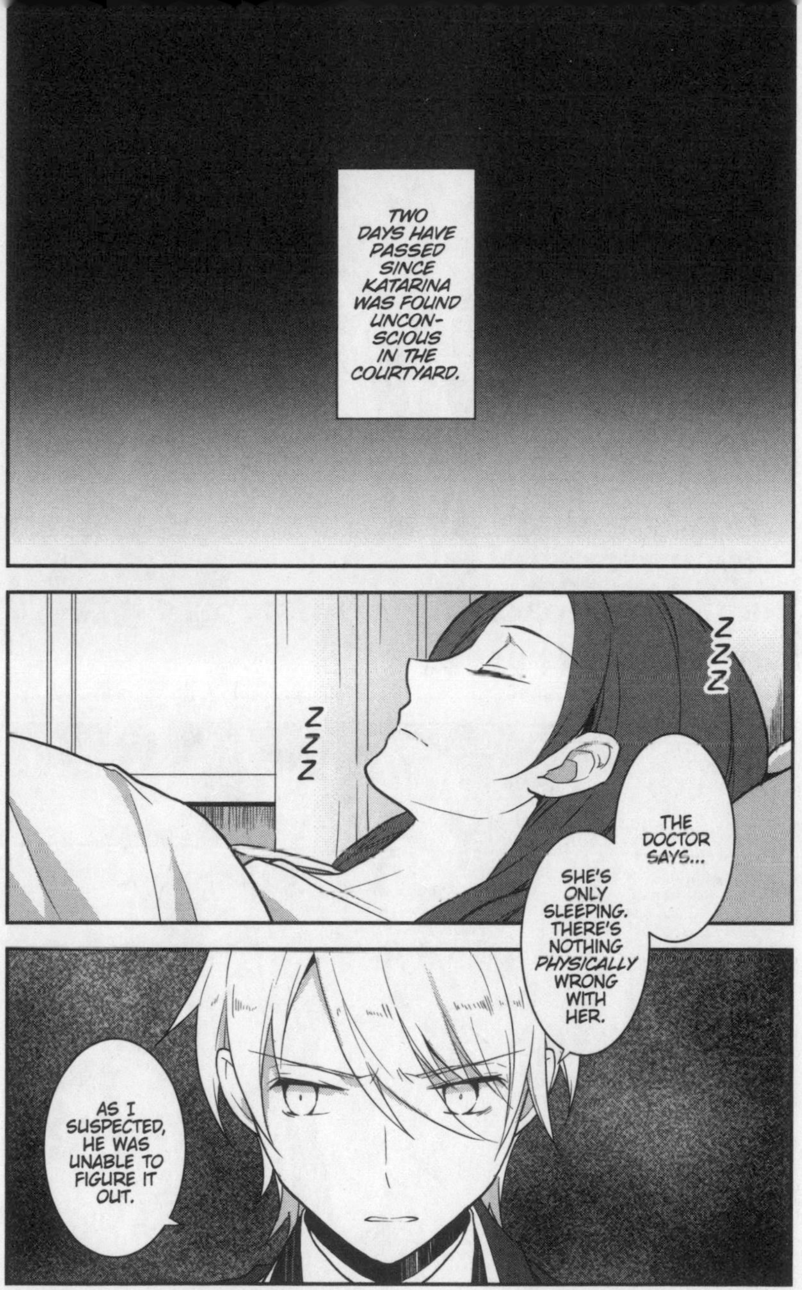
TWO DAYS HAVE PASSED SINCE KATARINA WAS FOUND UNCON-SCIOUS IN THE COURTYARD.
ZZZ
ZZZ
THE DOCTOR SAYS...
SHE'S ONLY SLEEPING. THERE'S NOTHING *PHYSICALLY* WRONG WITH HER.
AS I SUSPECTED, HE WAS UNABLE TO FIGURE IT OUT.

Chapter 18: The Approaching Footsteps of Doom (Part 6)

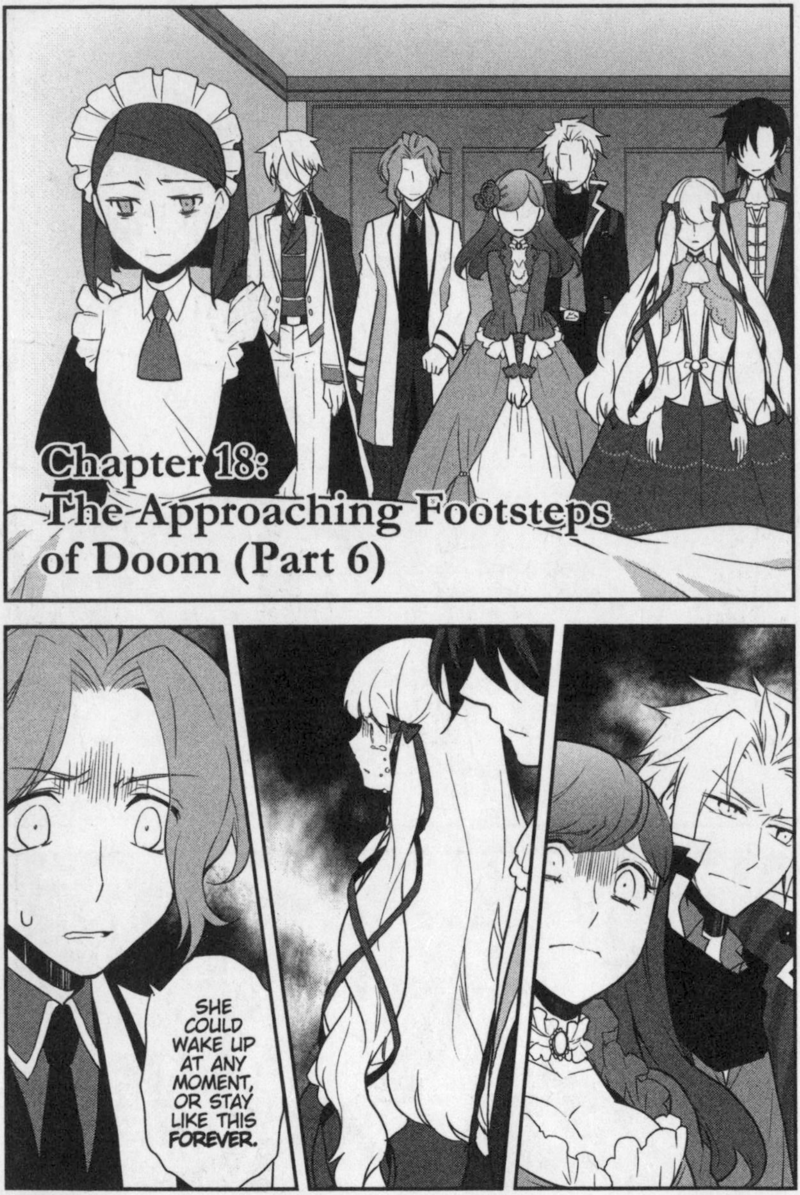
SHE COULD WAKE UP AT ANY MOMENT, OR STAY LIKE THIS FOREVER.

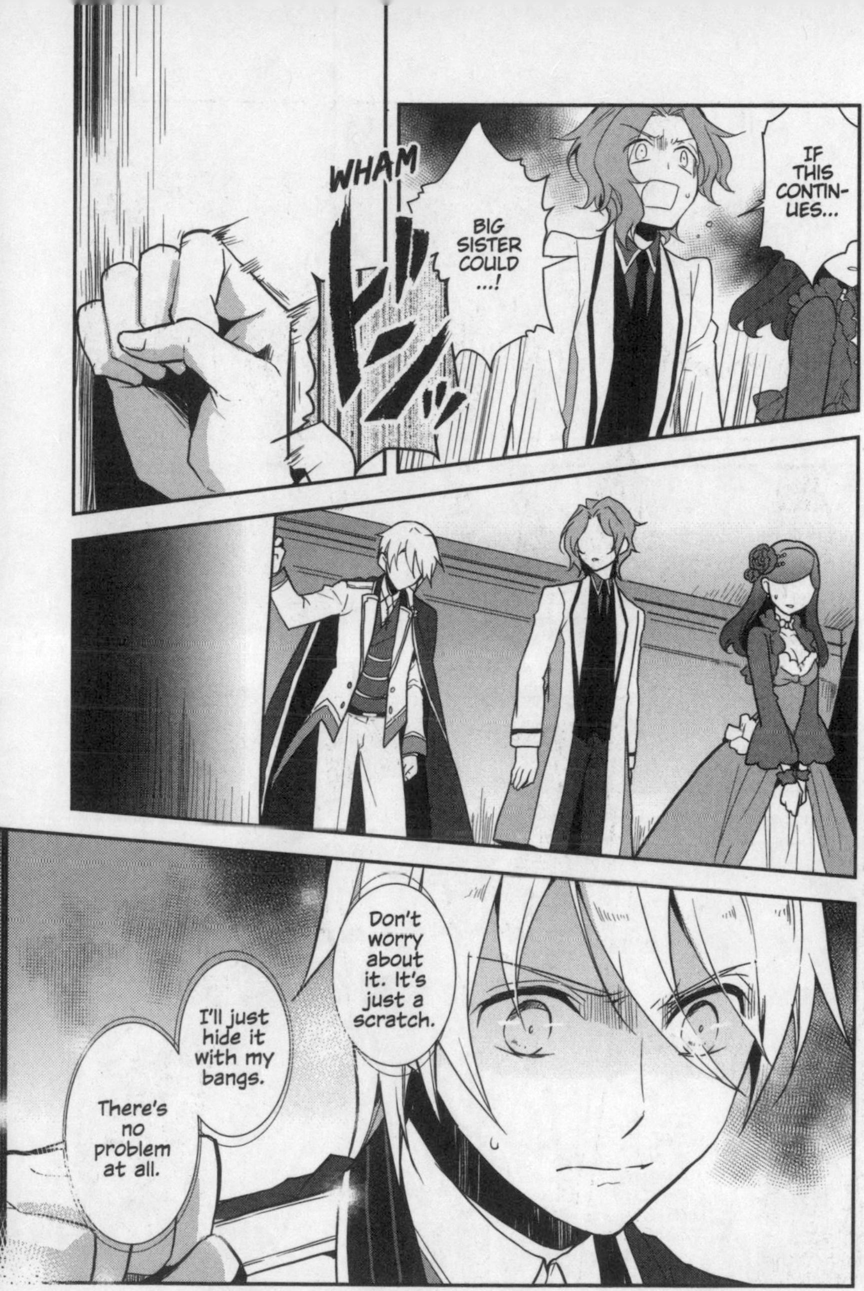
IF THIS CONTIN-UES...
BIG SISTER COULD ...!
WHAM
Don't worry about it. It's just a scratch.
I'll just hide it with my bangs.
There's no problem at all.

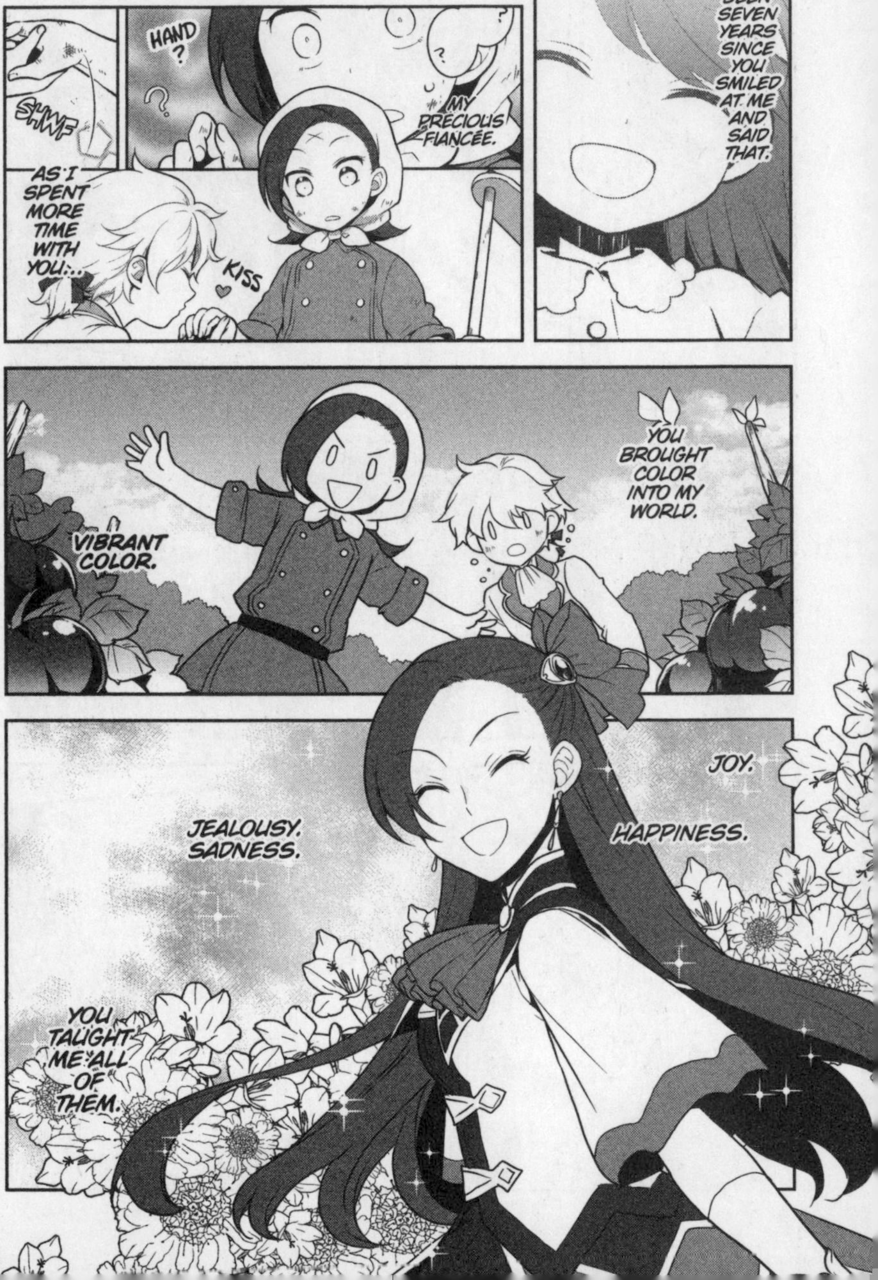
IT'S BEEN SEVEN YEARS SINCE YOU SMILED AT ME AND SAID THAT.
HAND?
MY PRECIOUS FIANCÉE.
SHWF SHWF
AS I SPENT MORE TIME WITH YOU...
KISS
YOU BROUGHT COLOR INTO MY WORLD.
VIBRANT COLOR.
JOY.
HAPPINESS.
JEALOUSY. SADNESS.
YOU TAUGHT ME ALL OF THEM.

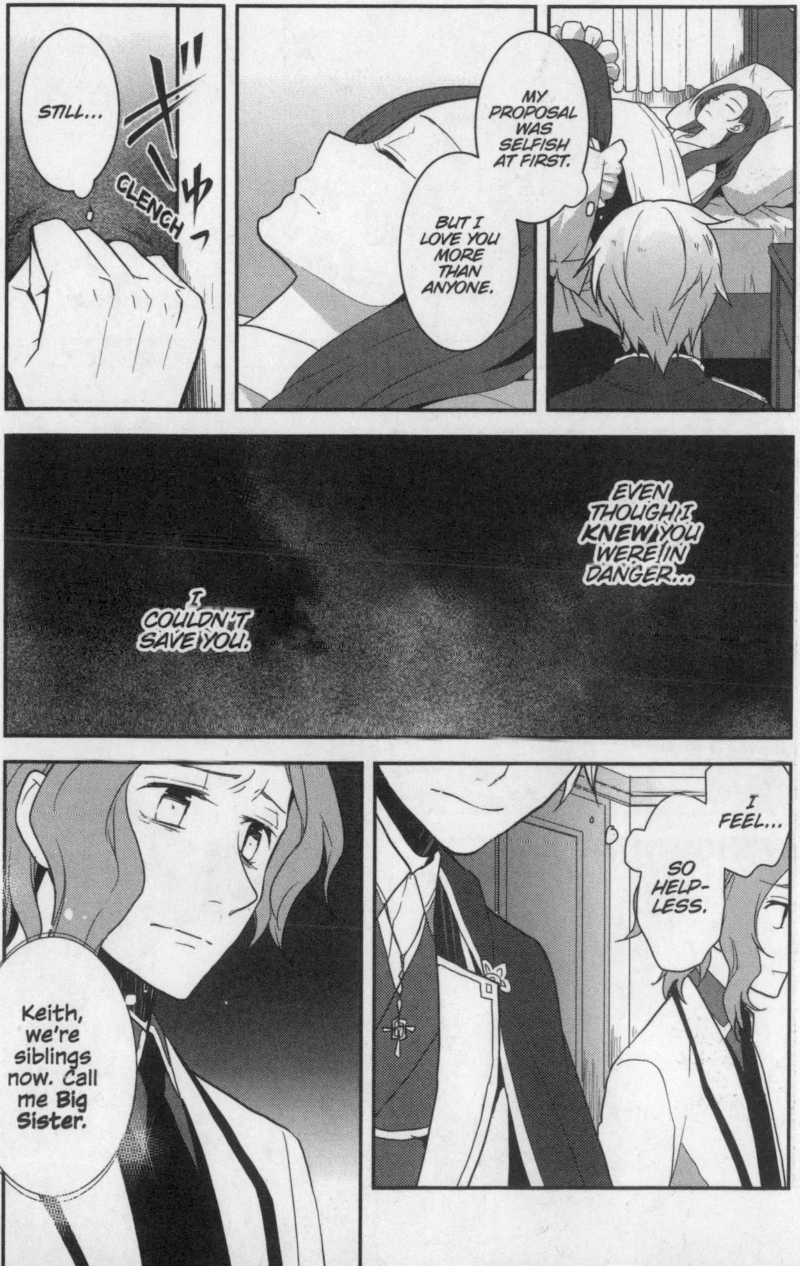
MY PROPOSAL WAS SELFISH AT FIRST.
BUT I LOVE YOU MORE THAN ANYONE.
STILL...
CLENCH
EVEN THOUGH I KNEW YOU WERE IN DANGER...
I COULDN'T SAVE YOU.
I FEEL...
SO HELP-LESS.
Keith, we're siblings now. Call me Big Sister.

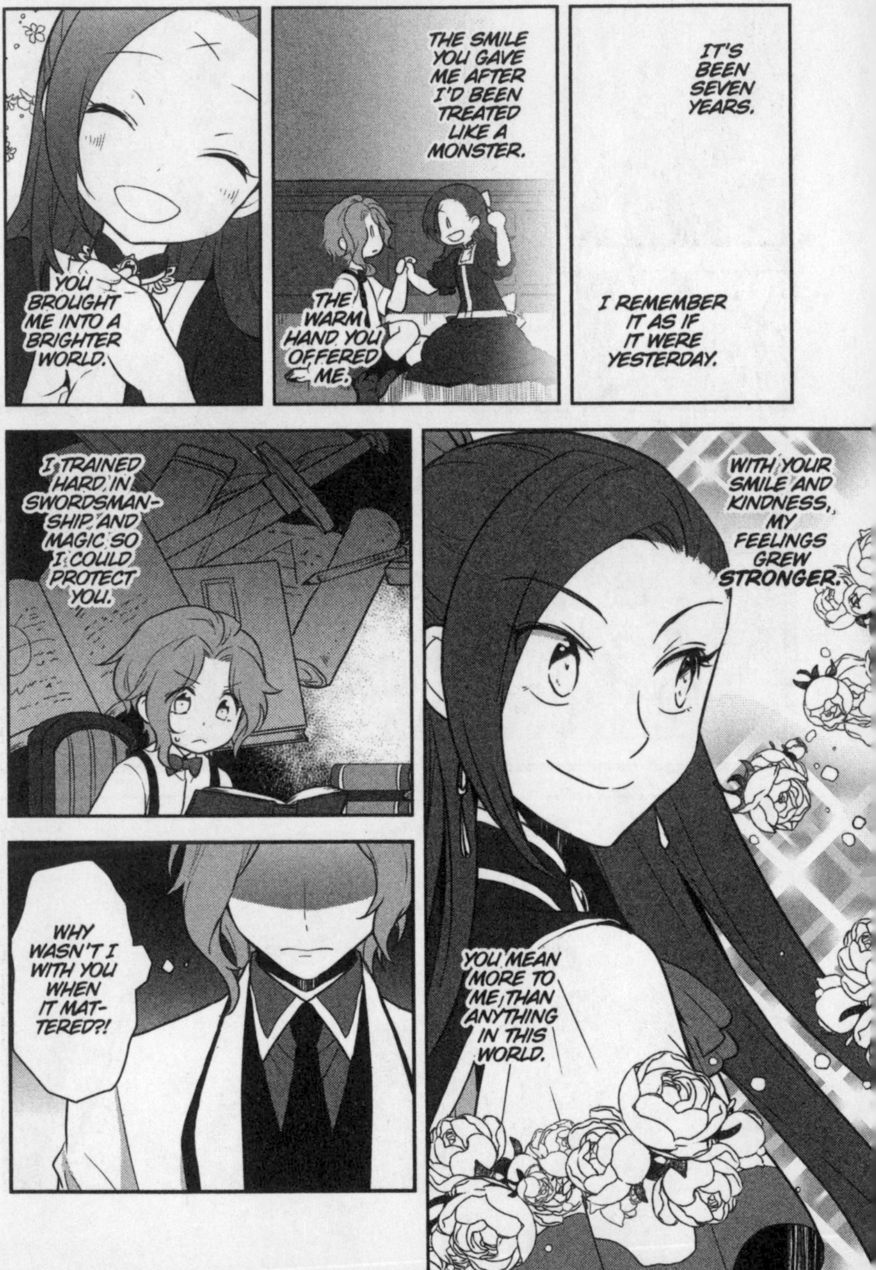
IT'S BEEN SEVEN YEARS.
I REMEMBER IT AS IF IT WERE YESTERDAY.
THE SMILE YOU GAVE ME AFTER I'D BEEN TREATED LIKE A MONSTER.
THE WARM HAND YOU OFFERED ME.
YOU BROUGHT ME INTO A BRIGHTER WORLD.
WITH YOUR SMILE AND KINDNESS, MY FEELINGS GREW STRONGER.
YOU MEAN MORE TO ME THAN ANYTHING IN THIS WORLD.
I TRAINED HARD IN SWORDSMAN-SHIP AND MAGIC SO I COULD PROTECT YOU.
WHY WASN'T I WITH YOU WHEN IT MAT-TERED?!

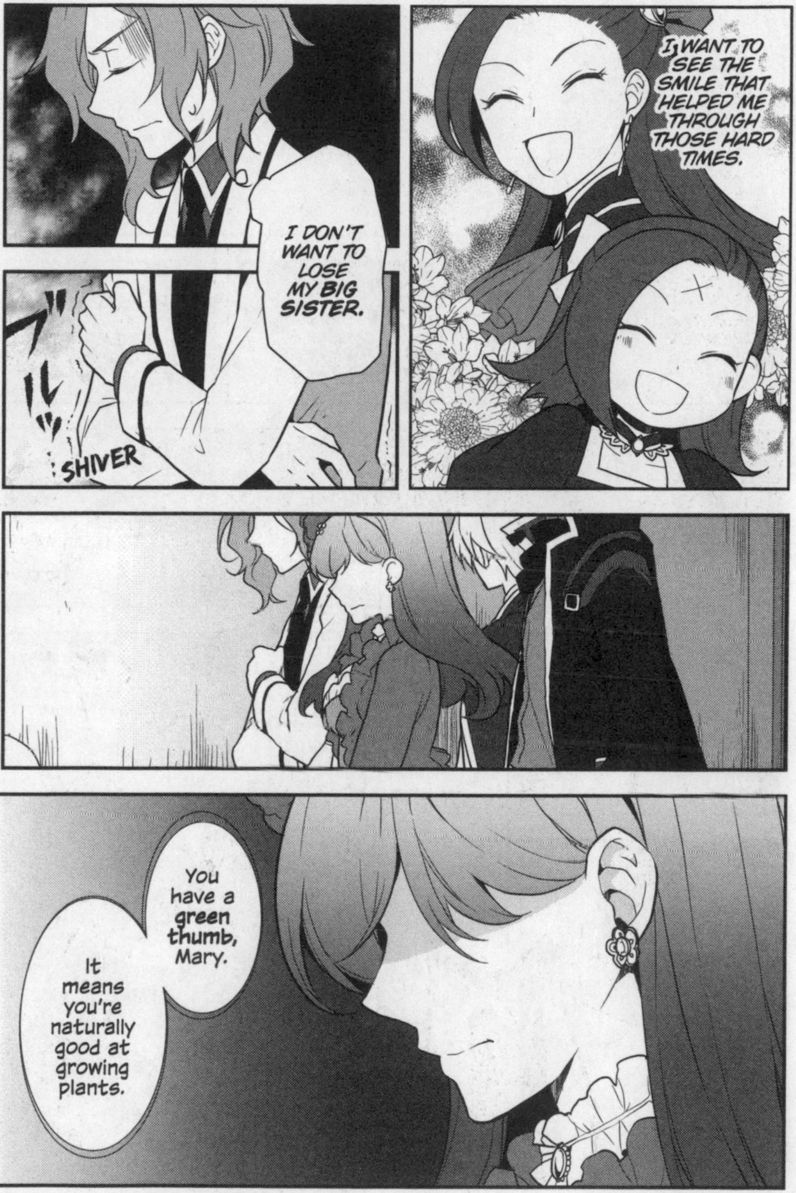
I WANT TO SEE THE SMILE THAT HELPED ME THROUGH THOSE HARD TIMES.
I DON'T WANT TO LOSE MY BIG SISTER.
SHIVER
You have a green thumb, Mary.
It means you're naturally good at growing plants.

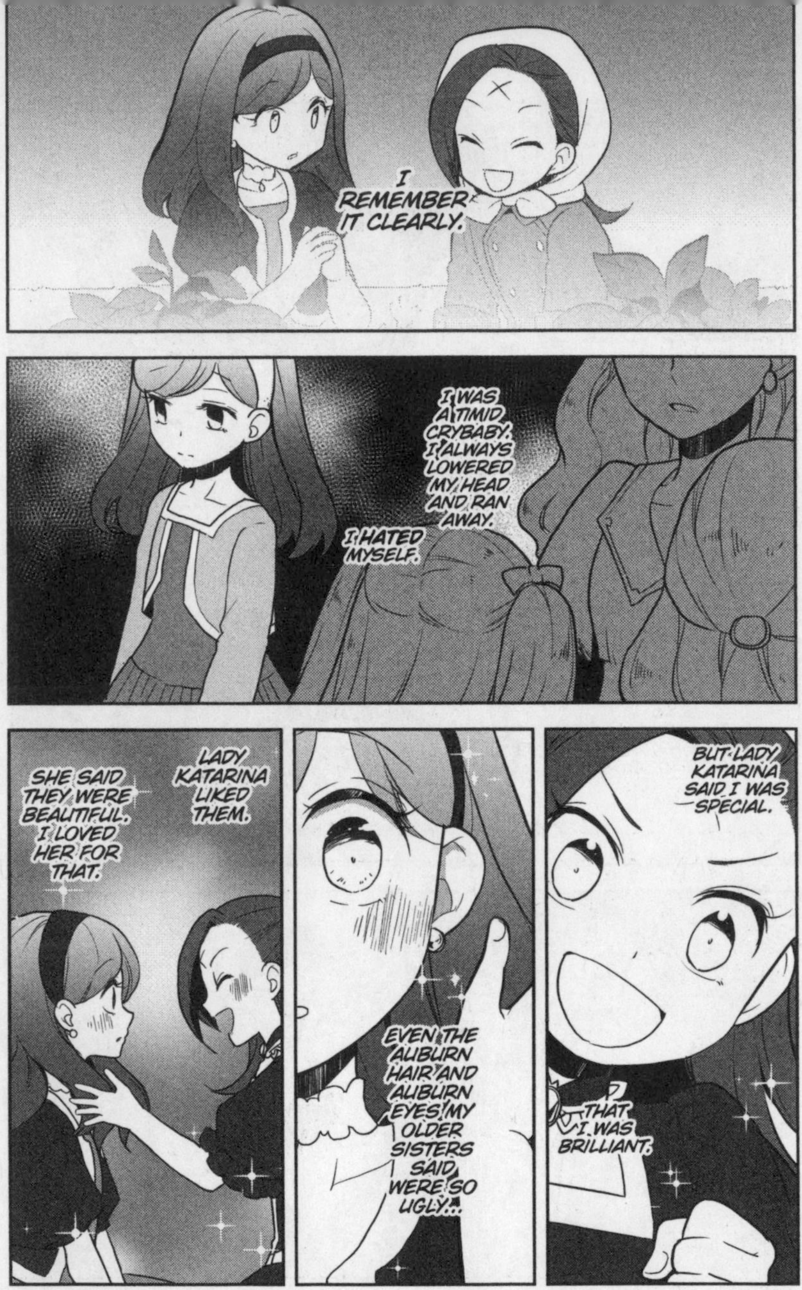
I REMEMBER IT CLEARLY.
I WAS A TIMID CRYBABY. I ALWAYS LOWERED MY HEAD AND RAN AWAY.
I HATED MYSELF.
BUT LADY KATARINA SAID I WAS SPECIAL.
THAT I WAS BRILLIANT.
EVEN THE AUBURN HAIR AND AUBURN EYES MY OLDER SISTERS SAID WERE SO UGLY...
LADY KATARINA LIKED THEM.
SHE SAID THEY WERE BEAUTIFUL. I LOVED HER FOR THAT.

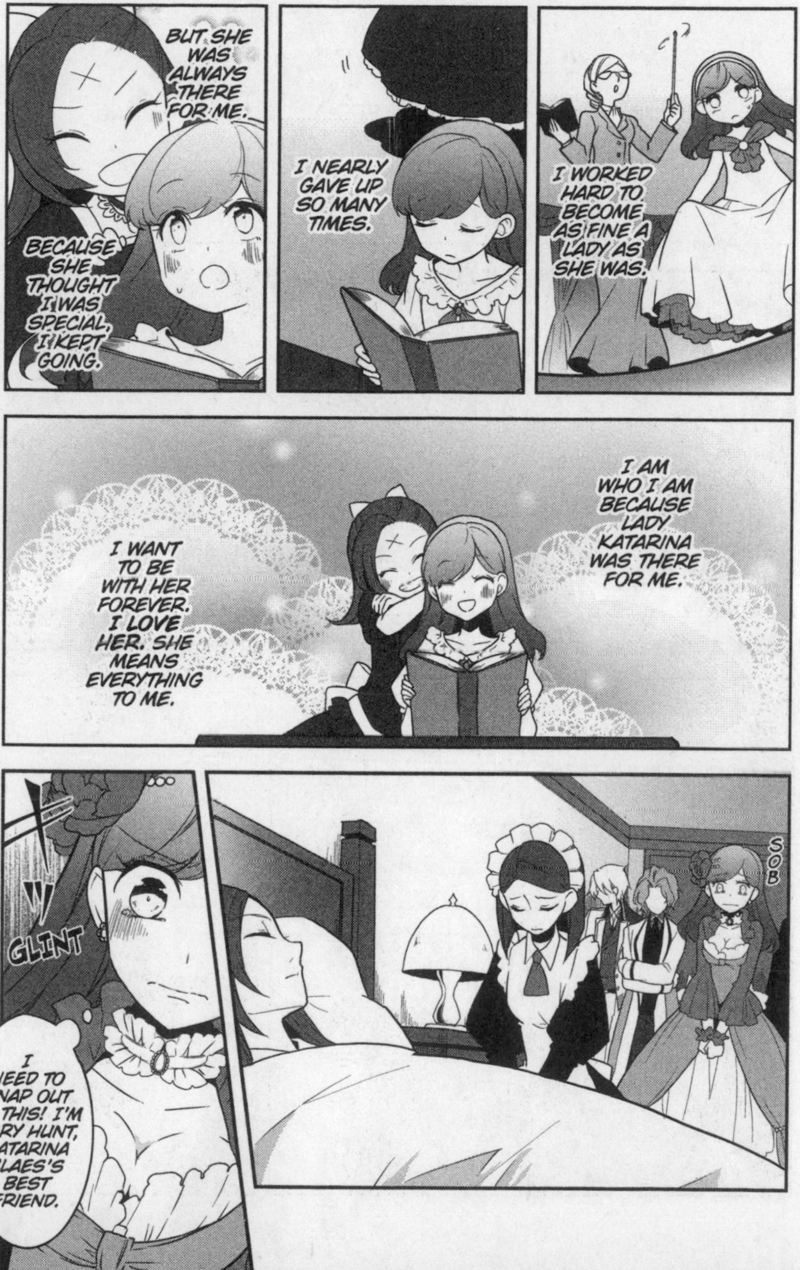
I WORKED HARD TO BECOME AS FINE A LADY AS SHE WAS.
I NEARLY GAVE UP SO MANY TIMES.
BUT SHE WAS ALWAYS THERE FOR ME.
BECAUSE SHE THOUGHT I WAS SPECIAL, I KEPT GOING.
I AM WHO I AM BECAUSE LADY KATARINA WAS THERE FOR ME.
I WANT TO BE WITH HER FOREVER. I LOVE HER. SHE MEANS EVERYTHING TO ME.
SOB
GLINT
I NEED TO SNAP OUT OF THIS! I'M MARY HUNT, KATARINA CLAES'S BEST FRIEND.

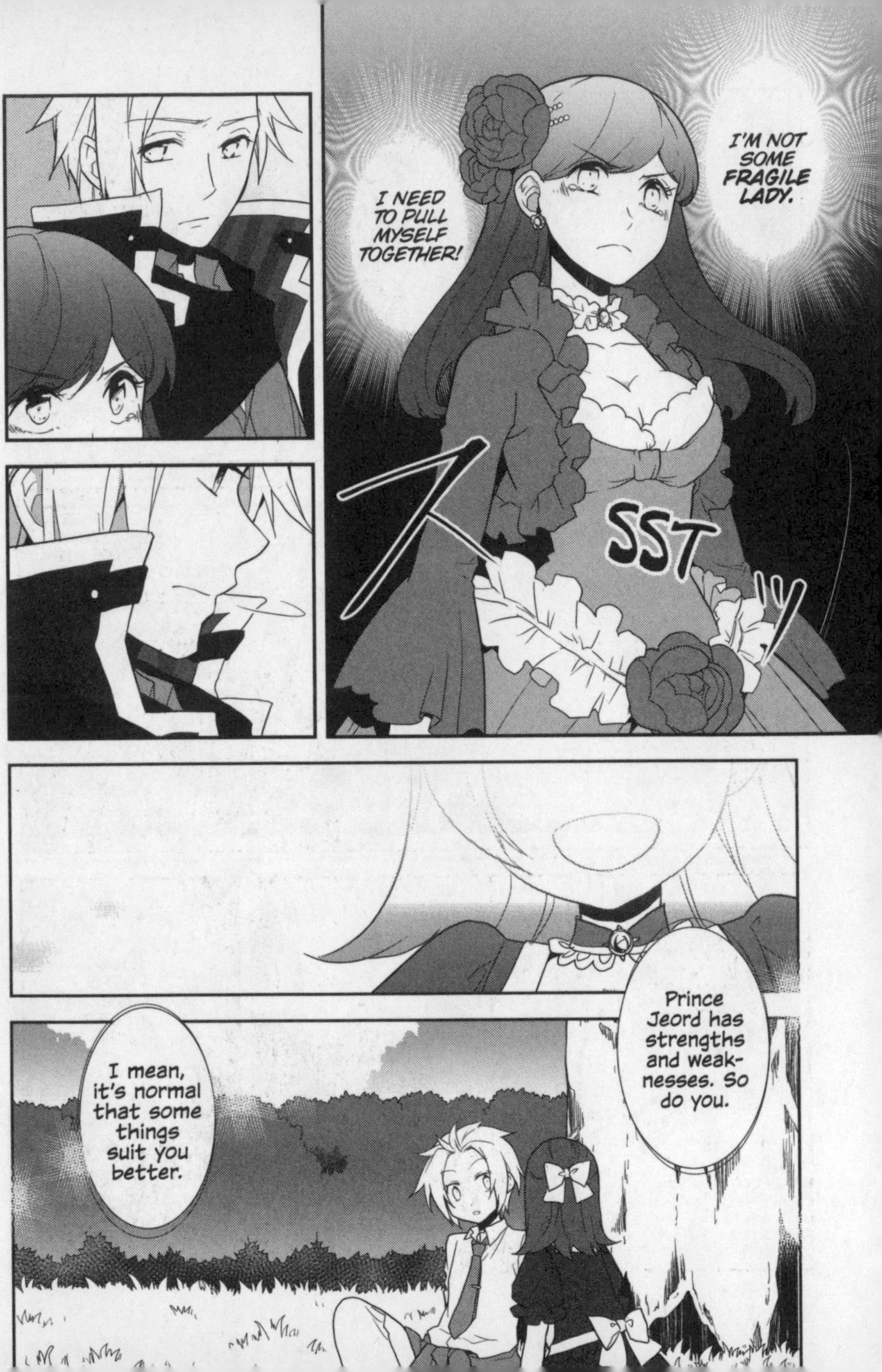
I'M NOT SOME FRAGILE LADY.
I NEED TO PULL MYSELF TOGETHER!
SST
Prince Jeord has strengths and weak-nesses. So do you.
I mean, it's normal that some things suit you better.

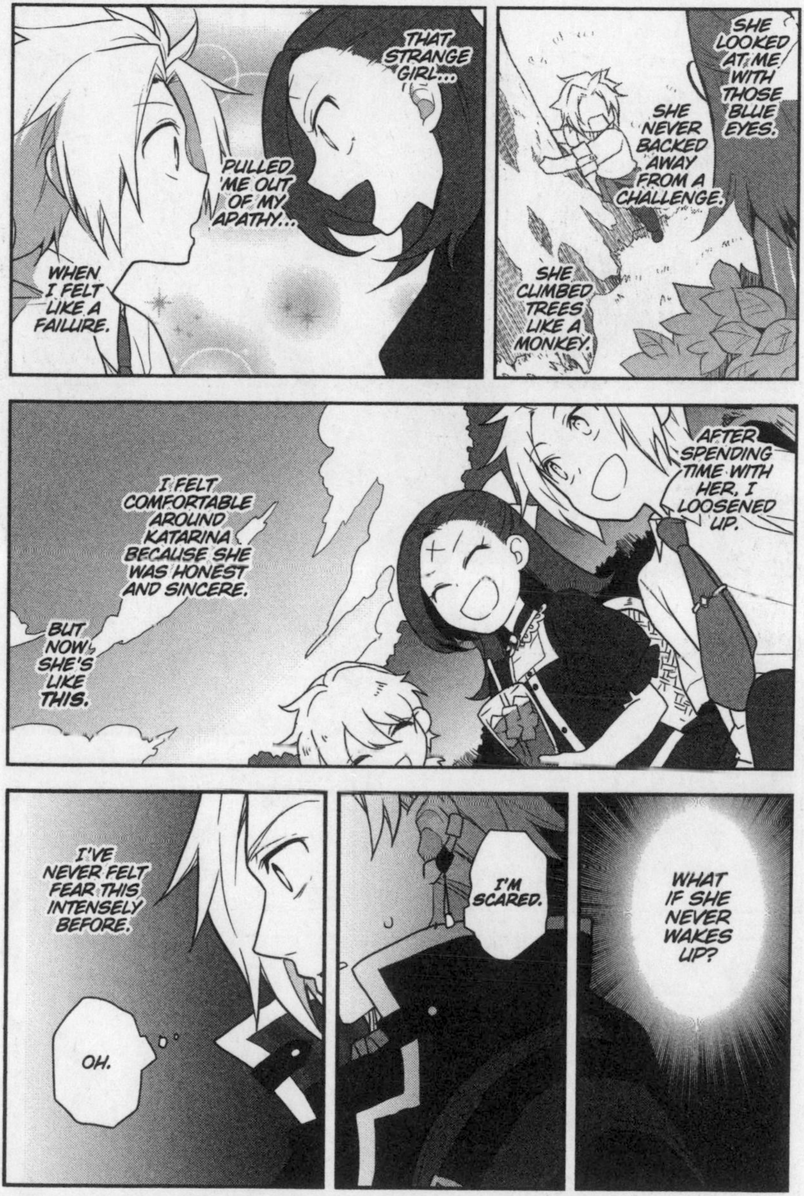
SHE LOOKED AT ME WITH THOSE BLUE EYES.
SHE NEVER BACKED AWAY FROM A CHALLENGE.
SHE CLIMBED TREES LIKE A MONKEY.
THAT STRANGE GIRL...
PULLED ME OUT OF MY APATHY...
WHEN I FELT LIKE A FAILURE.
AFTER SPENDING TIME WITH HER, I LOOSENED UP.
I FELT COMFORTABLE AROUND KATARINA BECAUSE SHE WAS HONEST AND SINCERE.
BUT NOW, SHE'S LIKE THIS.
WHAT IF SHE NEVER WAKES UP?
I'M SCARED.
I'VE NEVER FELT FEAR THIS INTENSELY BEFORE.
OH.

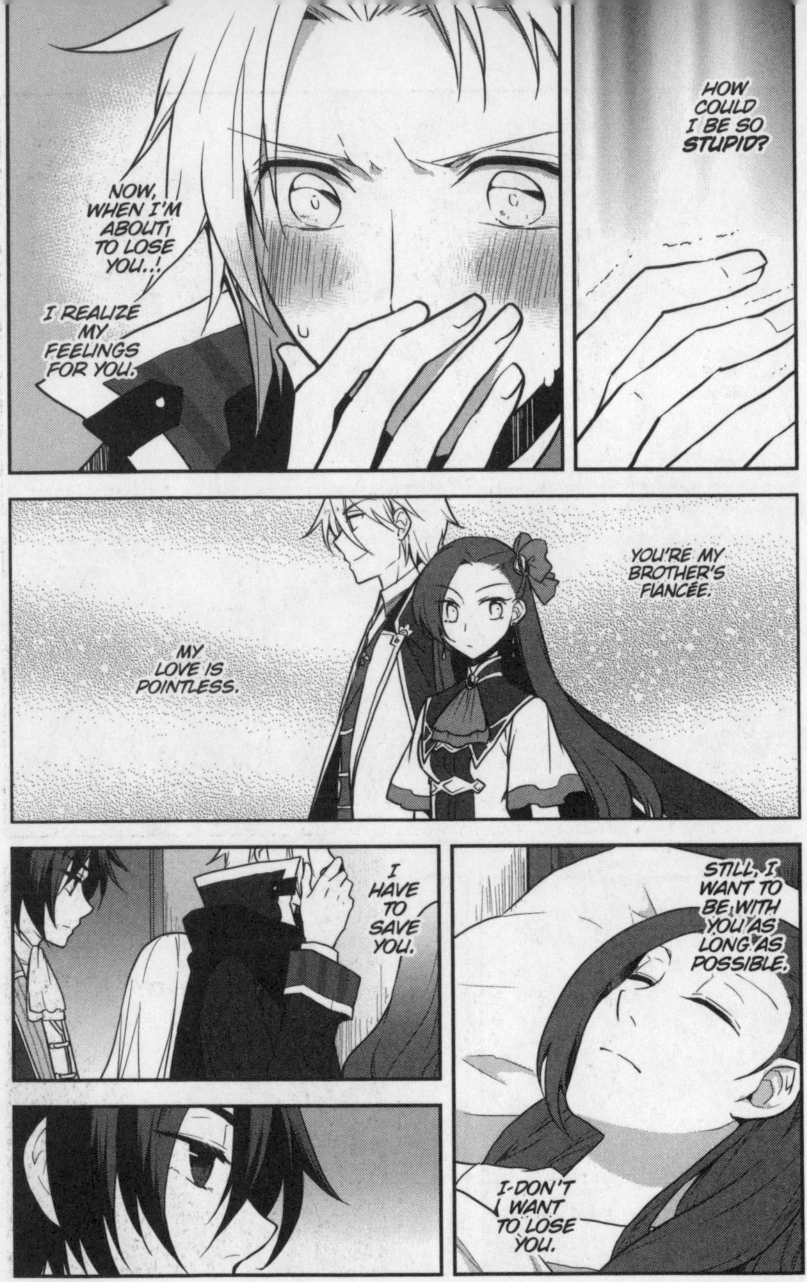
HOW COULD I BE SO STUPID?
NOW, WHEN I'M ABOUT TO LOSE YOU..!
I REALIZE MY FEELINGS FOR YOU.
YOU'RE MY BROTHER'S FIANCÉE.
MY LOVE IS POINTLESS.
STILL, I WANT TO BE WITH YOU AS LONG AS POSSIBLE.
I-DON'T I WANT TO LOSE YOU.
I HAVE TO SAVE YOU.

You have such amazing parents and a lovely sister.
You're very fortunate, Lord Nicol.
SHE SMILED WHEN SHE SAID THAT.
I'LL NEVER FORGET IT.
PEOPLE ASSUMED MY
CURSED. THEY PITIED ME.
BUT I AM FORTUNATE!
I COULDN'T GET THEM TO UNDERSTAND. I WAS READY TO GIVE UP ON THEM.
BUT SHE UNDERSTOOD.

LADY KATARINA'S KINDNESS ENVELOPED ME.

WHEN PEOPLE'S MISCONCEPTIONS FRUSTRATED ME...

FROM THAT DAY ON, SHE BECAME MY EVERYTHING.

PEOPLE REFUSED TO MAKE EYE CONTACT WITH ME.

MAYBE I WASN'T GOOD AT SOCIALIZING.

BUT... KATARINA ALWAYS LOOKED ME STRAIGHT IN THE EYE.

SHE'D FLASH A SMILE AS BRIGHT AS THE SUN.

PEOPLE WANT ME TO BE THE NEXT PRIME MINISTER, BUT WHAT GOOD IS THAT IF I CAN'T HELP HER?

I HATE MYSELF.

I CAN'T BE WITH HER, DESPITE HOW I FEEL.

SHE'S ENGAGED TO MY CHILD-HOOD FRIEND.

BUT I WANT TO BE HER FRIEND FOR AS LONG AS POSSIBLE.

WHAT'S THE POINT OF ANYTHING IF I CAN'T SAVE SOME-ONE WHO MEANS THIS MUCH TO ME?

CLENCH

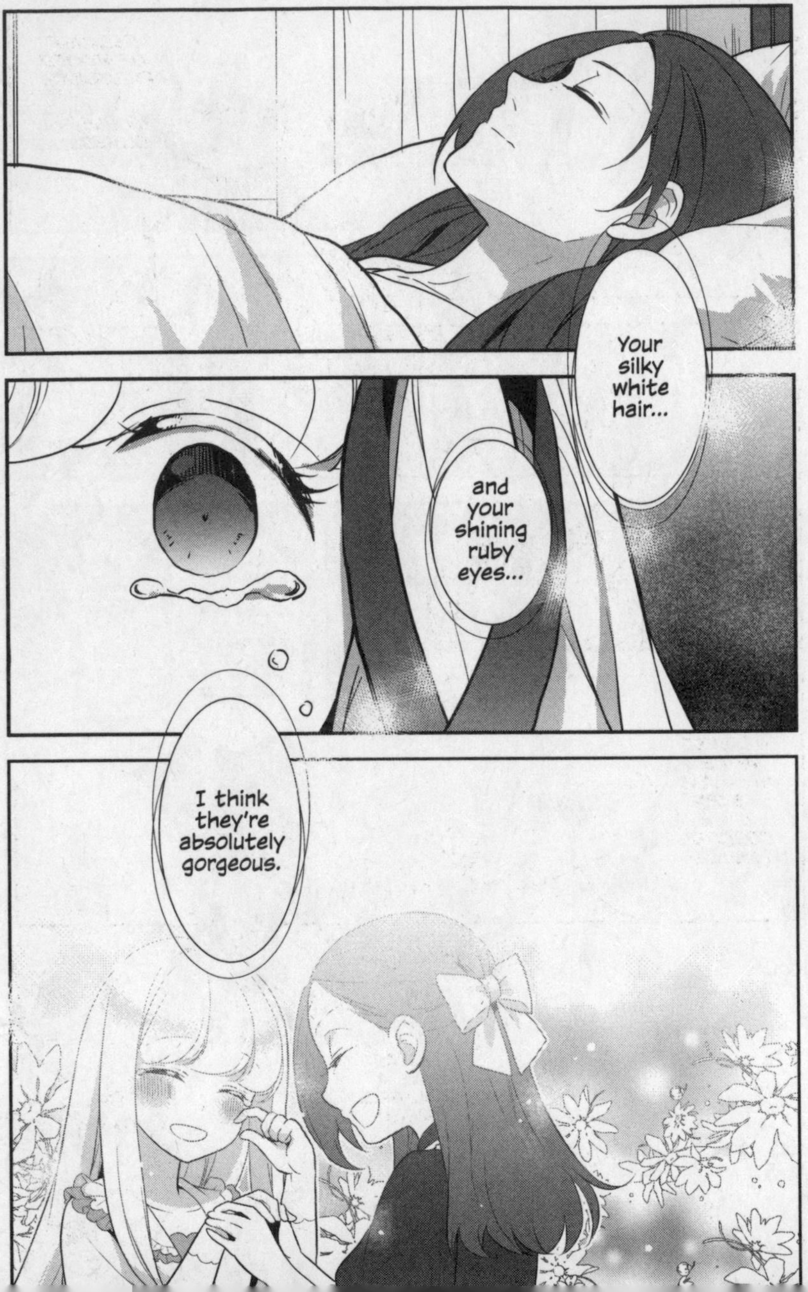
Your silky white hair...
and your shining ruby eyes...
I think they're absolutely gorgeous.

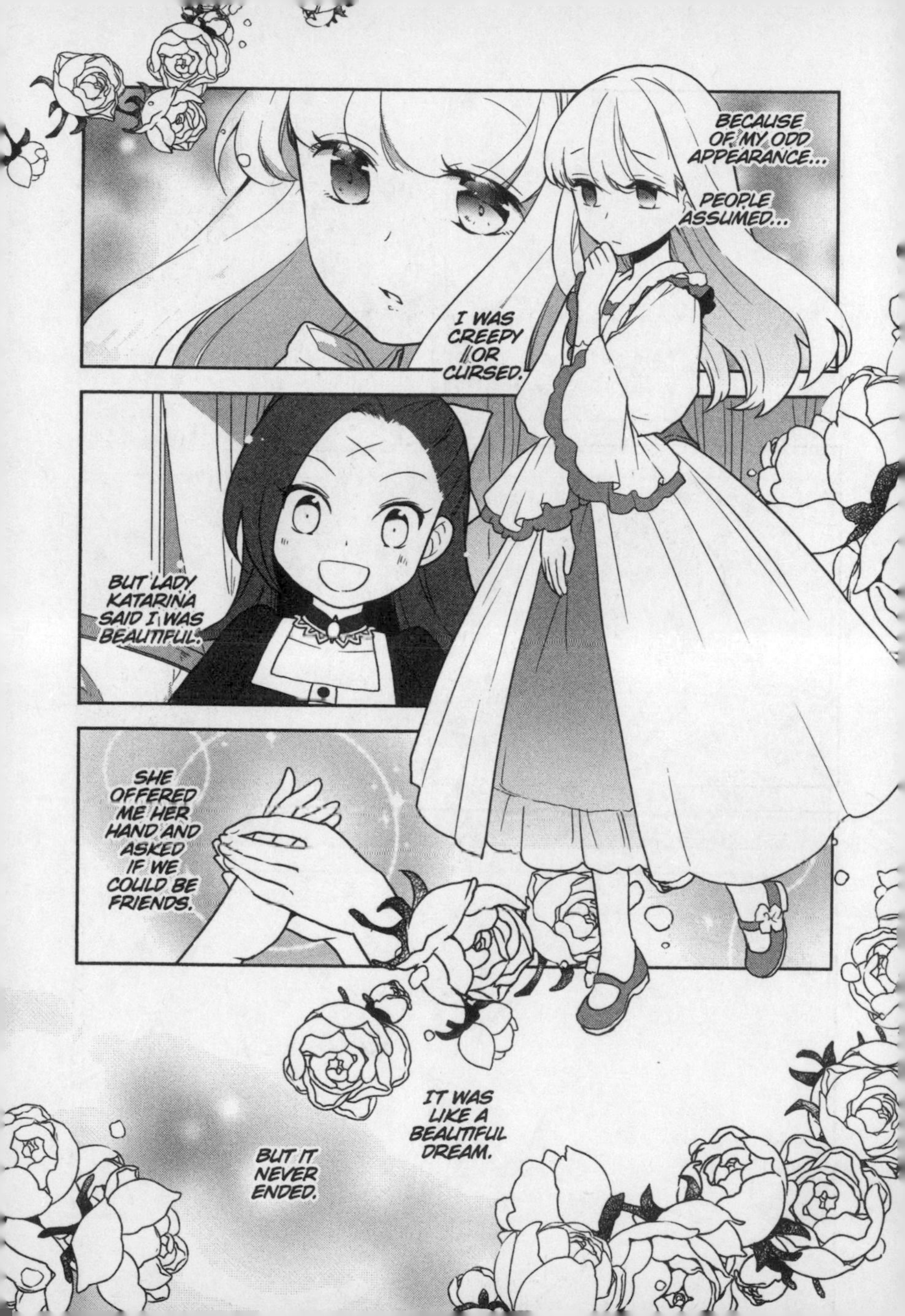
BECAUSE OF MY ODD APPEARANCE...
PEOPLE ASSUMED...
I WAS CREEPY OR CURSED.
BUT LADY KATARINA SAID I WAS BEAUTIFUL.
SHE OFFERED ME HER HAND AND ASKED IF WE COULD BE FRIENDS.
IT WAS LIKE A BEAUTIFUL DREAM.
BUT IT NEVER ENDED.

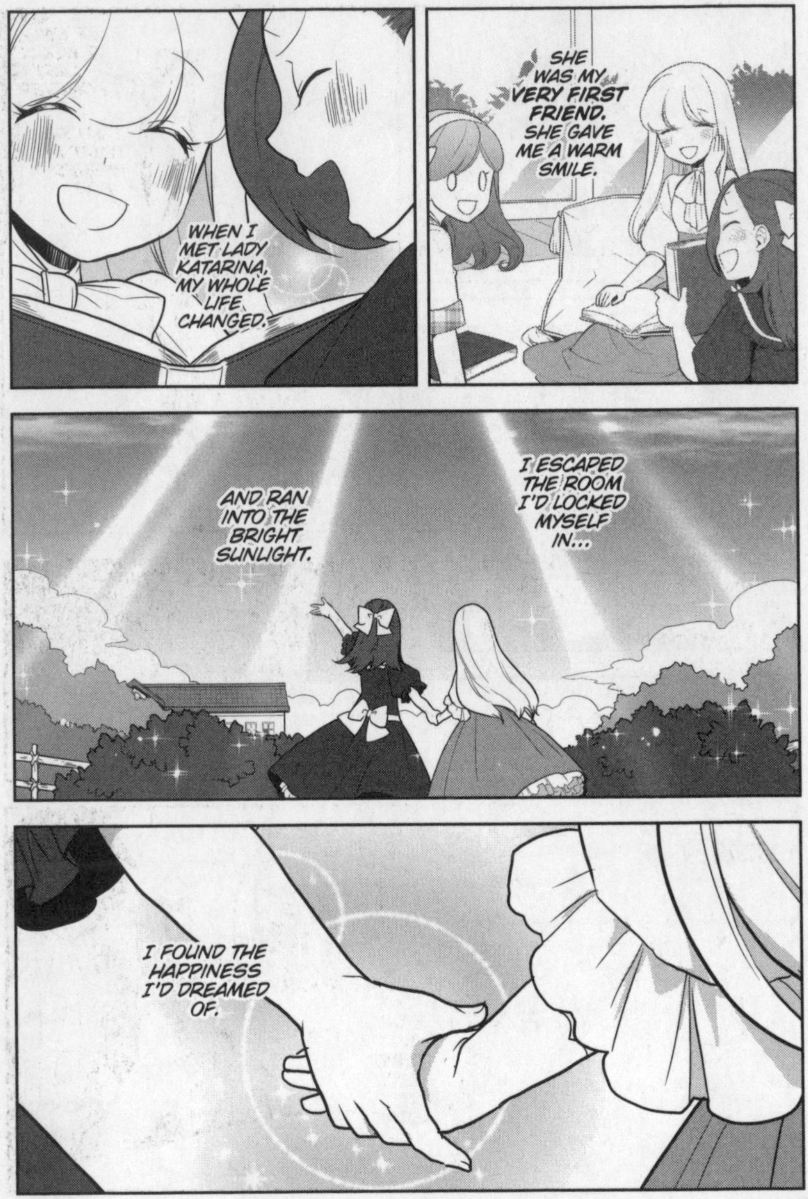
SHE WAS MY VERY FIRST FRIEND. SHE GAVE ME A WARM SMILE.
WHEN I MET LADY KATARINA, MY WHOLE LIFE CHANGED.
I ESCAPED THE ROOM I'D LOCKED MYSELF IN...
AND RAN INTO THE BRIGHT SUNLIGHT.
I FOUND THE HAPPINESS I'D DREAMED OF.

I'VE BEEN HERE FOR TWO DAYS.

EVERY TIME, I CALL HER NAME.

BUT KATARINA NEVER WAKES UP.

IF ONLY IT WOULD LAST FOREVER.

THAT'S WHAT I WISHED FOR.

PLIP

PLIP

WHY?

WHY DID THIS HAVE TO HAPPEN TO HER?

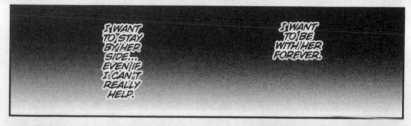

I WANT TO STAY BY HER SIDE... EVEN IF I CAN'T REALLY HELP.

I WANT TO BE WITH HER FOREVER.

PLIP

PLIP

GULP

MY BROTHER WANTED TO TAKE ME BACK TO MY ROOM.

BUT I'M TOO FRIGHT-ENED TO LEAVE HER.

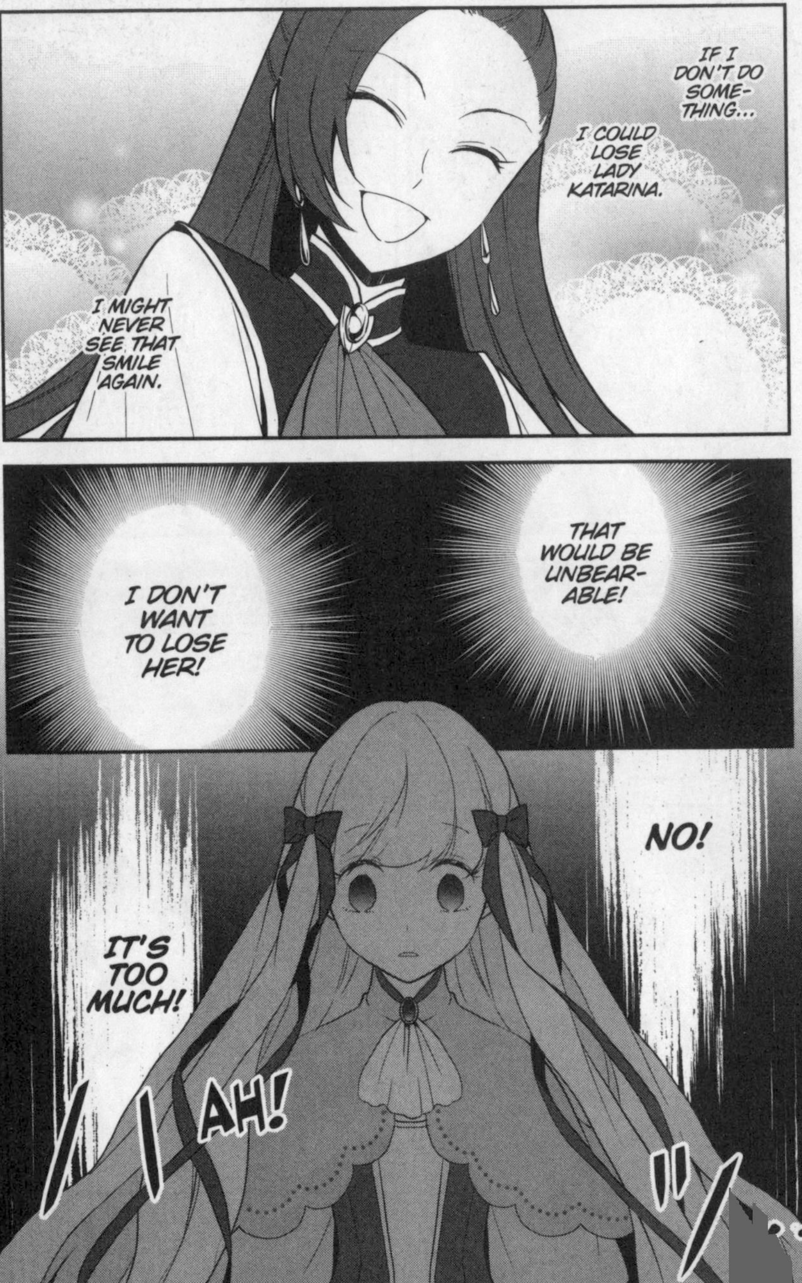
IF I DON'T DO SOME-THING...
I COULD LOSE LADY KATARINA.
I MIGHT NEVER SEE THAT SMILE AGAIN.
THAT WOULD BE UNBEAR-ABLE!
I DON'T WANT TO LOSE HER!
NO!
IT'S TOO MUCH!
AH!

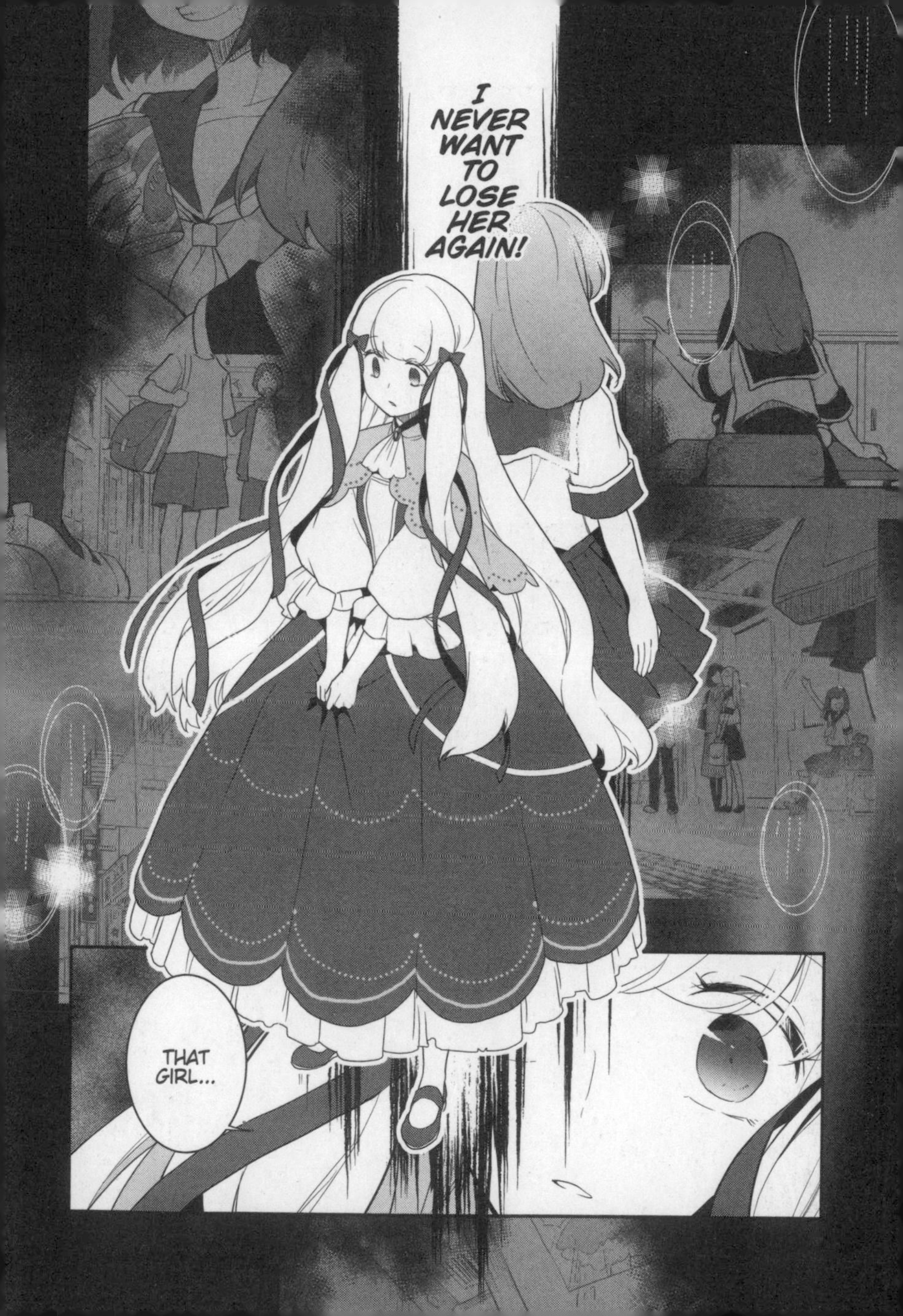
I NEVER WANT TO LOSE HER AGAIN!
THAT GIRL...

My Next Life
as a VILLAINESS:
ALL ROUTES
LEAD TO DOOM!

Chapter 19

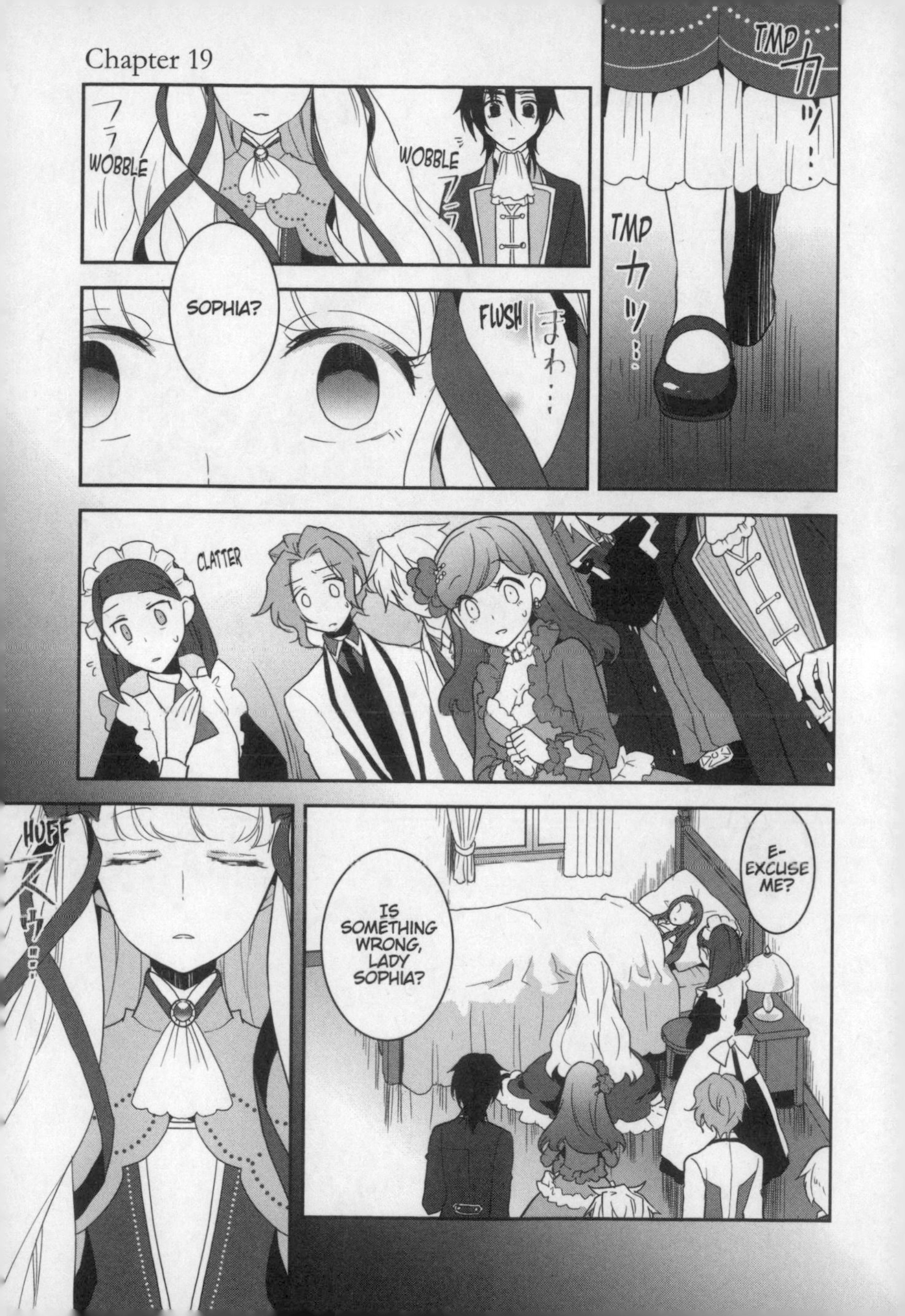
TMP
カッ…
TMP
カッ…
WOBBLE
フラ
フラ
WOBBLE
FLUSH
ほわ…
SOPHIA?
CLATTER
E-EXCUSE ME?
IS SOMETHING WRONG, LADY SOPHIA?
HUFF
スゥ…

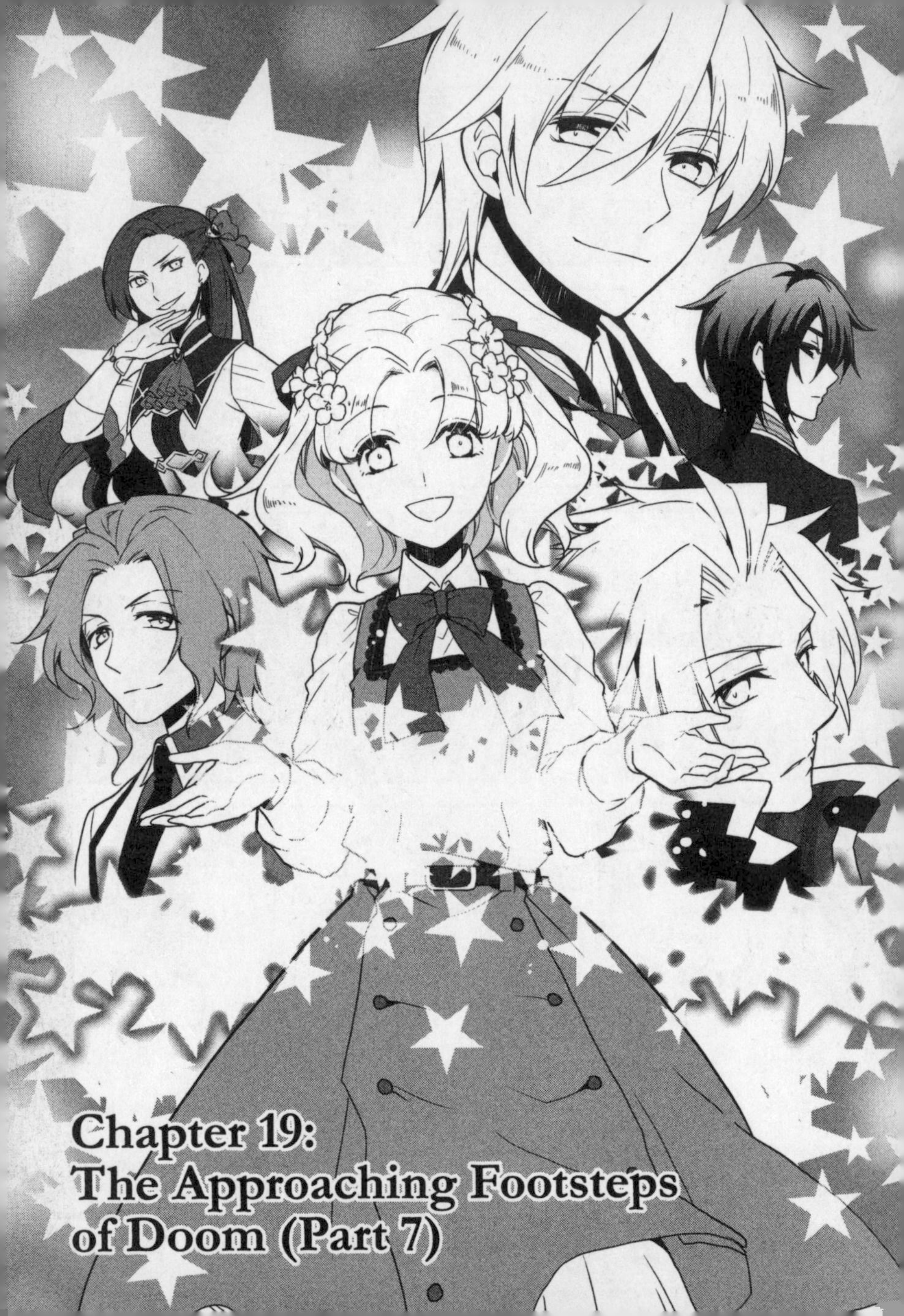

Chapter 19: The Approaching Footsteps of Doom (Part 7)

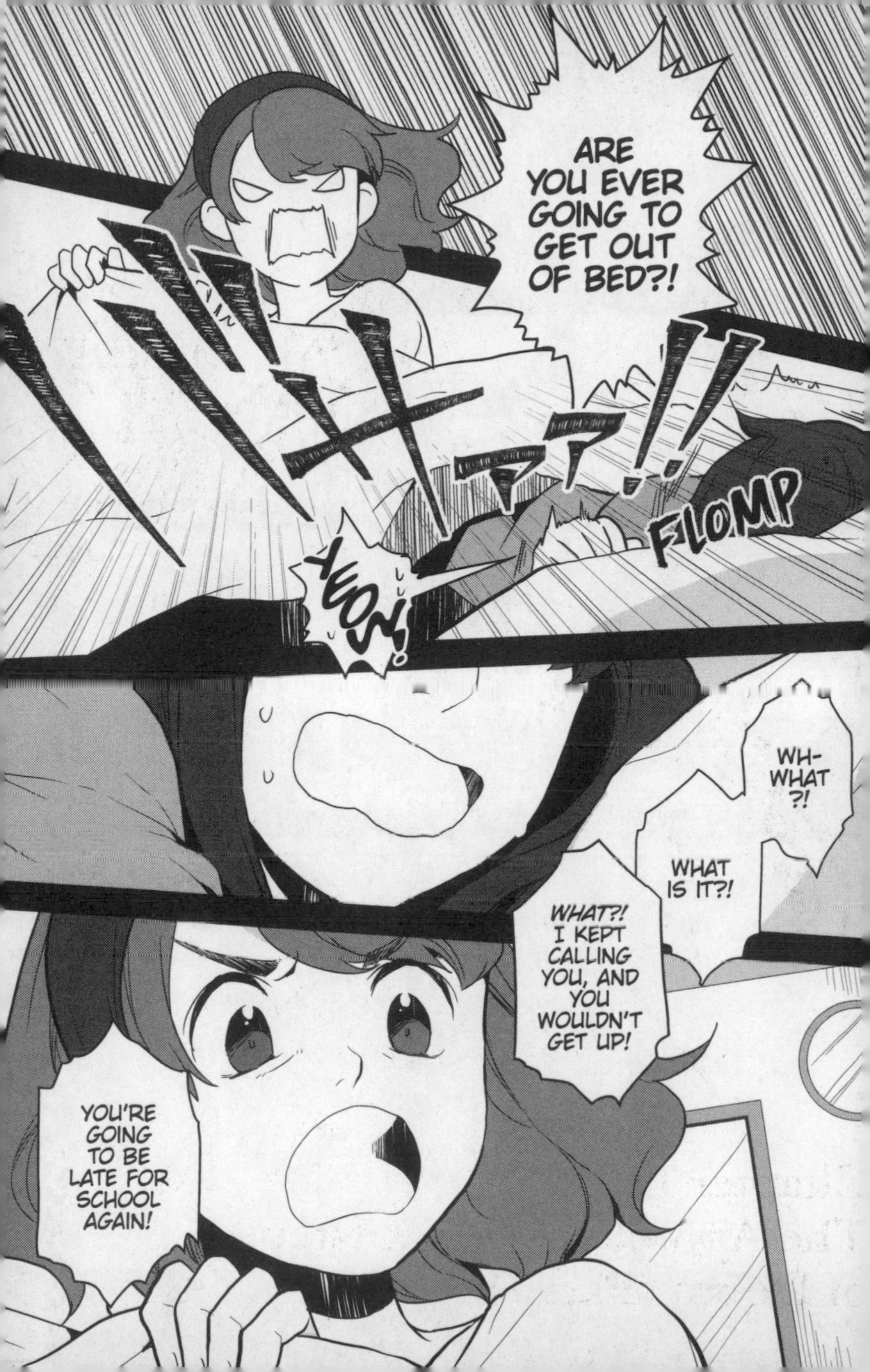
ARE YOU EVER GOING TO GET OUT OF BED?!
FLOMP
WOOSH!
WH- WHAT?!
WHAT IS IT?!
WHAT?! I KEPT CALLING YOU, AND YOU WOULDN'T GET UP!
YOU'RE GOING TO BE LATE FOR SCHOOL AGAIN!

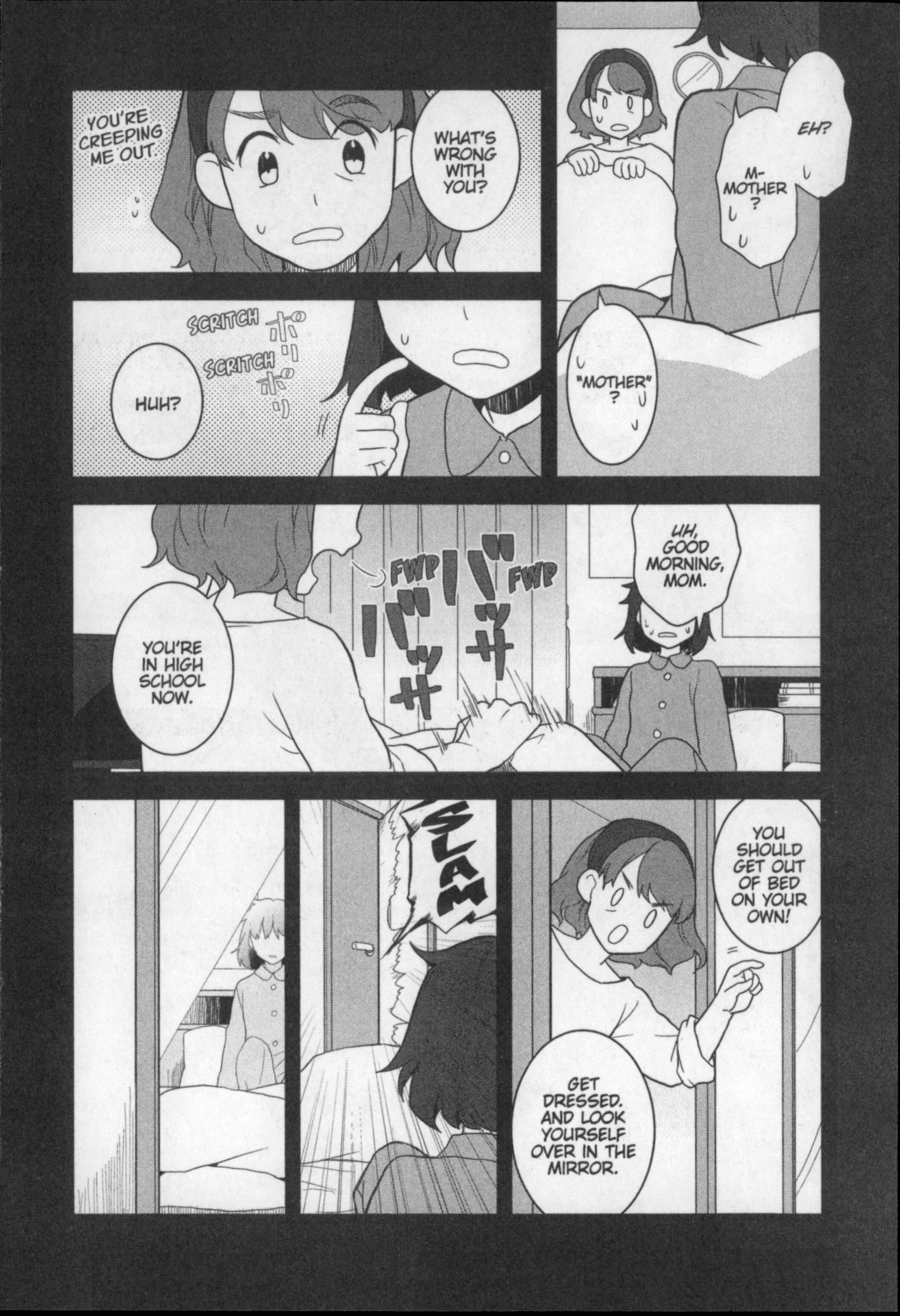
EH?
M-MOTHER?
"MOTHER"?
WHAT'S WRONG WITH YOU?
YOU'RE CREEPING ME OUT.
SCRITCH ポリ
SCRITCH ポリ
HUH?
UH, GOOD MORNING, MOM.
FWP バッサ
FWP バッサ
YOU'RE IN HIGH SCHOOL NOW.
YOU SHOULD GET OUT OF BED ON YOUR OWN!
GET DRESSED. AND LOOK YOURSELF OVER IN THE MIRROR.
SLAM

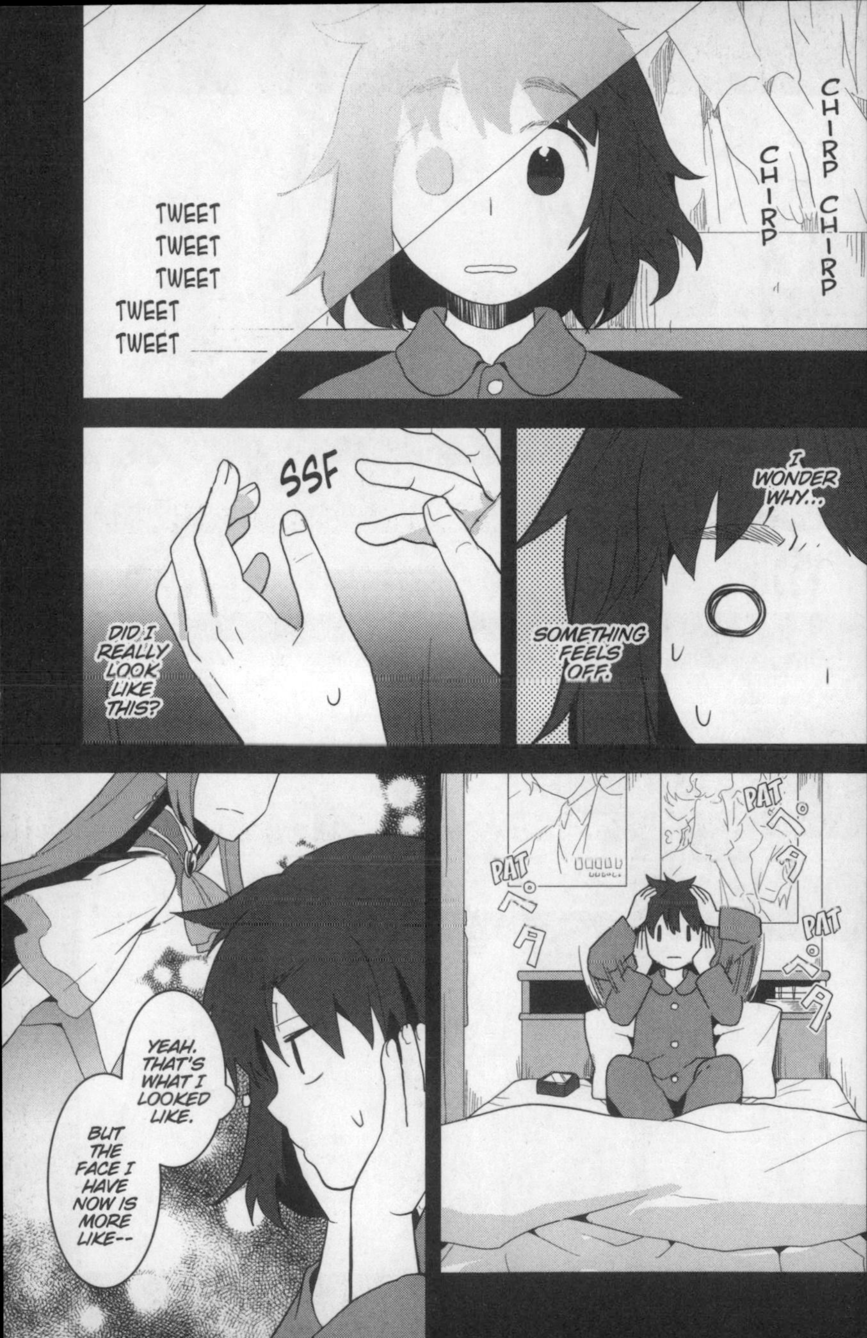
CHIRP CHIRP
CHIRP
TWEET TWEET TWEET TWEET TWEET
I WONDER WHY...
SOMETHING FEELS OFF.
SSF
DID I REALLY LOOK LIKE THIS?
PAT ペタ
PAT ペタ
PAT ペタ
YEAH. THAT'S WHAT I LOOKED LIKE.
BUT THE FACE I HAVE NOW IS MORE LIKE--

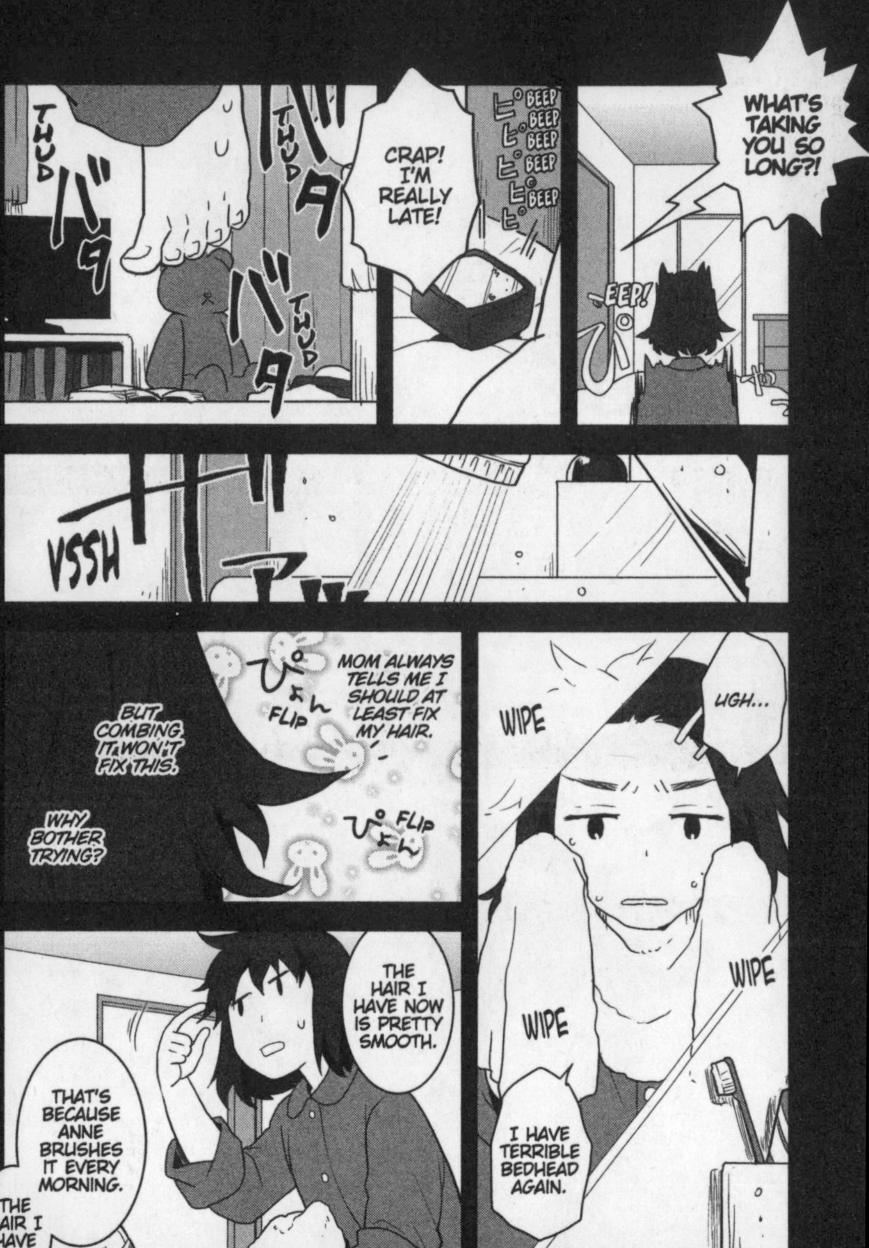
WHAT'S TAKING YOU SO LONG?!
EEP!
BEEP BEEP BEEP BEEP BEEP
CRAP! I'M REALLY LATE!
THUD
THUD
THUD
VSSH
UGH...
WIPE
WIPE
WIPE
I HAVE TERRIBLE BEDHEAD AGAIN.
MOM ALWAYS TELLS ME I SHOULD AT LEAST FIX MY HAIR.
FLIP
BUT COMBING IT WON'T FIX THIS.
FLIP
WHY BOTHER TRYING?
THE HAIR I HAVE NOW IS PRETTY SMOOTH.
THAT'S BECAUSE ANNE BRUSHES IT EVERY MORNING.
THE HAIR I HAVE NOW?

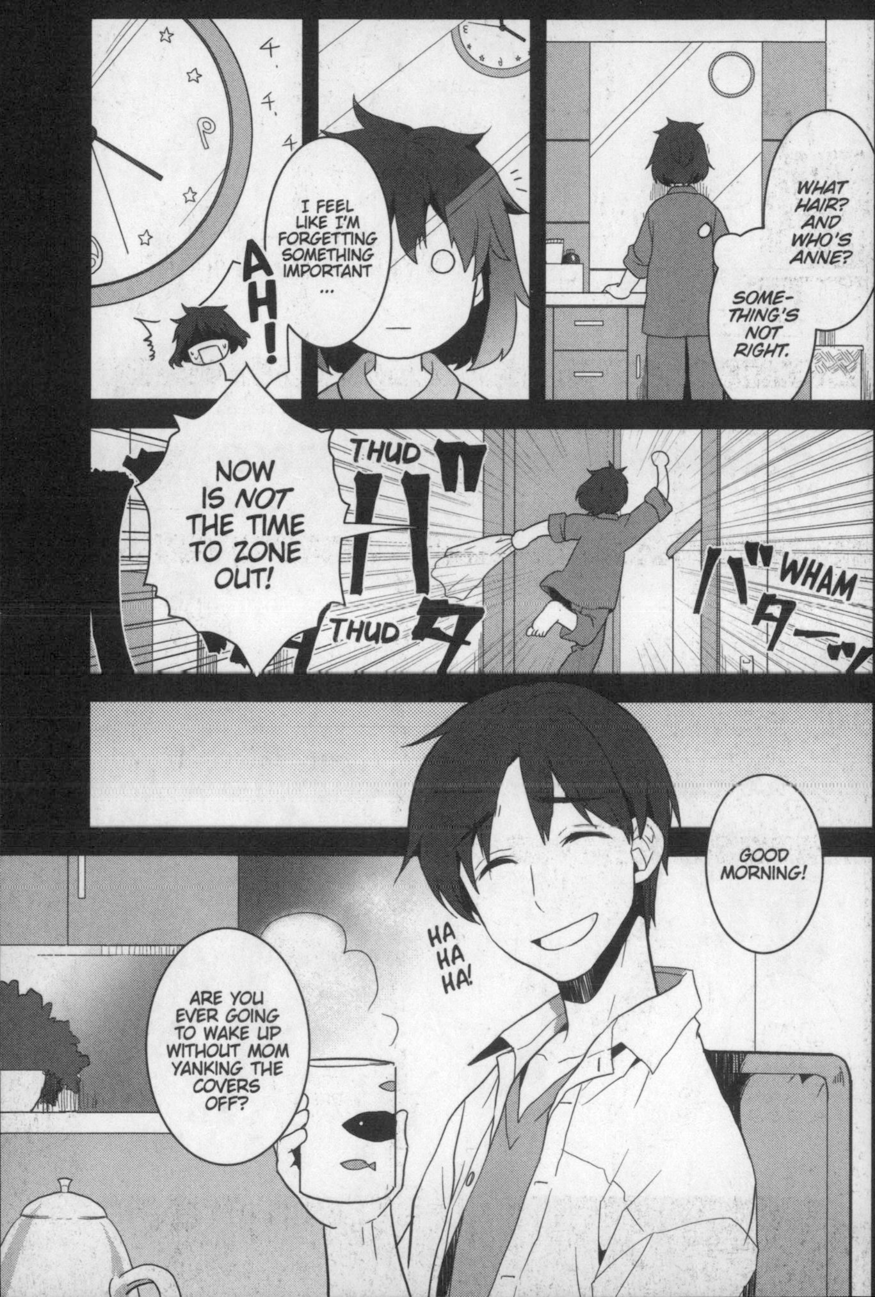
WHAT HAIR? AND WHO'S ANNE?
SOME-THING'S NOT RIGHT.
I FEEL LIKE I'M FORGETTING SOMETHING IMPORTANT ...
AH!
WHAM
THUD
THUD
NOW IS NOT THE TIME TO ZONE OUT!
GOOD MORNING!
HA HA HA!
ARE YOU EVER GOING TO WAKE UP WITHOUT MOM YANKING THE COVERS OFF?

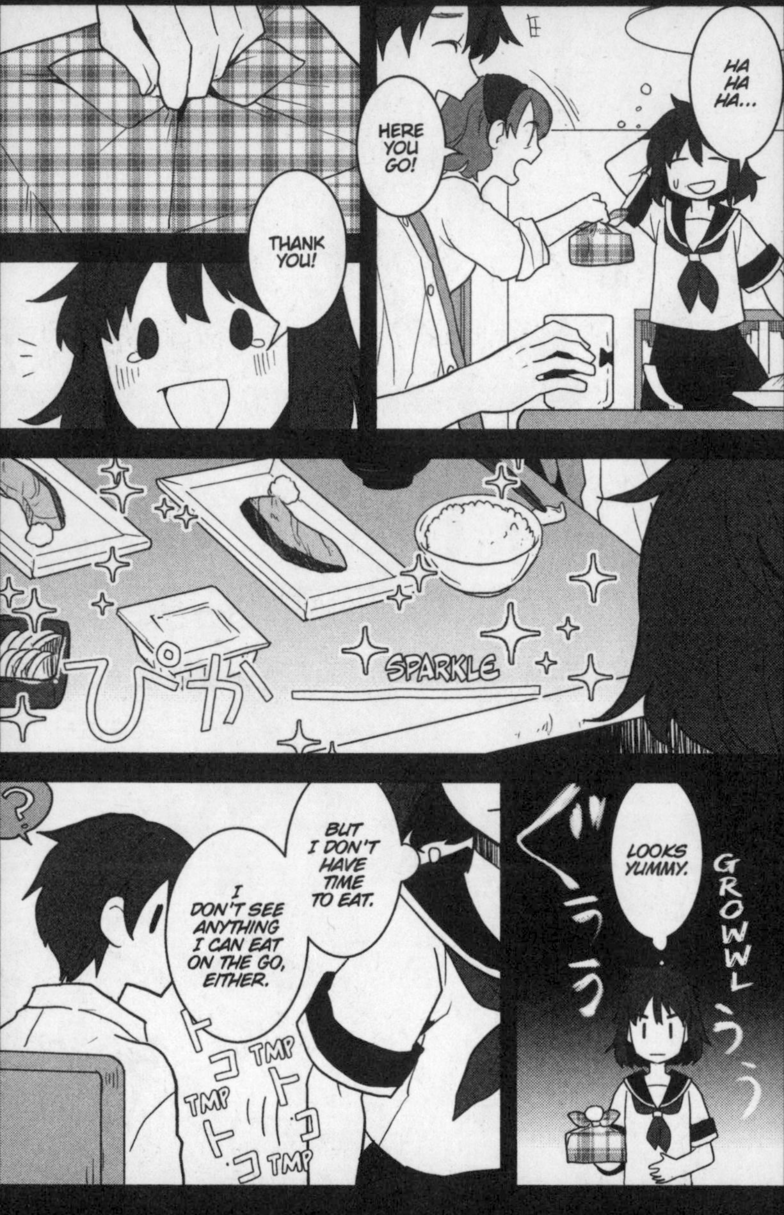
HA HA HA...
HERE YOU GO!
THANK YOU!
ぴか
SPARKLE
LOOKS YUMMY.
GROWL
?
BUT I DON'T HAVE TIME TO EAT.
I DON'T SEE ANYTHING I CAN EAT ON THE GO, EITHER.
TMP
TMP
TMP

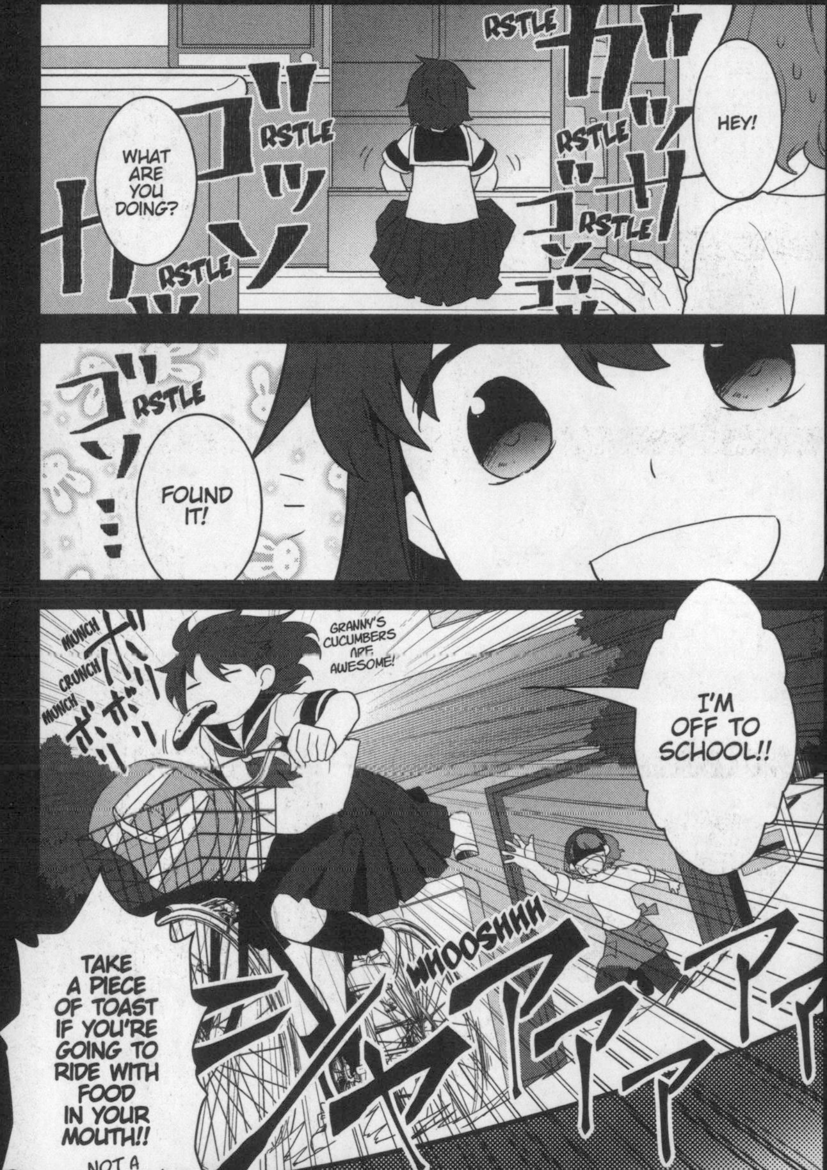
HEY!
RSTLE
RSTLE
RSTLE
WHAT ARE YOU DOING?
RSTLE
RSTLE
RSTLE
FOUND IT!
I'M OFF TO SCHOOL!!
GRANNY'S CUCUMBERS NPF, AWESOME!
MUNCH
CRUNCH
MUNCH
WHOOSHHH
TAKE A PIECE OF TOAST IF YOU'RE GOING TO RIDE WITH FOOD IN YOUR MOUTH!!
NOT A CUCUMBER!

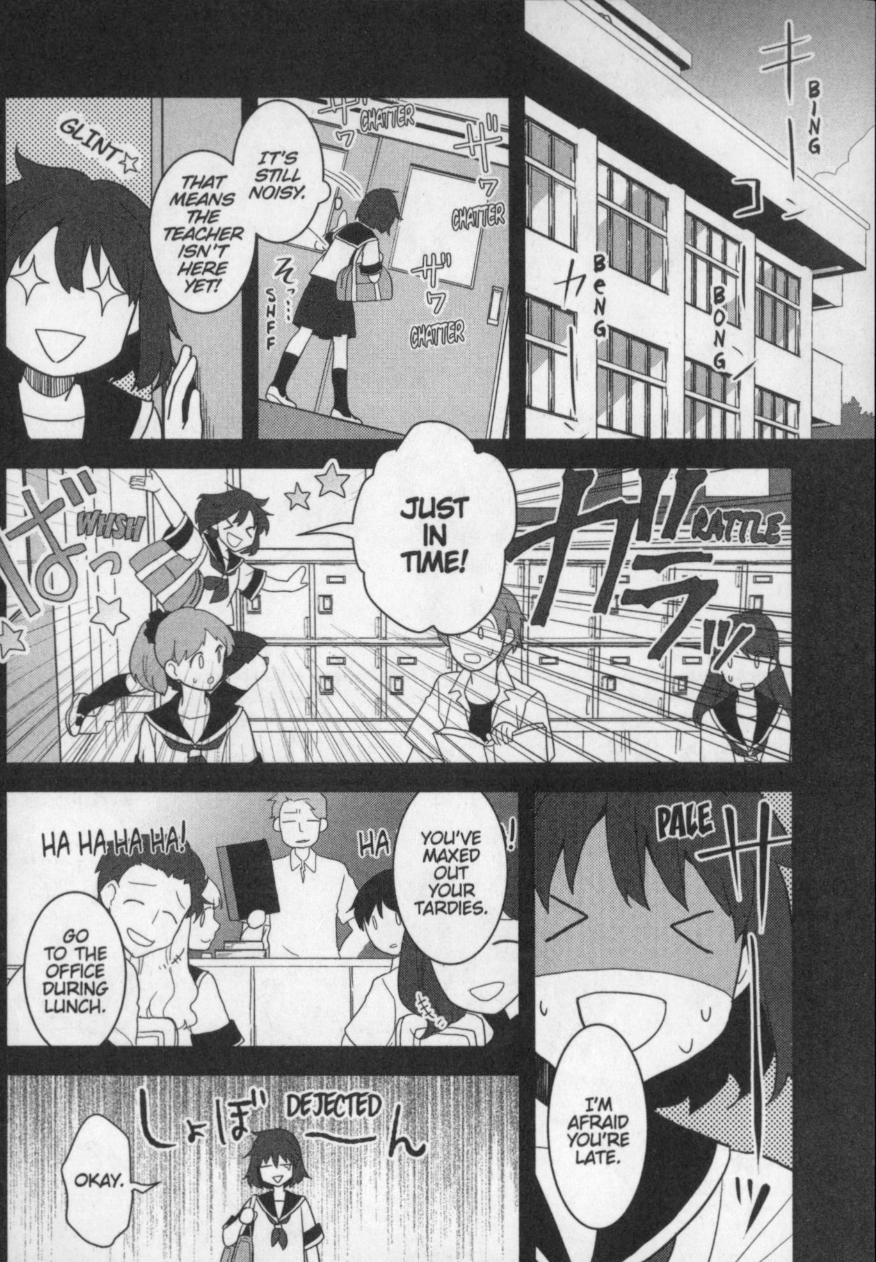
BING
BONG
BeNG
CHATTER
CHATTER
CHATTER
IT'S STILL NOISY.
SNFF
GLINT☆
THAT MEANS THE TEACHER ISN'T HERE YET!
RATTLE
JUST IN TIME!
WHSH
PALE
I'M AFRAID YOU'RE LATE.
HA HA HA HA!
YOU'VE MAXED OUT YOUR TARDIES.
GO TO THE OFFICE DURING LUNCH.
DEJECTED
OKAY.

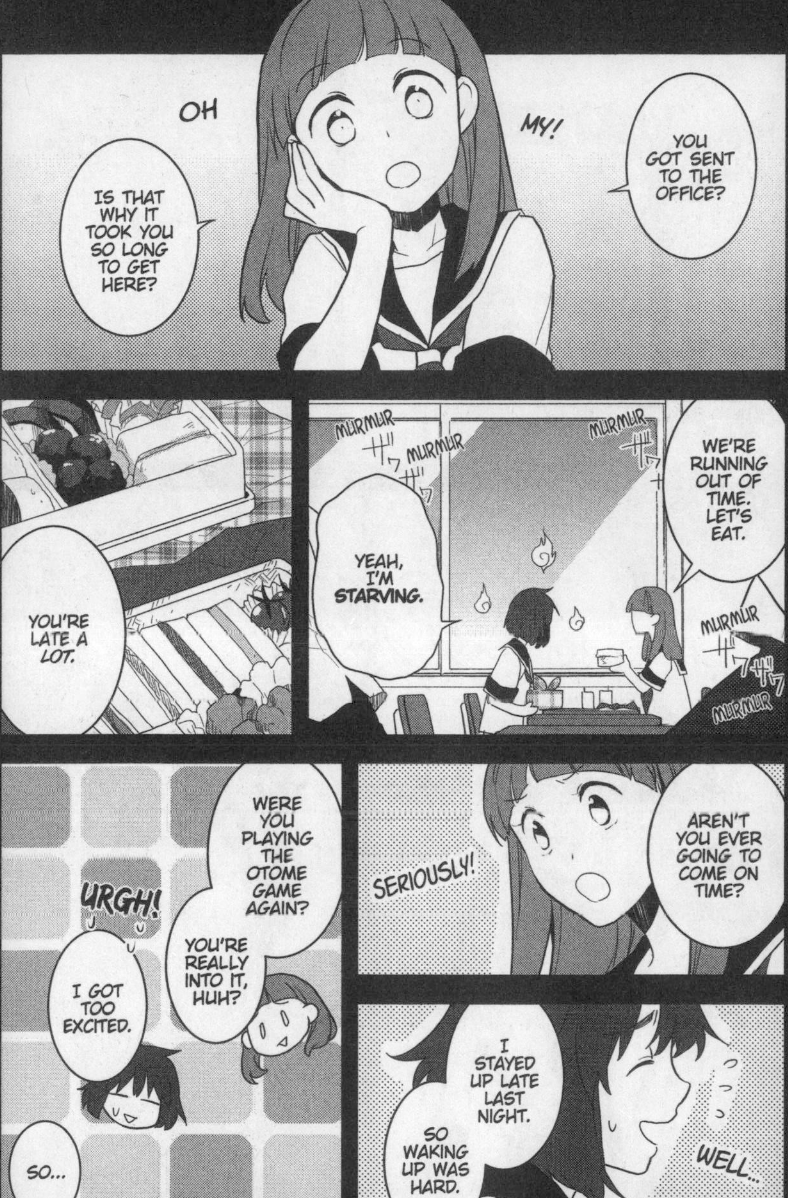
OH
MY!
YOU GOT SENT TO THE OFFICE?
IS THAT WHY IT TOOK YOU SO LONG TO GET HERE?
MURMUR
MURMUR
MURMUR
WE'RE RUNNING OUT OF TIME. LET'S EAT.
YEAH, I'M STARVING.
MURMUR
MURMUR
YOU'RE LATE A LOT.
AREN'T YOU EVER GOING TO COME ON TIME?
SERIOUSLY!
WELL...
I STAYED UP LATE LAST NIGHT.
SO WAKING UP WAS HARD.
WERE YOU PLAYING THE OTOME GAME AGAIN?
URGH!
YOU'RE REALLY INTO IT, HUH?
I GOT TOO EXCITED.
SO...

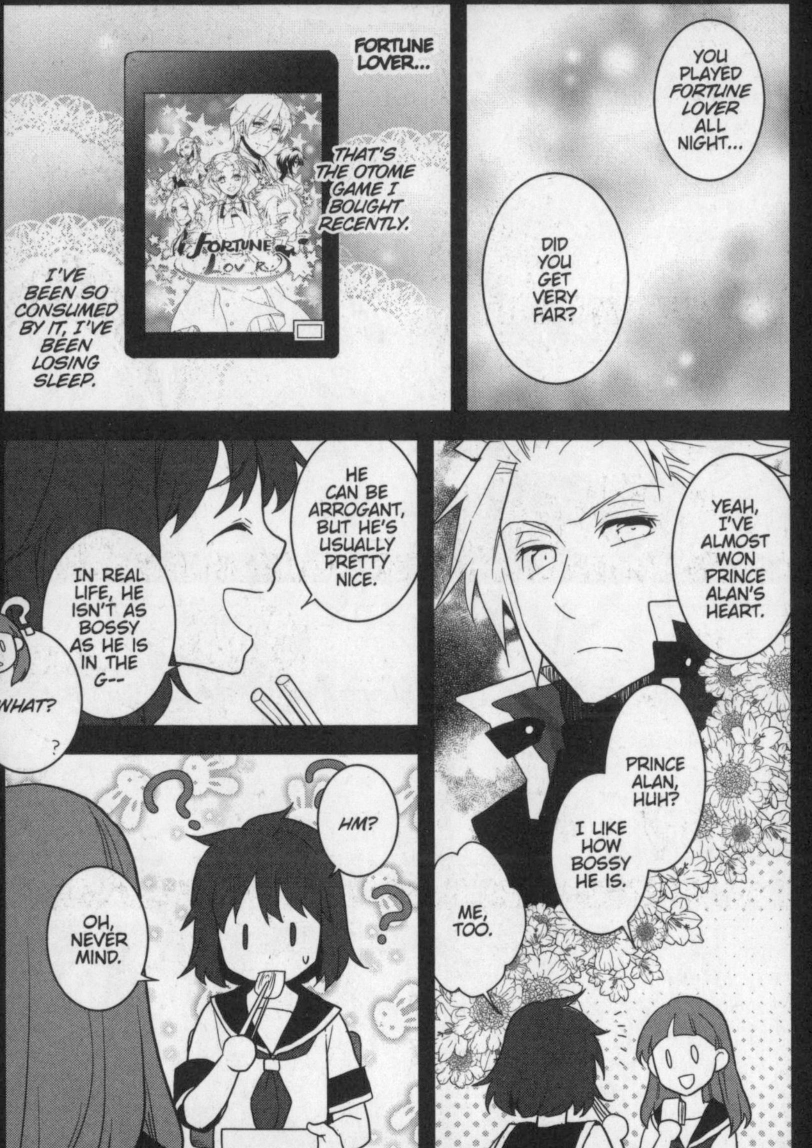
YOU PLAYED FORTUNE LOVER ALL NIGHT...
DID YOU GET VERY FAR?
FORTUNE LOVER...
THAT'S THE OTOME GAME I BOUGHT RECENTLY.
I'VE BEEN SO CONSUMED BY IT, I'VE BEEN LOSING SLEEP.
YEAH, I'VE ALMOST WON PRINCE ALAN'S HEART.
PRINCE ALAN, HUH? I LIKE HOW BOSSY HE IS.
ME, TOO.
HE CAN BE ARROGANT, BUT HE'S USUALLY PRETTY NICE.
IN REAL LIFE, HE ISN'T AS BOSSY AS HE IS IN THE G--
WHAT?
HM?
OH, NEVER MIND.

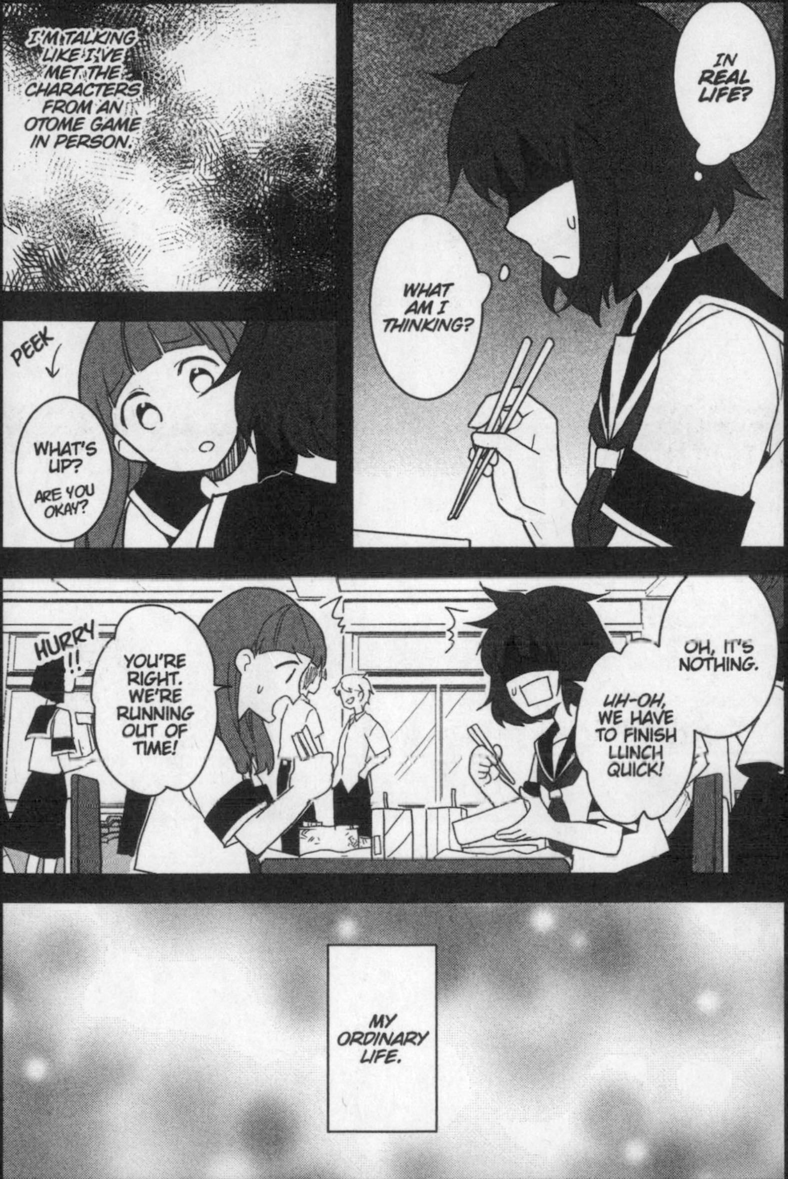
IN REAL LIFE?
WHAT AM I THINKING?
I'M TALKING LIKE I'VE MET THE CHARACTERS FROM AN OTOME GAME IN PERSON.
PEEK
WHAT'S UP?
ARE YOU OKAY?
OH, IT'S NOTHING.
UH-OH, WE HAVE TO FINISH LUNCH QUICK!
YOU'RE RIGHT. WE'RE RUNNING OUT OF TIME!
HURRY!!
MY ORDINARY LIFE.

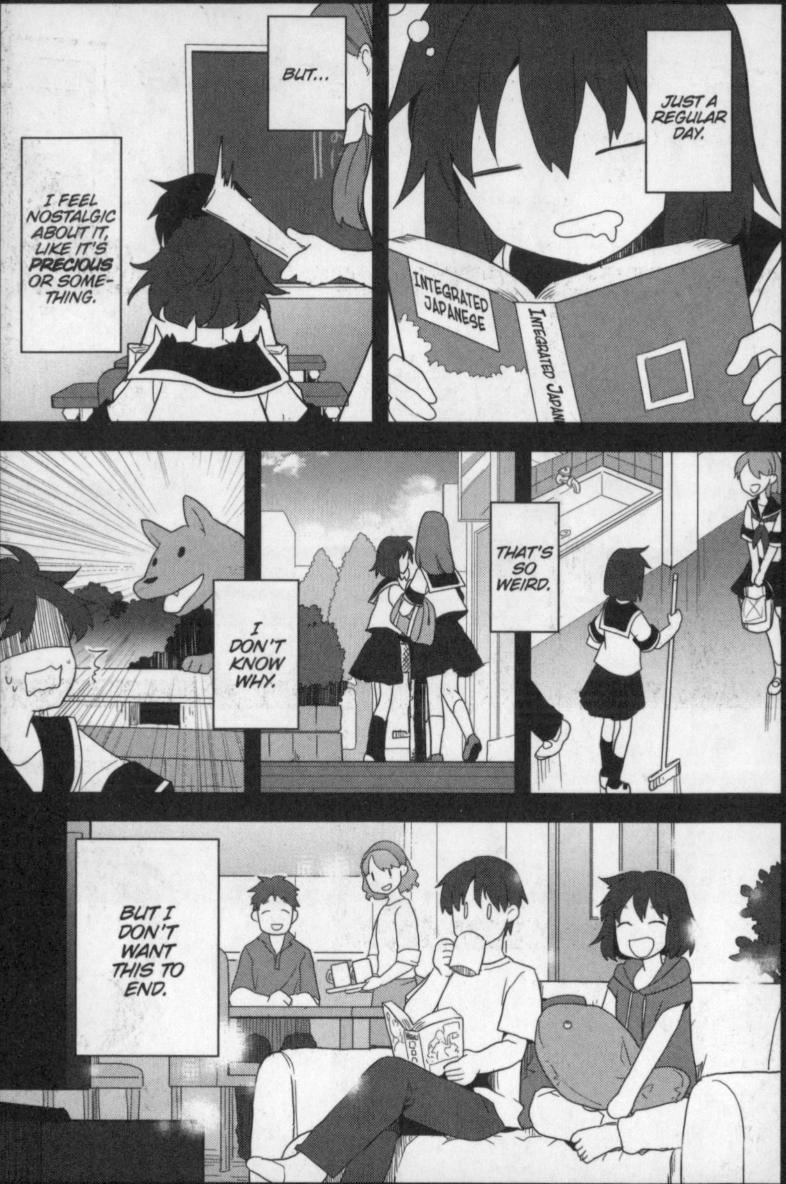
JUST A REGULAR DAY.
INTEGRATED JAPANESE
BUT...
I FEEL NOSTALGIC ABOUT IT, LIKE IT'S PRECIOUS OR SOMETHING.
THAT'S SO WEIRD.
I DON'T KNOW WHY.
BUT I DON'T WANT THIS TO END.

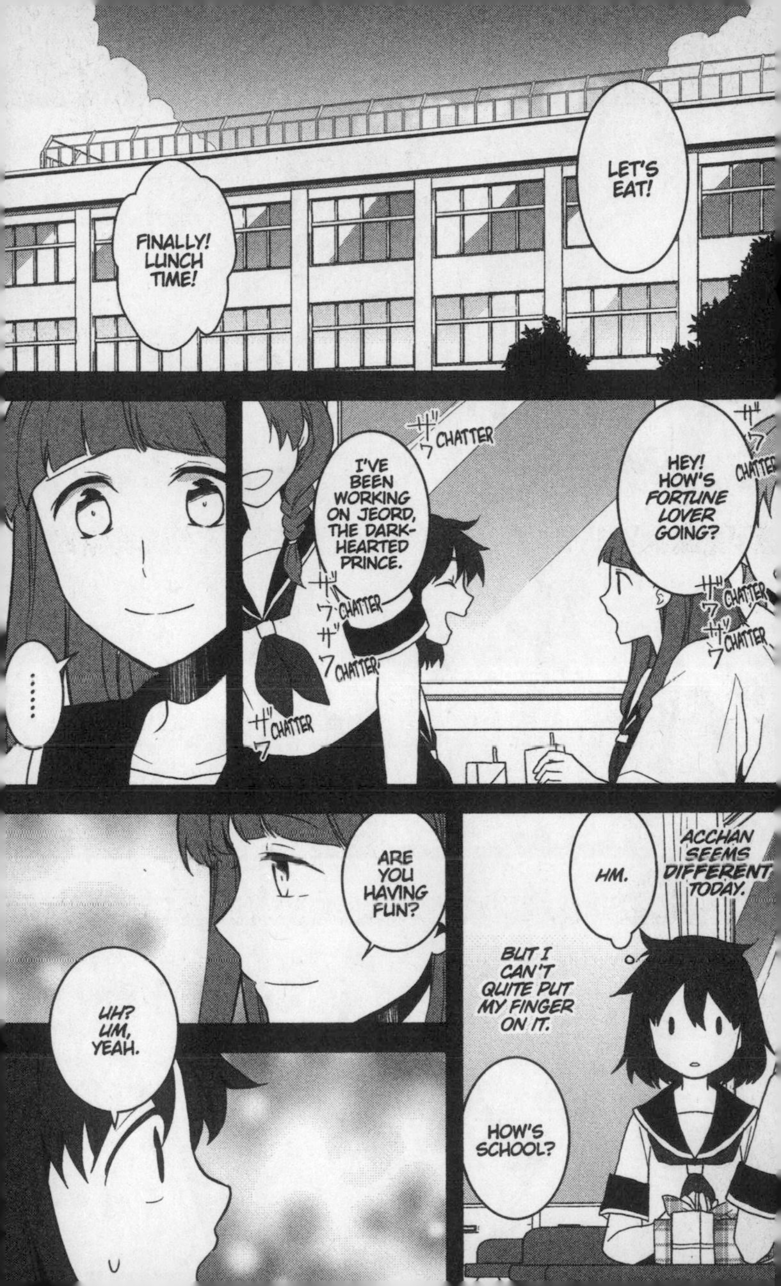
LET'S EAT!
FINALLY! LUNCH TIME!
ザワ CHATTER
HEY! HOW'S FORTUNE LOVER GOING?
ザワ CHATTER
ザワ CHATTER
ザワ CHATTER
I'VE BEEN WORKING ON JEORD, THE DARK-HEARTED PRINCE.
ザワ CHATTER
ザワ CHATTER
ザワ CHATTER
......
ACCHAN SEEMS DIFFERENT TODAY.
HM.
BUT I CAN'T QUITE PUT MY FINGER ON IT.
HOW'S SCHOOL?
ARE YOU HAVING FUN?
UH? UM, YEAH.

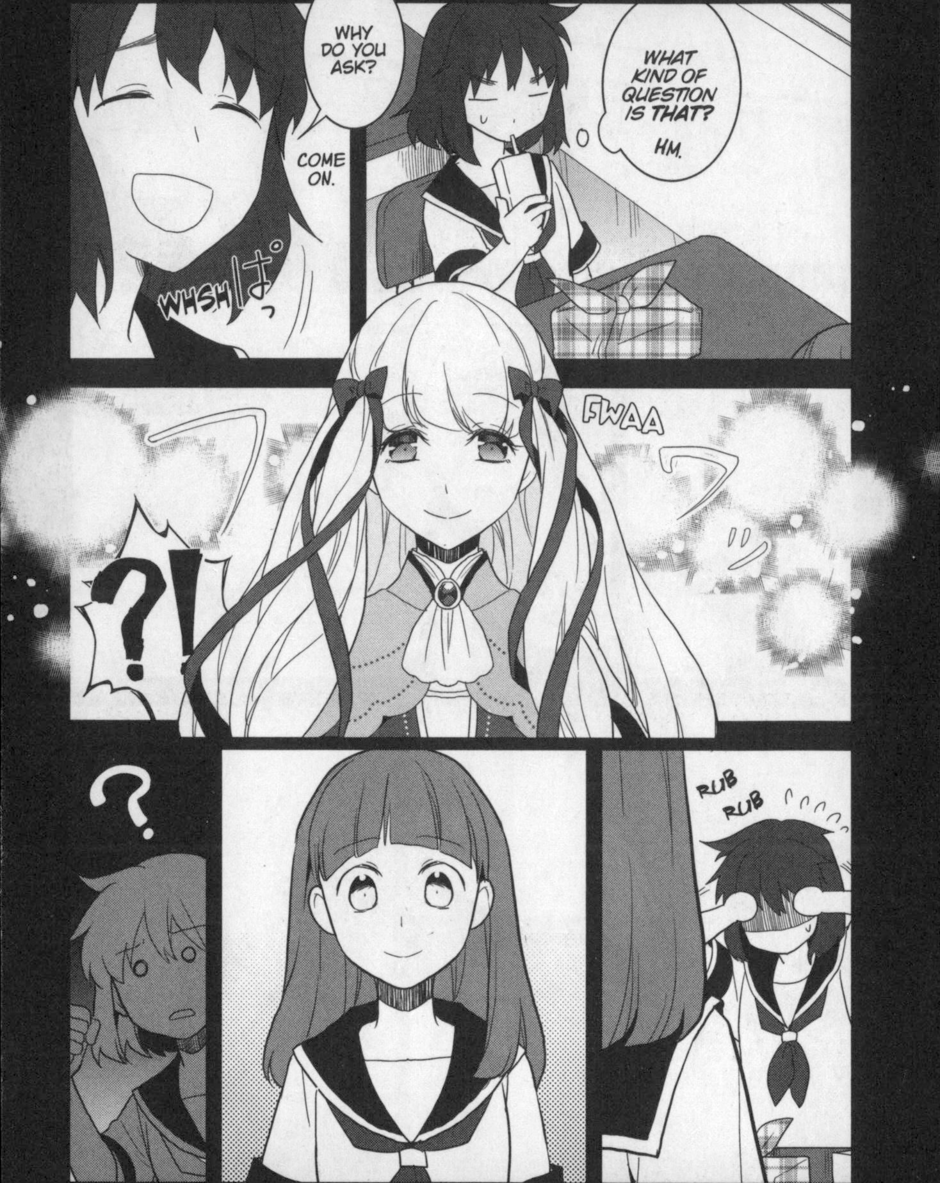
WHAT KIND OF QUESTION IS THAT?
HM.
WHY DO YOU ASK?
COME ON.
WHSH ぱっ
FWAA
?!
?
RUB RUB

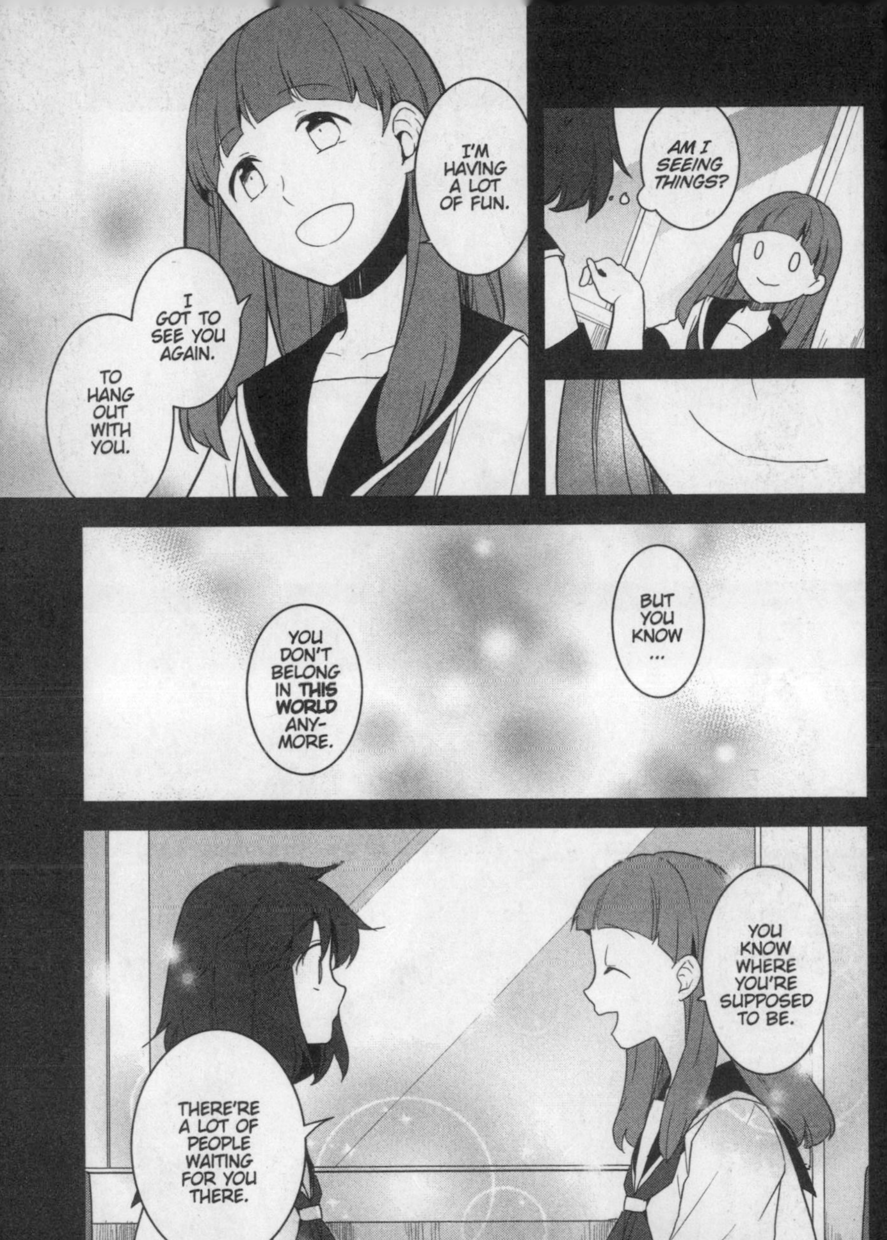
AM I SEEING THINGS?
I'M HAVING A LOT OF FUN.
I GOT TO SEE YOU AGAIN.
TO HANG OUT WITH YOU.
BUT YOU KNOW...
YOU DON'T BELONG IN THIS WORLD ANYMORE.
YOU KNOW WHERE YOU'RE SUPPOSED TO BE.
THERE'RE A LOT OF PEOPLE WAITING FOR YOU THERE.

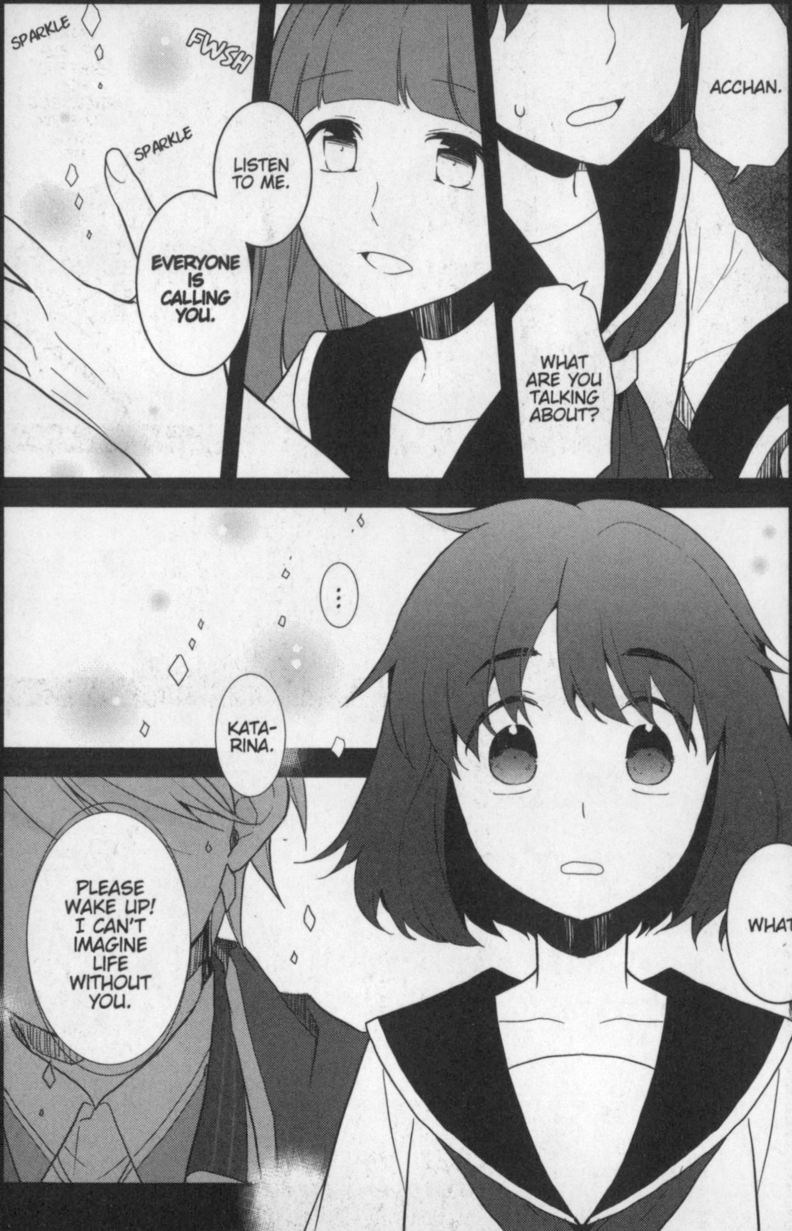
ACCHAN.
WHAT ARE YOU TALKING ABOUT?
FWSH
SPARKLE
LISTEN TO ME.
SPARKLE
EVERYONE IS CALLING YOU.
…
KATA-RINA.
PLEASE WAKE UP! I CAN'T IMAGINE LIFE WITHOUT YOU.
WHAT?

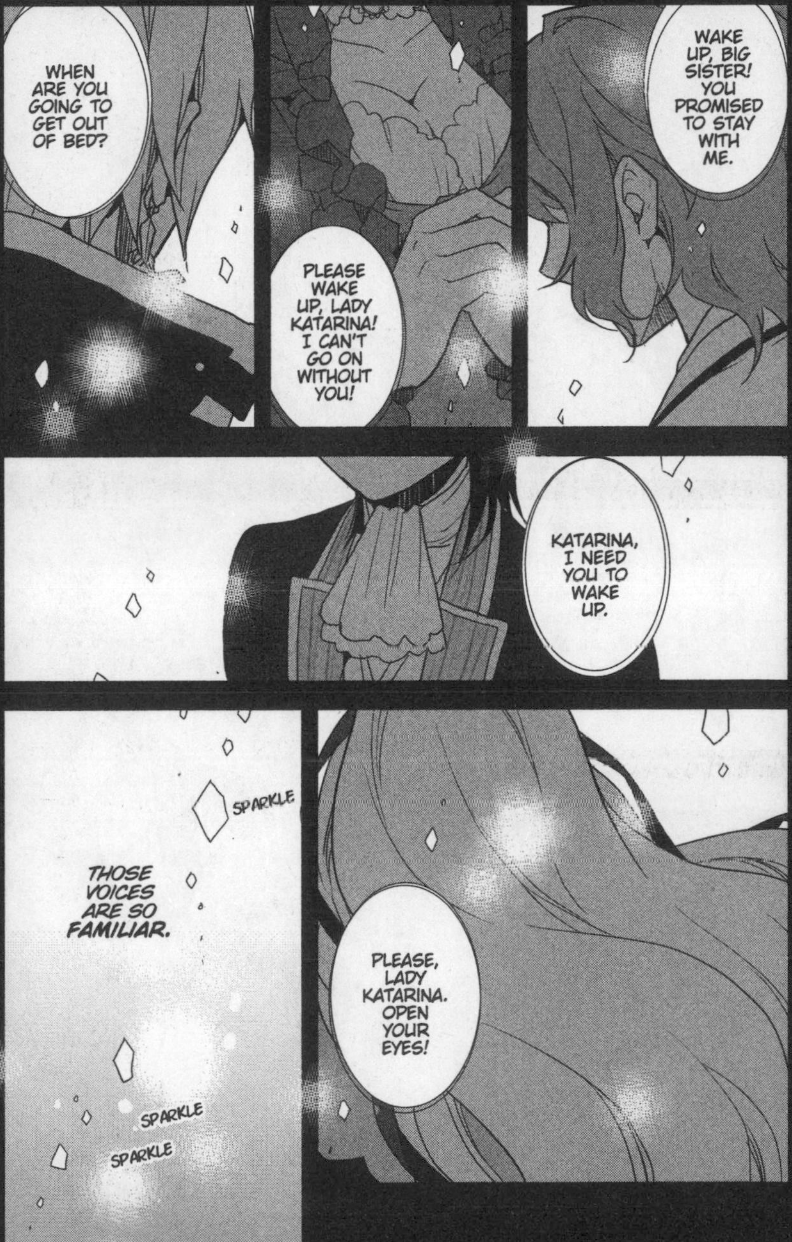
WAKE UP, BIG SISTER! YOU PROMISED TO STAY WITH ME.
PLEASE WAKE UP, LADY KATARINA! I CAN'T GO ON WITHOUT YOU!
WHEN ARE YOU GOING TO GET OUT OF BED?
KATARINA, I NEED YOU TO WAKE UP.
PLEASE, LADY KATARINA. OPEN YOUR EYES!
SPARKLE
THOSE VOICES ARE SO FAMILIAR.
SPARKLE
SPARKLE

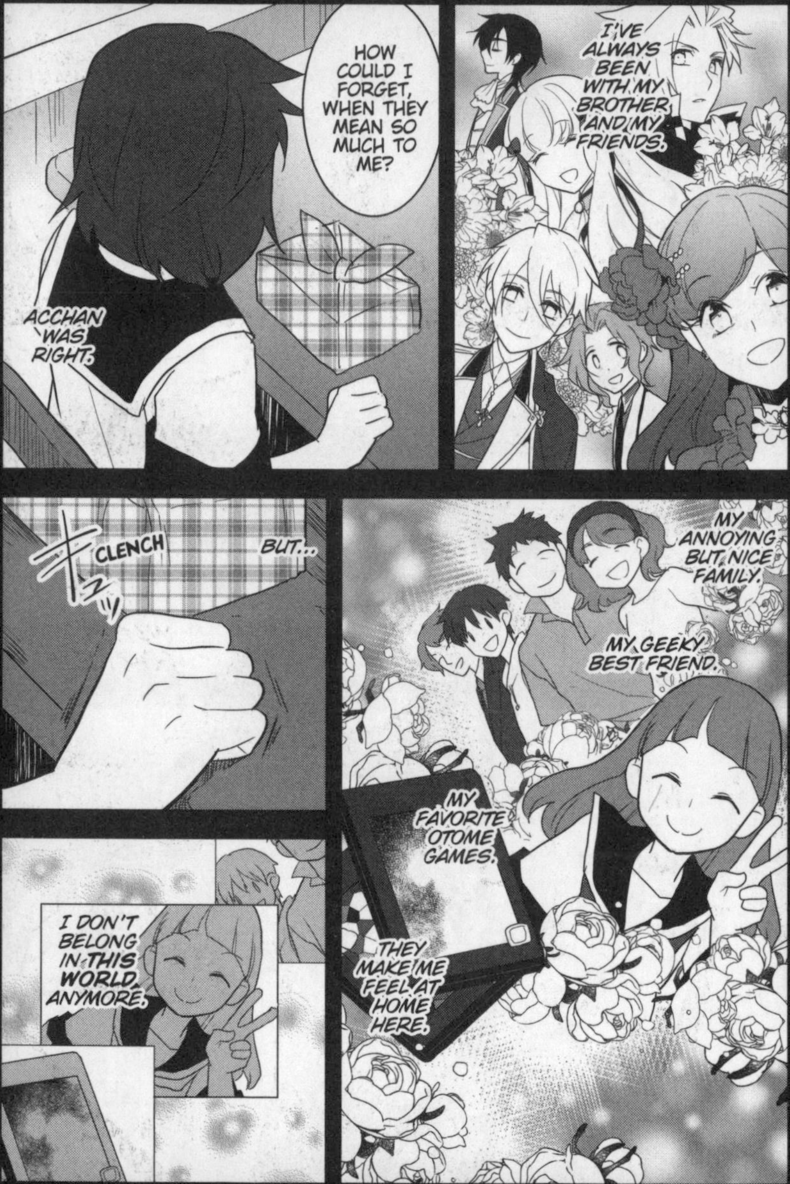
I'VE ALWAYS BEEN WITH MY BROTHER AND MY FRIENDS.
HOW COULD I FORGET, WHEN THEY MEAN SO MUCH TO ME?
ACCHAN WAS RIGHT.
MY ANNOYING BUT NICE FAMILY.
MY GEEKY BEST FRIEND.
MY FAVORITE OTOME GAMES.
THEY MAKE ME FEEL AT HOME HERE.
BUT...
CLENCH
I DON'T BELONG IN THIS WORLD ANYMORE.

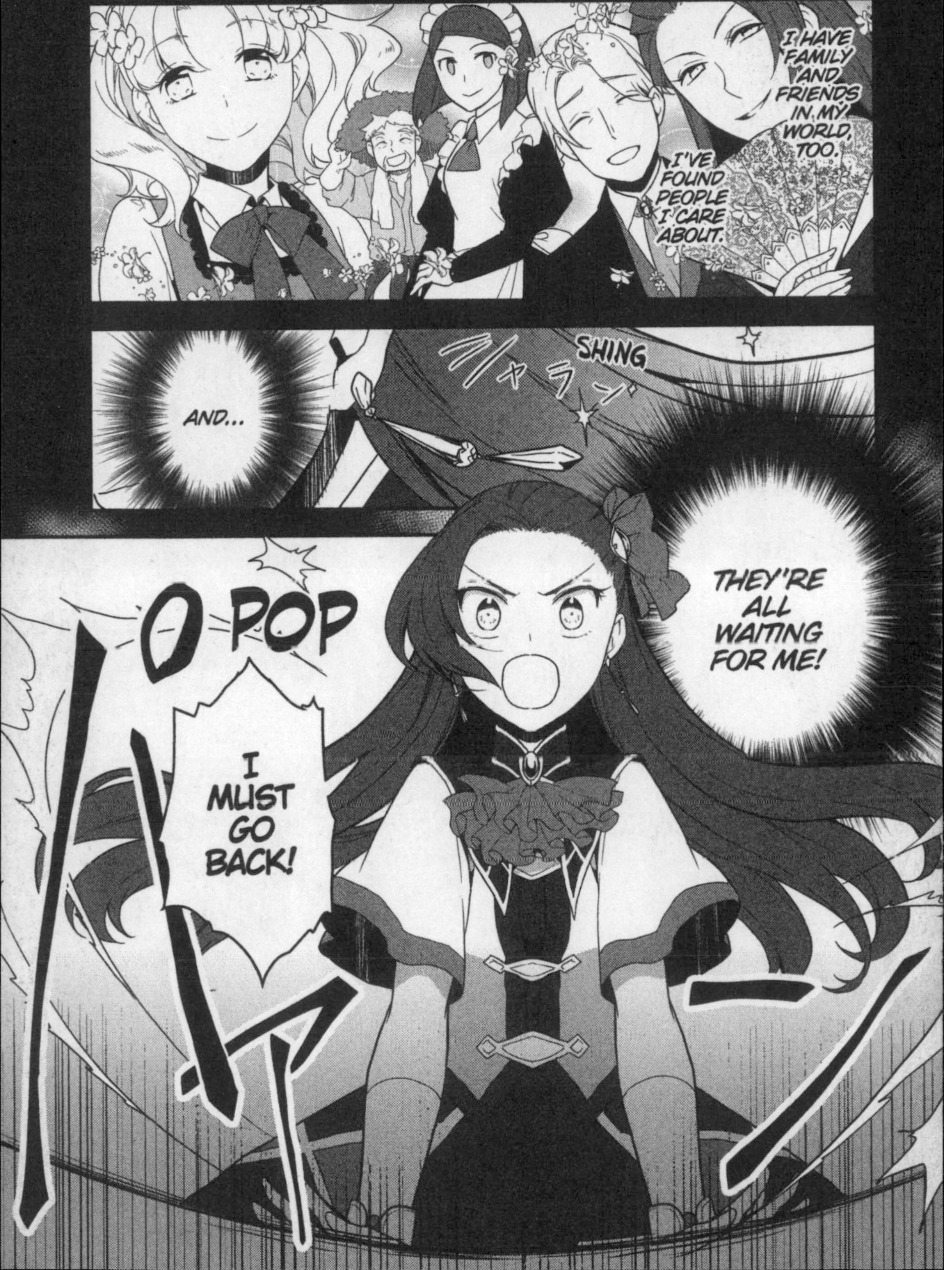
I HAVE FAMILY AND FRIENDS IN MY WORLD, TOO.
I'VE FOUND PEOPLE I CARE ABOUT.
SHING
AND...
THEY'RE ALL WAITING FOR ME!
POP
I MUST GO BACK!

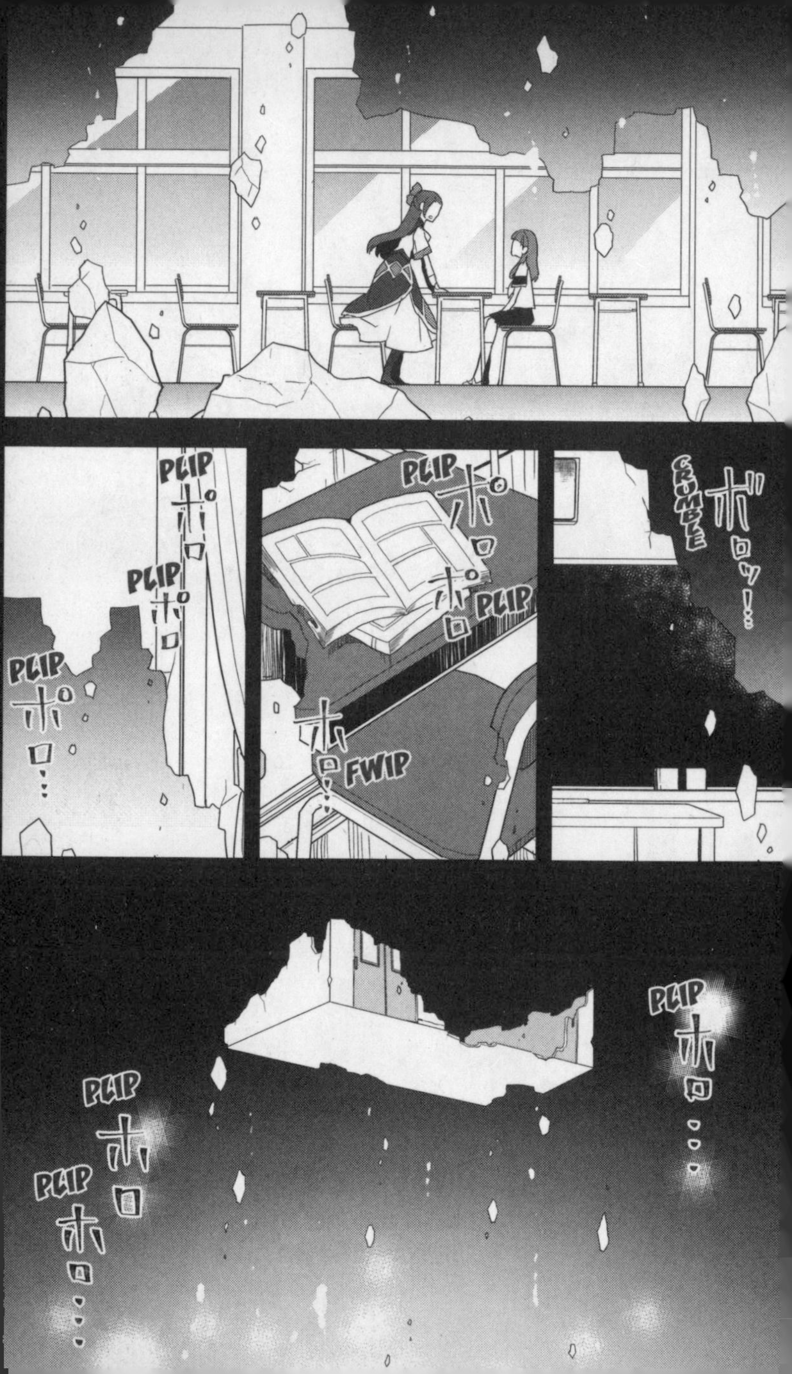
CRUMBLE
ボロッ…!!
PLIP
ポロ
ポロ
PLIP
ポロ…
FWIP
PLIP
ポロ
PLIP
ポロ
PLIP
ポロ…
PLIP
ポロ…
PLIP
ポロ
PLIP
ポロ…

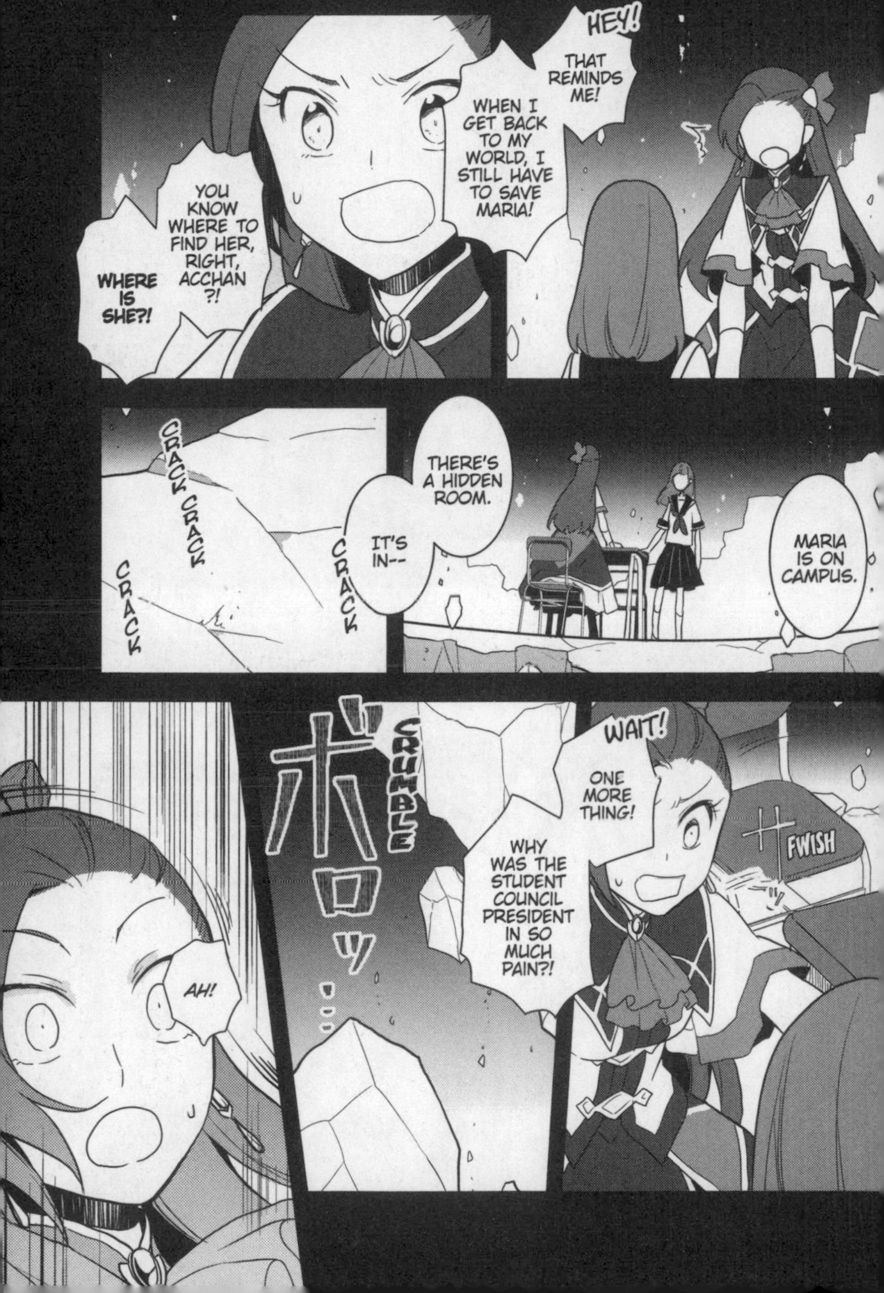
HEY!
THAT REMINDS ME!
WHEN I GET BACK TO MY WORLD, I STILL HAVE TO SAVE MARIA!
YOU KNOW WHERE TO FIND HER, RIGHT, ACCHAN?!
WHERE IS SHE?!
MARIA IS ON CAMPUS.
THERE'S A HIDDEN ROOM.
IT'S IN--
CRACK
CRACK CRACK
CRACK
WAIT!
ONE MORE THING!
WHY WAS THE STUDENT COUNCIL PRESIDENT IN SO MUCH PAIN?!
FWISH
ボロッ
CRUMBLE
AH!

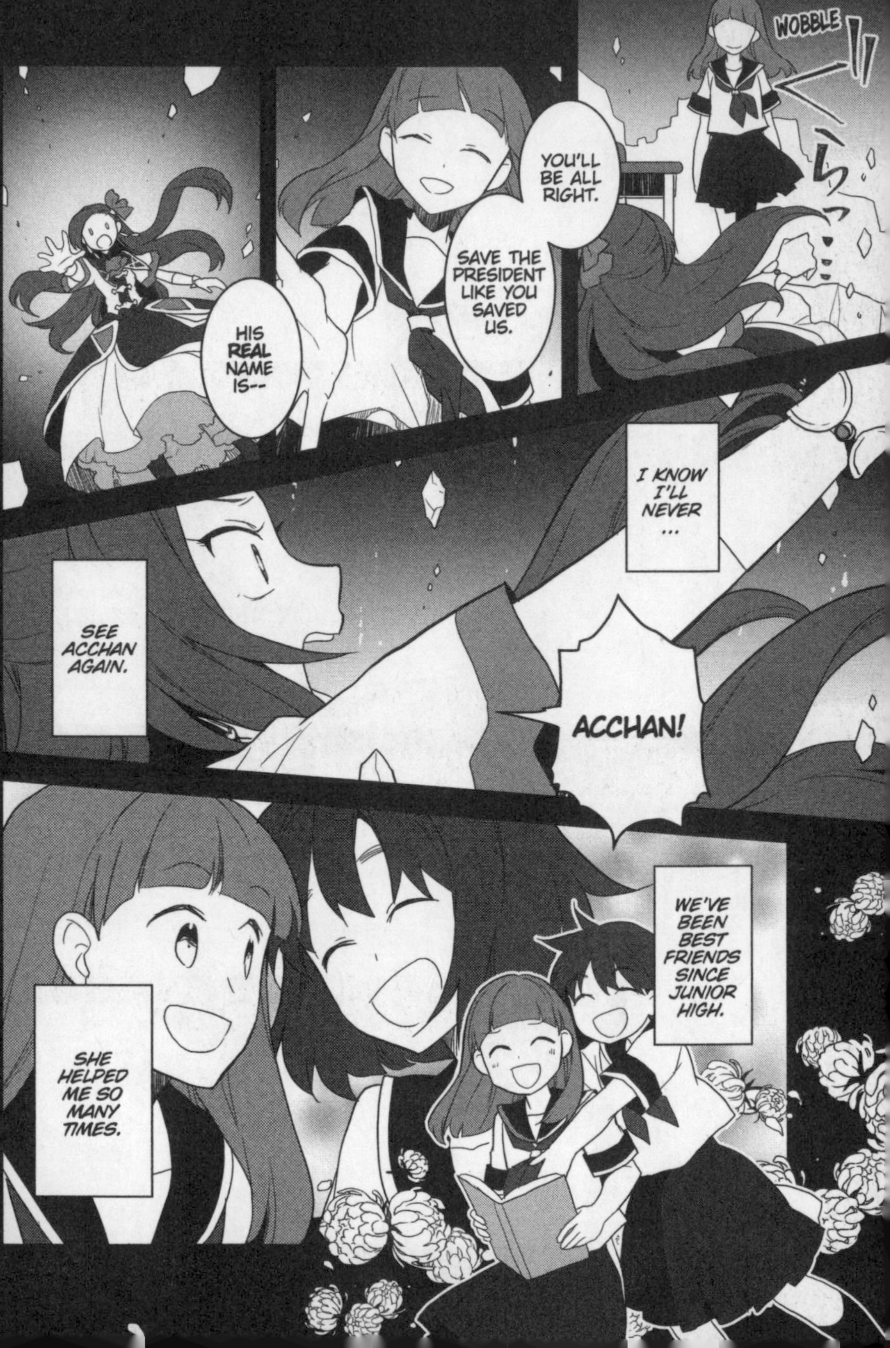
WOBBLE
YOU'LL BE ALL RIGHT.
SAVE THE PRESIDENT LIKE YOU SAVED US.
HIS REAL NAME IS--
I KNOW I'LL NEVER ...
SEE ACCHAN AGAIN.
ACCHAN!
WE'VE BEEN BEST FRIENDS SINCE JUNIOR HIGH.
SHE HELPED ME SO MANY TIMES.

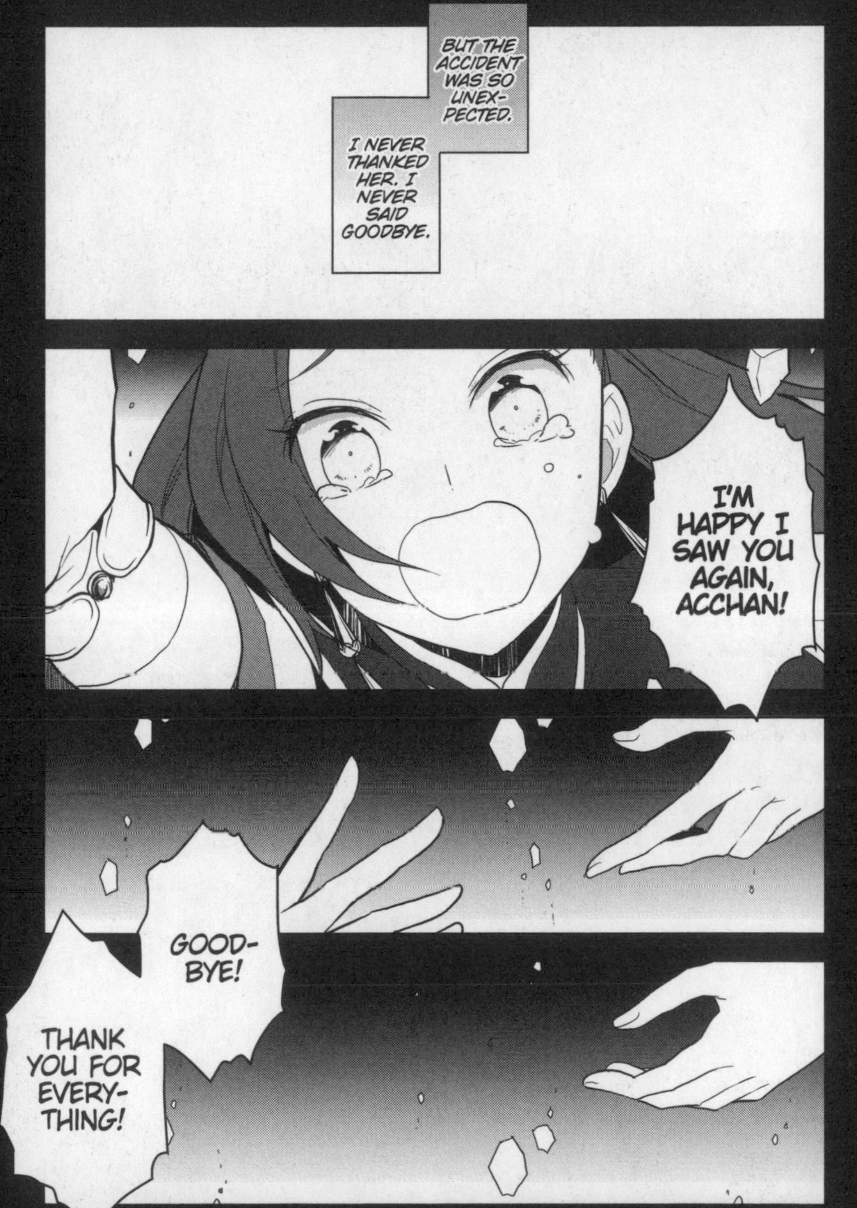
BUT THE ACCIDENT WAS SO UNEXPECTED.
I NEVER THANKED HER. I NEVER SAID GOODBYE.
I'M HAPPY I SAW YOU AGAIN, ACCHAN!
GOODBYE!
THANK YOU FOR EVERYTHING!

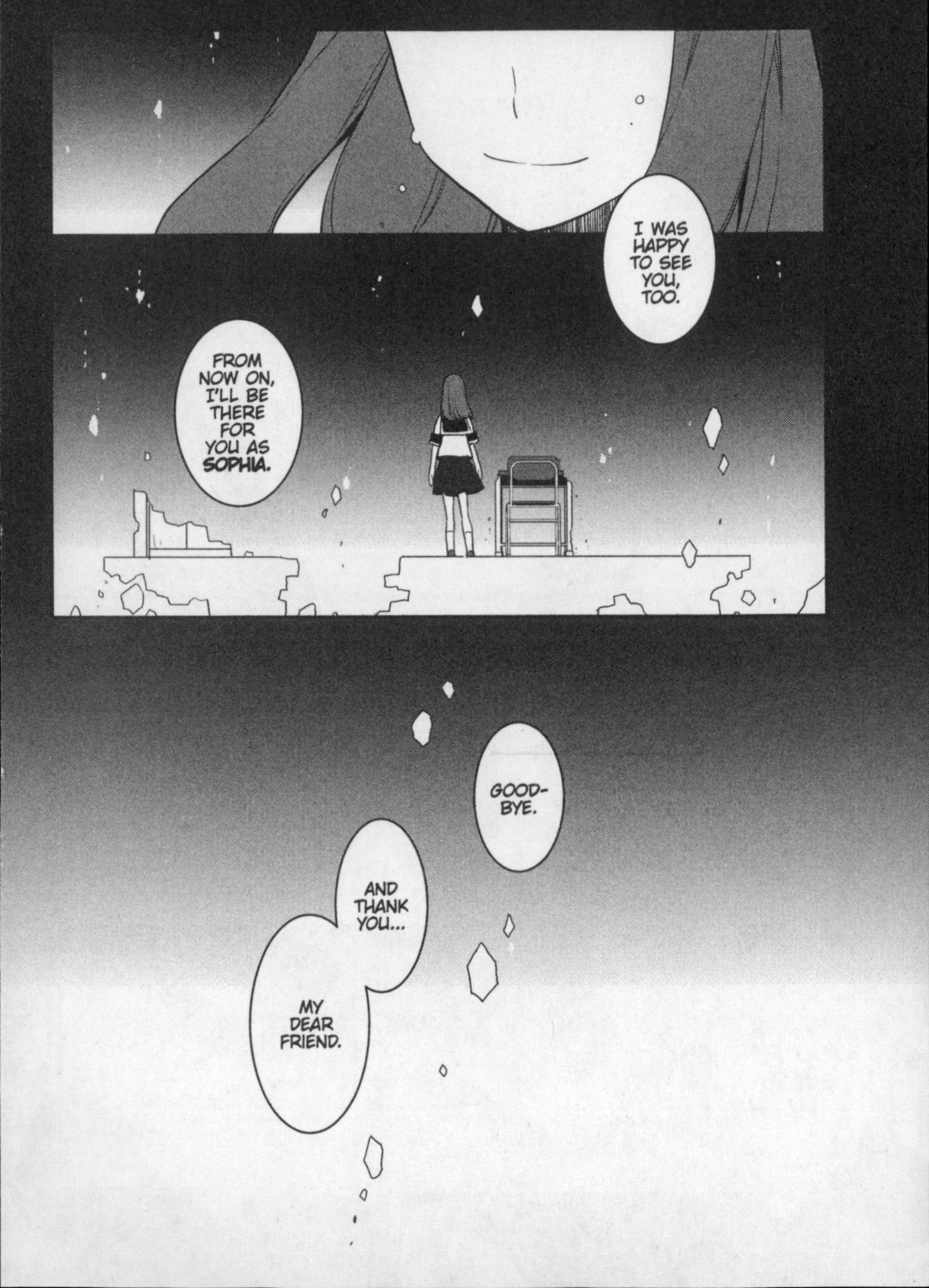
I WAS HAPPY TO SEE YOU, TOO.
FROM NOW ON, I'LL BE THERE FOR YOU AS SOPHIA.
GOOD-BYE.
AND THANK YOU...
MY DEAR FRIEND.

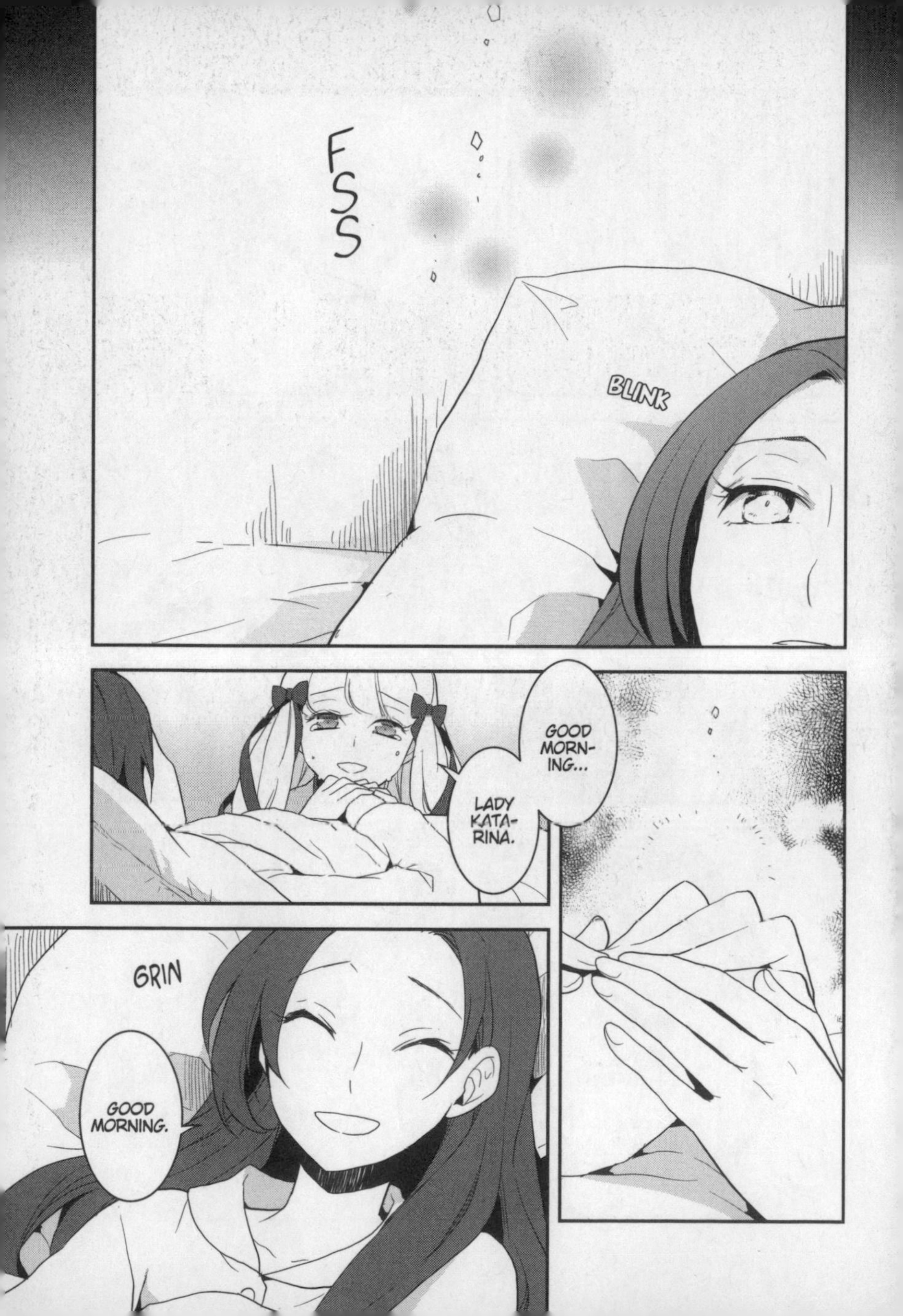
FSS
BLINK
GOOD MORNING...
LADY KATARINA.
GRIN
GOOD MORNING.

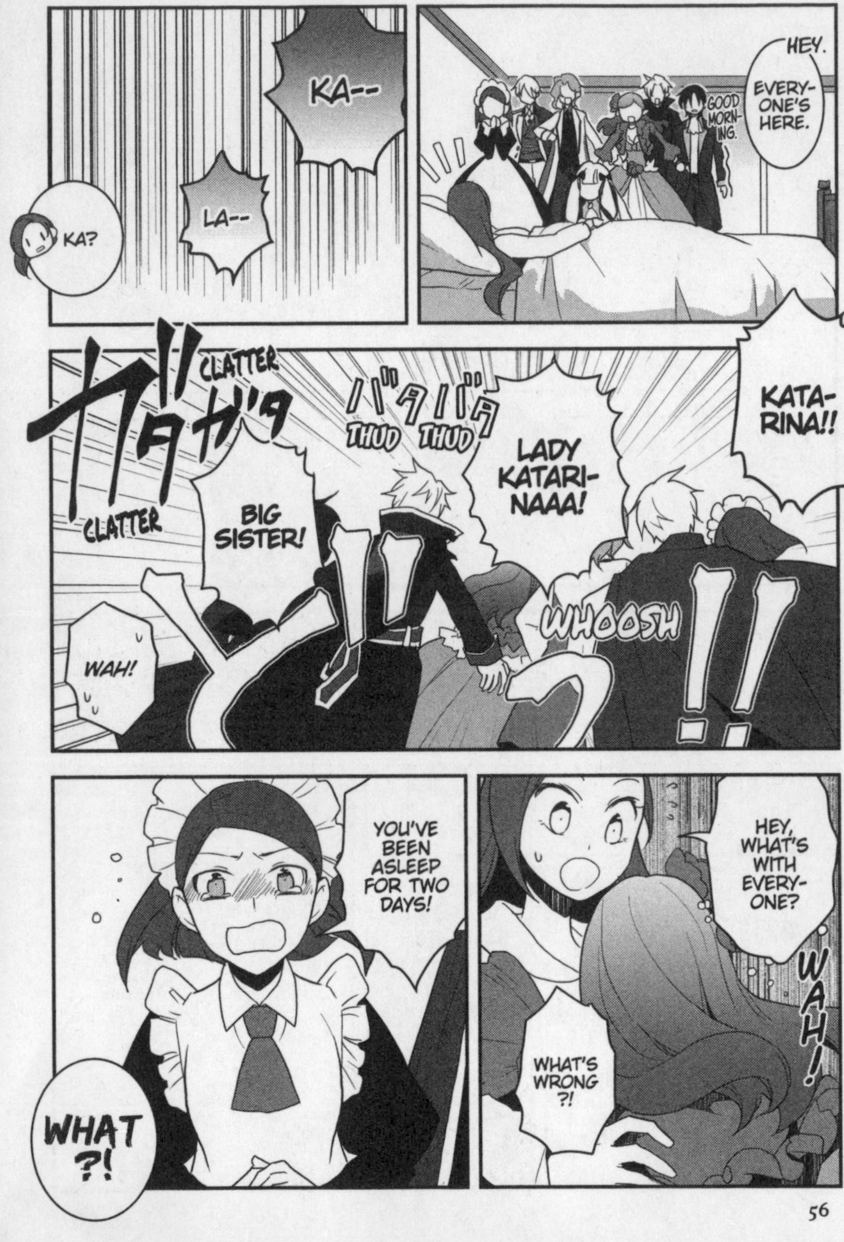
HEY.
EVERY-ONE'S HERE.
GOOD MORN-ING.
KA--
LA--
KA?
KATA-RINA!!
LADY KATARI-NAAA!
バタバタ
THUD THUD
BIG SISTER!
ガタガタ
CLATTER
CLATTER
WHOOSH
WAH!
HEY, WHAT'S WITH EVERY-ONE?
WAH!
WHAT'S WRONG?!
YOU'VE BEEN ASLEEP FOR TWO DAYS!
WHAT?!

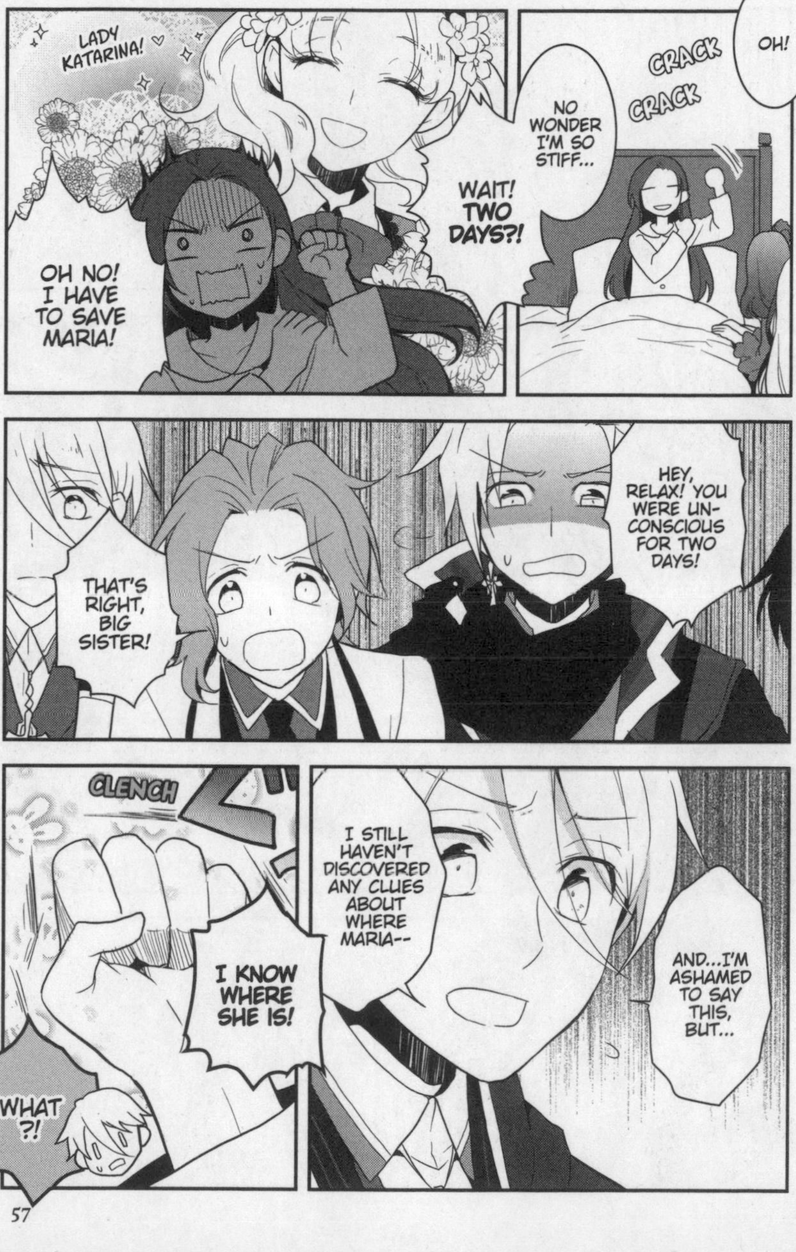
OH!
CRACK
CRACK
NO WONDER I'M SO STIFF...
WAIT! TWO DAYS?!
LADY KATARINA! ♡
OH NO! I HAVE TO SAVE MARIA!
HEY, RELAX! YOU WERE UN-CONSCIOUS FOR TWO DAYS!
THAT'S RIGHT, BIG SISTER!
AND...I'M ASHAMED TO SAY THIS, BUT...
I STILL HAVEN'T DISCOVERED ANY CLUES ABOUT WHERE MARIA--
CLENCH
I KNOW WHERE SHE IS!
WHAT ?!

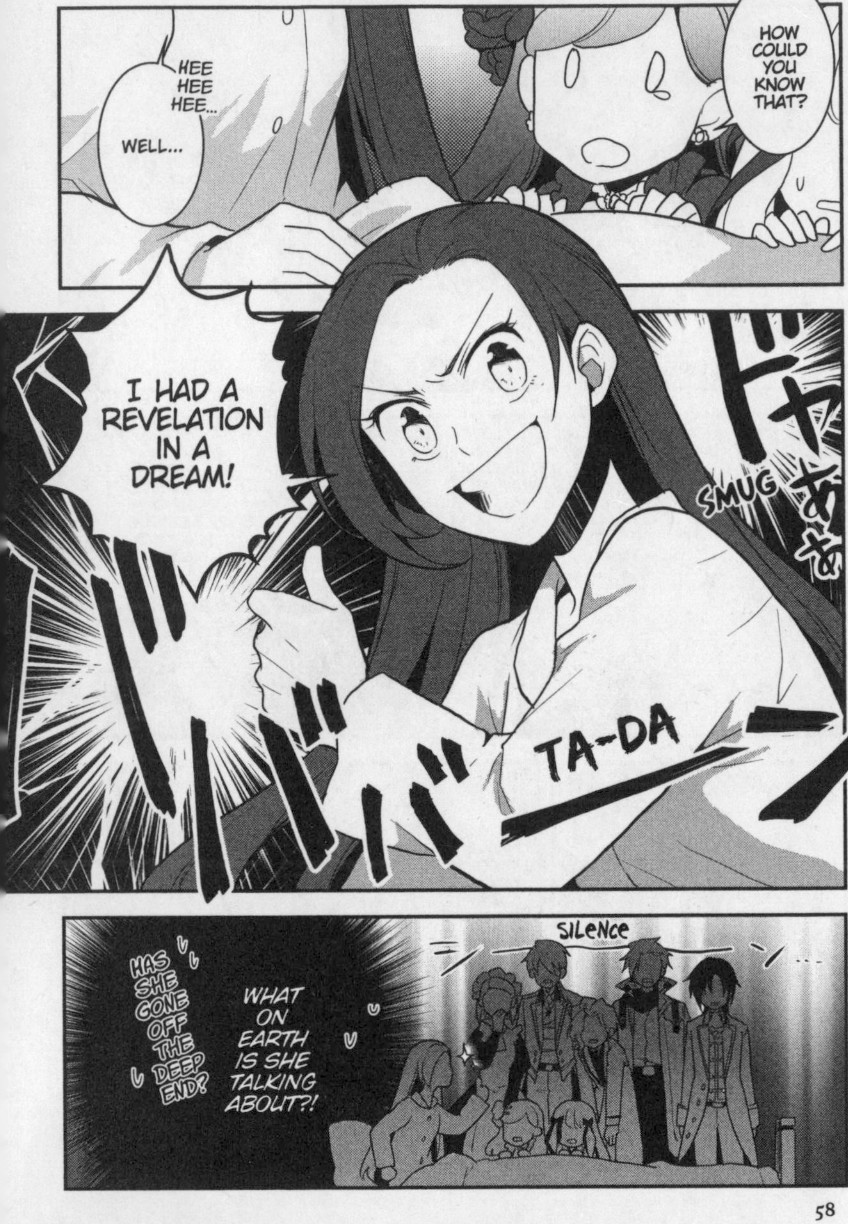
HOW COULD YOU KNOW THAT?
HEE HEE HEE...
WELL...
I HAD A REVELATION IN A DREAM!
SMUG
TA-DA
SILENCE
WHAT ON EARTH IS SHE TALKING ABOUT?!
HAS SHE GONE OFF THE DEEP END?

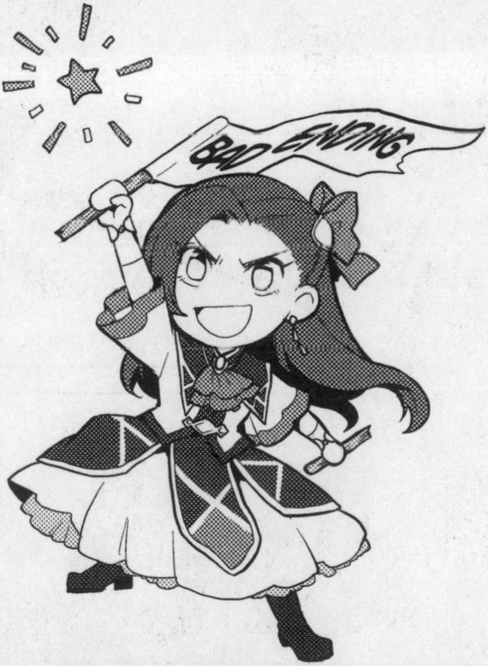
BAD ENDING

My Next Life
as a VILLAINESS:
ALL ROUTES
LEAD TO DOOM!

Chapter 20

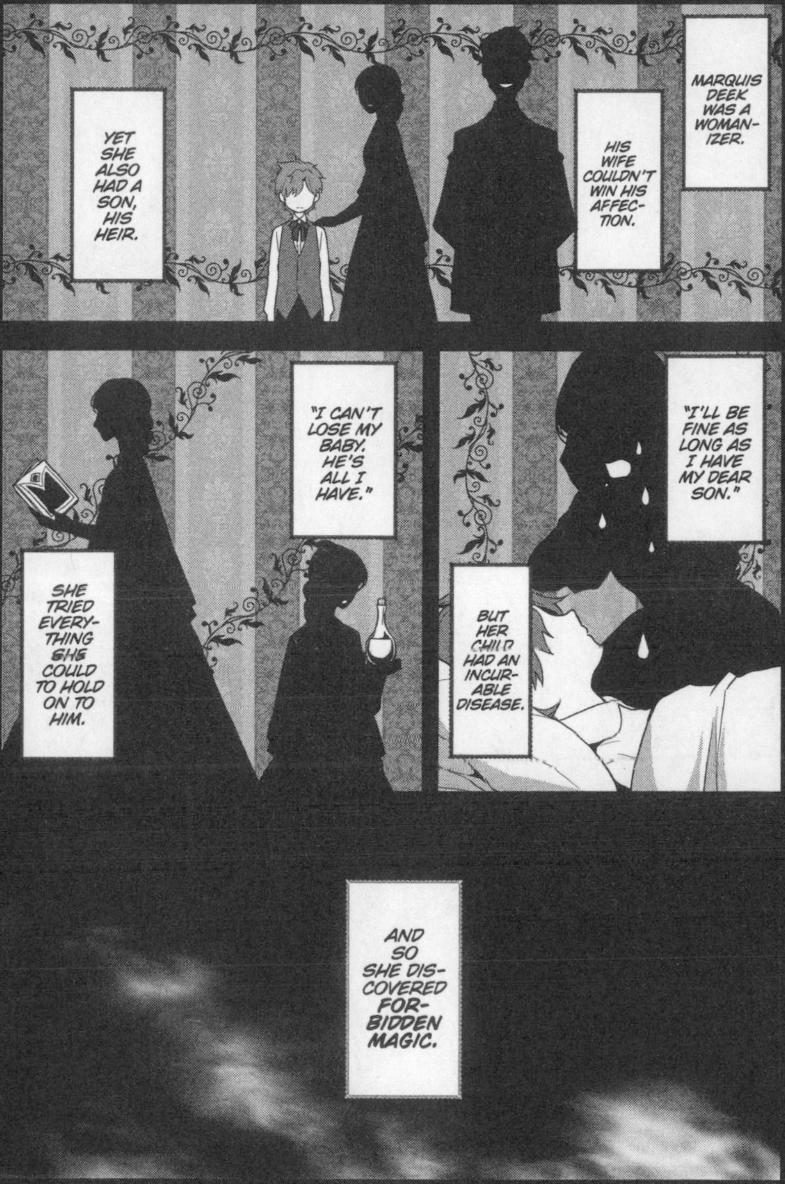

MARQUIS DEEK WAS A WOMANIZER.
HIS WIFE COULDN'T WIN HIS AFFECTION.
YET SHE ALSO HAD A SON, HIS HEIR.
"I'LL BE FINE AS LONG AS I HAVE MY DEAR SON."
BUT HER CHILD HAD AN INCURABLE DISEASE.
"I CAN'T LOSE MY BABY. HE'S ALL I HAVE."
SHE TRIED EVERYTHING SHE COULD TO HOLD ON TO HIM.
AND SO SHE DISCOVERED FORBIDDEN MAGIC.

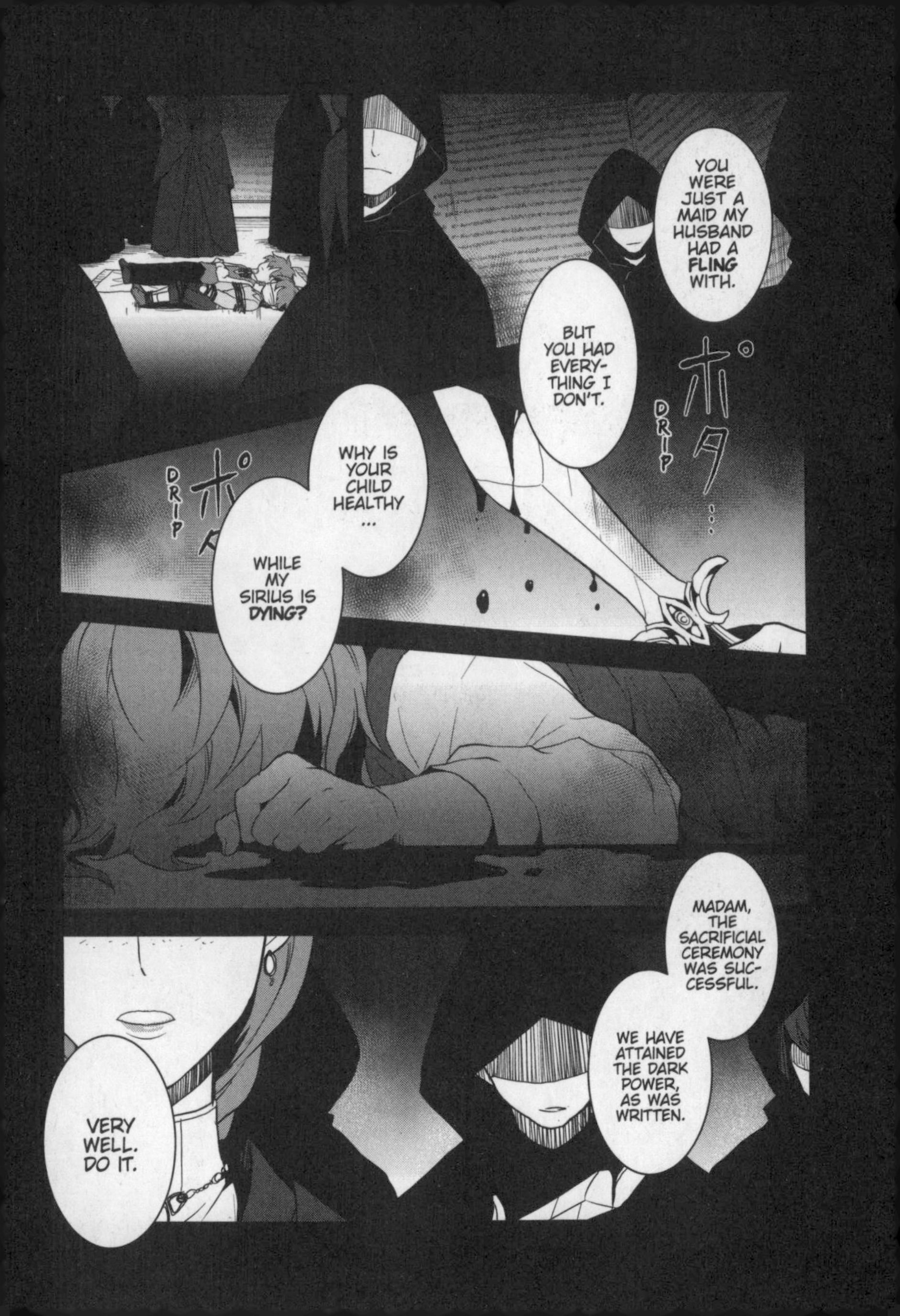
YOU WERE JUST A MAID MY HUSBAND HAD A **FLING** WITH.
BUT YOU HAD EVERY-THING I DON'T.
ポタ…
DRIP
WHY IS YOUR CHILD HEALTHY ...
WHILE MY SIRIUS IS **DYING?**
ポタ
DRIP
MADAM, THE SACRIFICIAL CEREMONY WAS SUC-CESSFUL.
WE HAVE ATTAINED THE DARK POWER, AS WAS WRITTEN.
VERY WELL. DO IT.

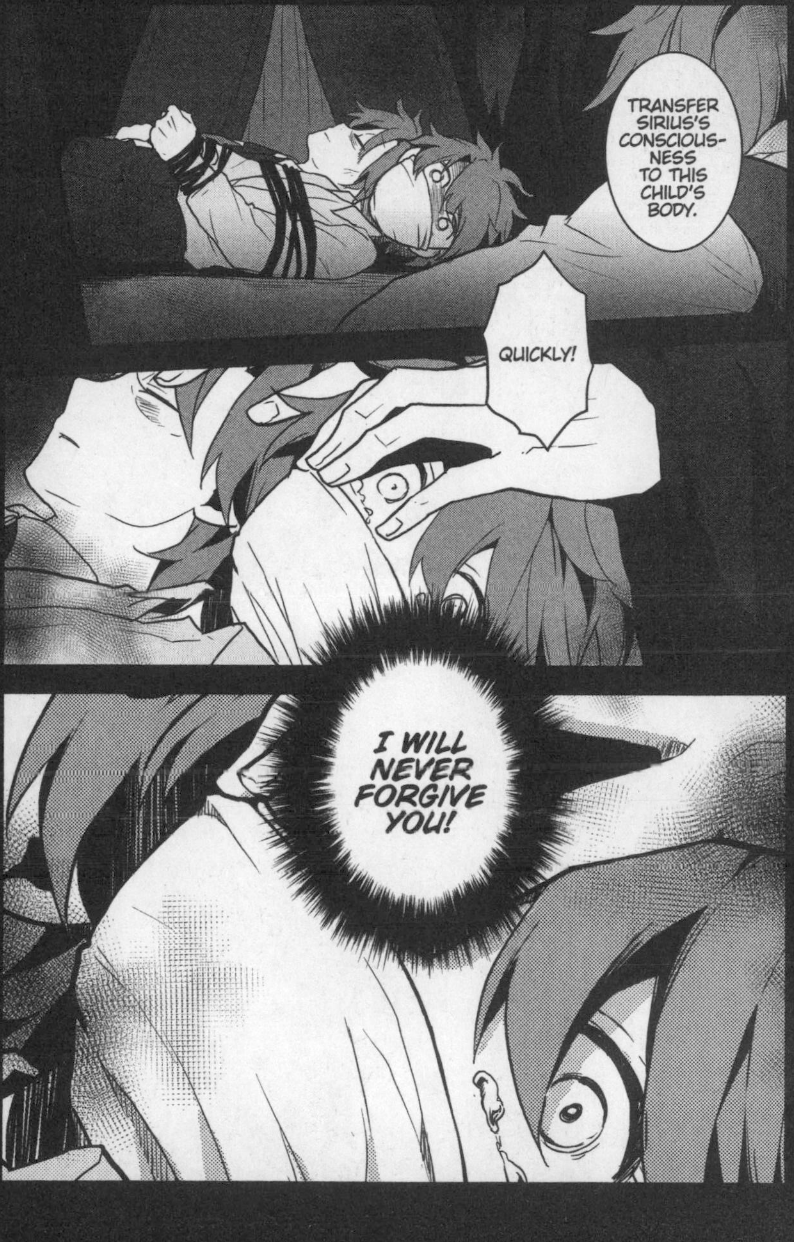
TRANSFER SIRIUS'S CONSCIOUS-NESS TO THIS CHILD'S BODY.
QUICKLY!
I WILL NEVER FORGIVE YOU!

Chapter 20: The Approaching Footsteps of Doom (Part 8)

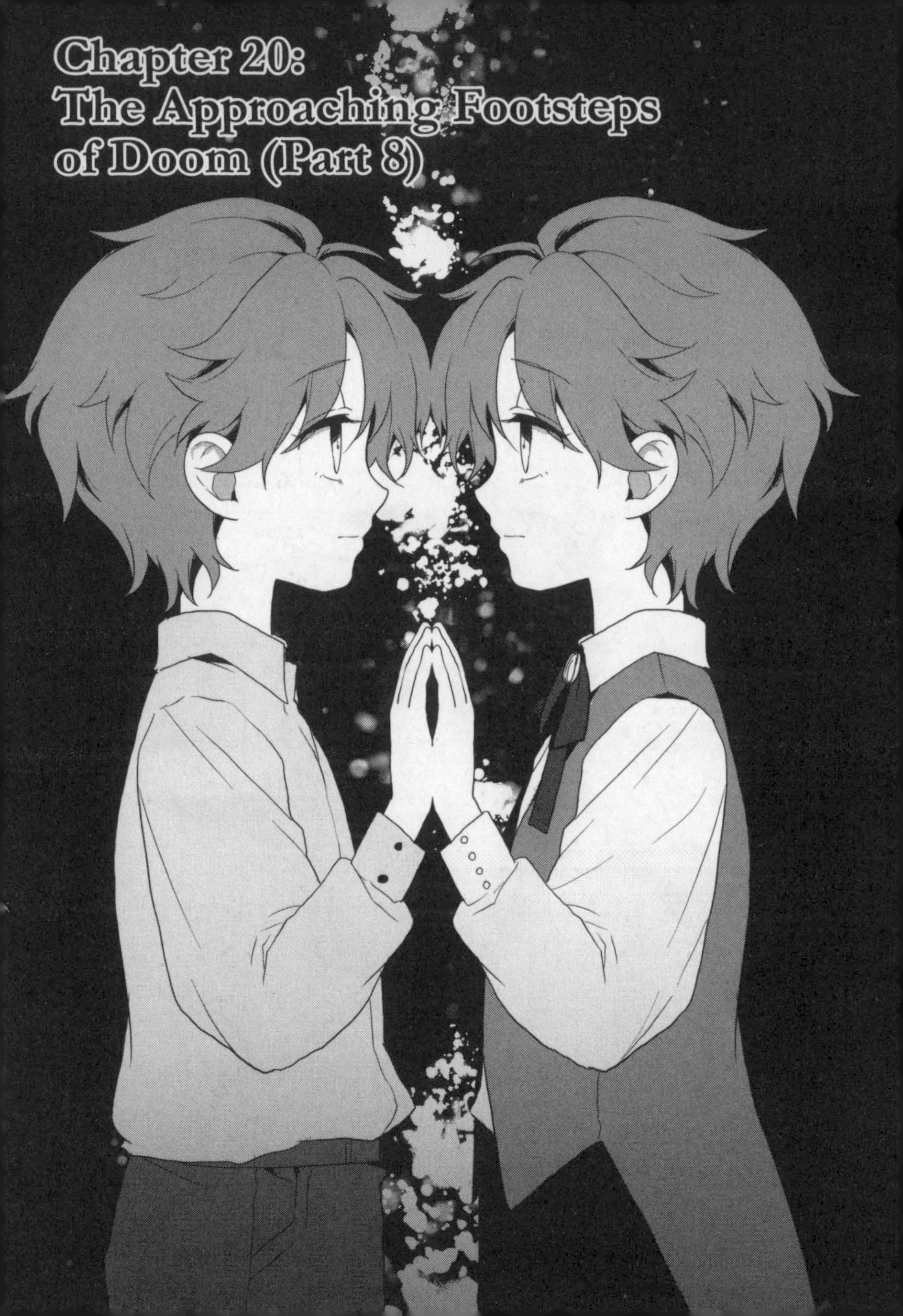

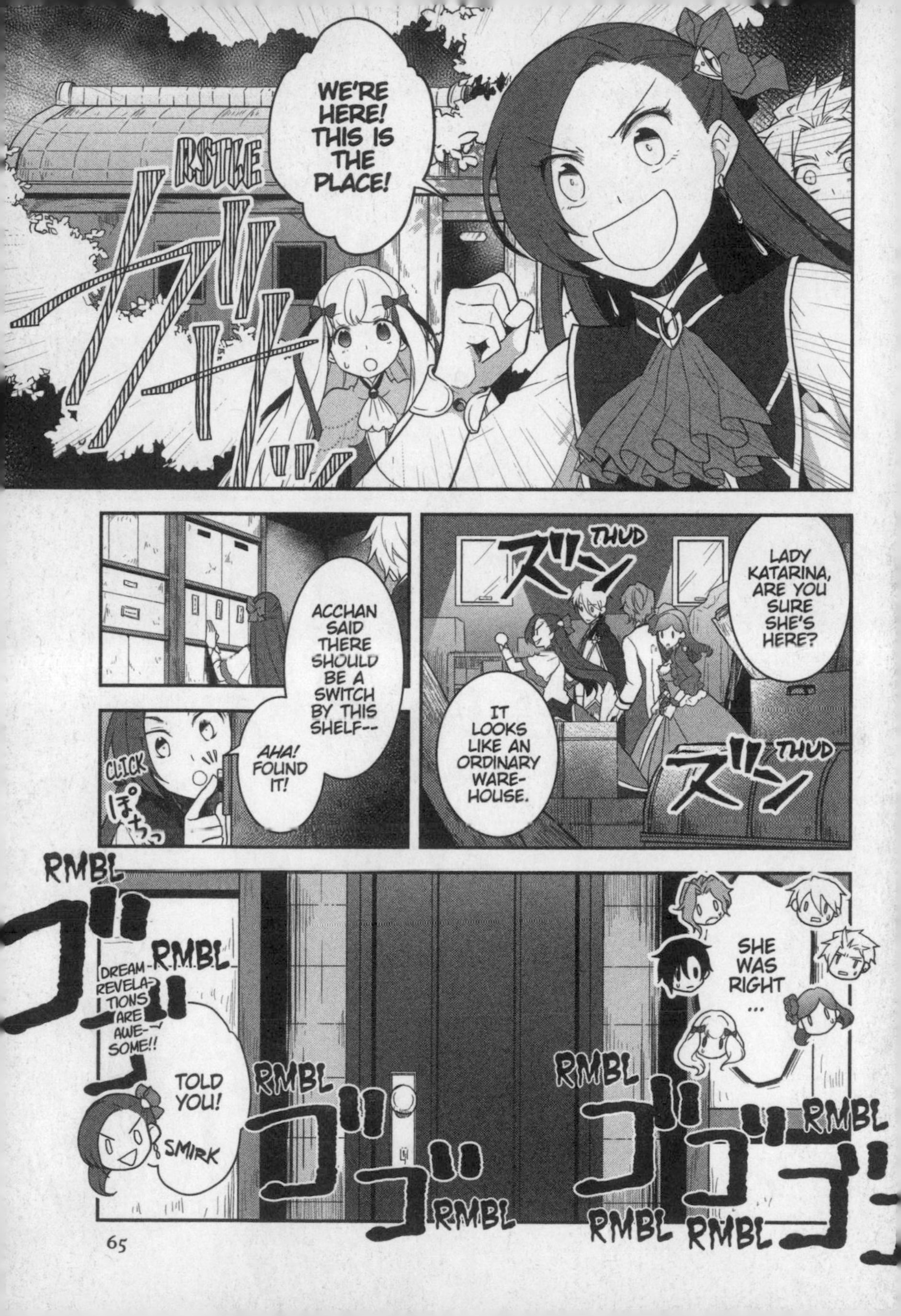
WE'RE HERE! THIS IS THE PLACE!
RSTLE
THUD
LADY KATARINA, ARE YOU SURE SHE'S HERE?
IT LOOKS LIKE AN ORDINARY WAREHOUSE.
THUD
ACCHAN SAID THERE SHOULD BE A SWITCH BY THIS SHELF--
AHA! FOUND IT!
CLICK
SHE WAS RIGHT ...
RMBL
RMBL
RMBL
RMBL
RMBL
RMBL
RMBL
RMBL
DREAM-REVELATIONS ARE AWESOME!!
TOLD YOU!
SMIRK

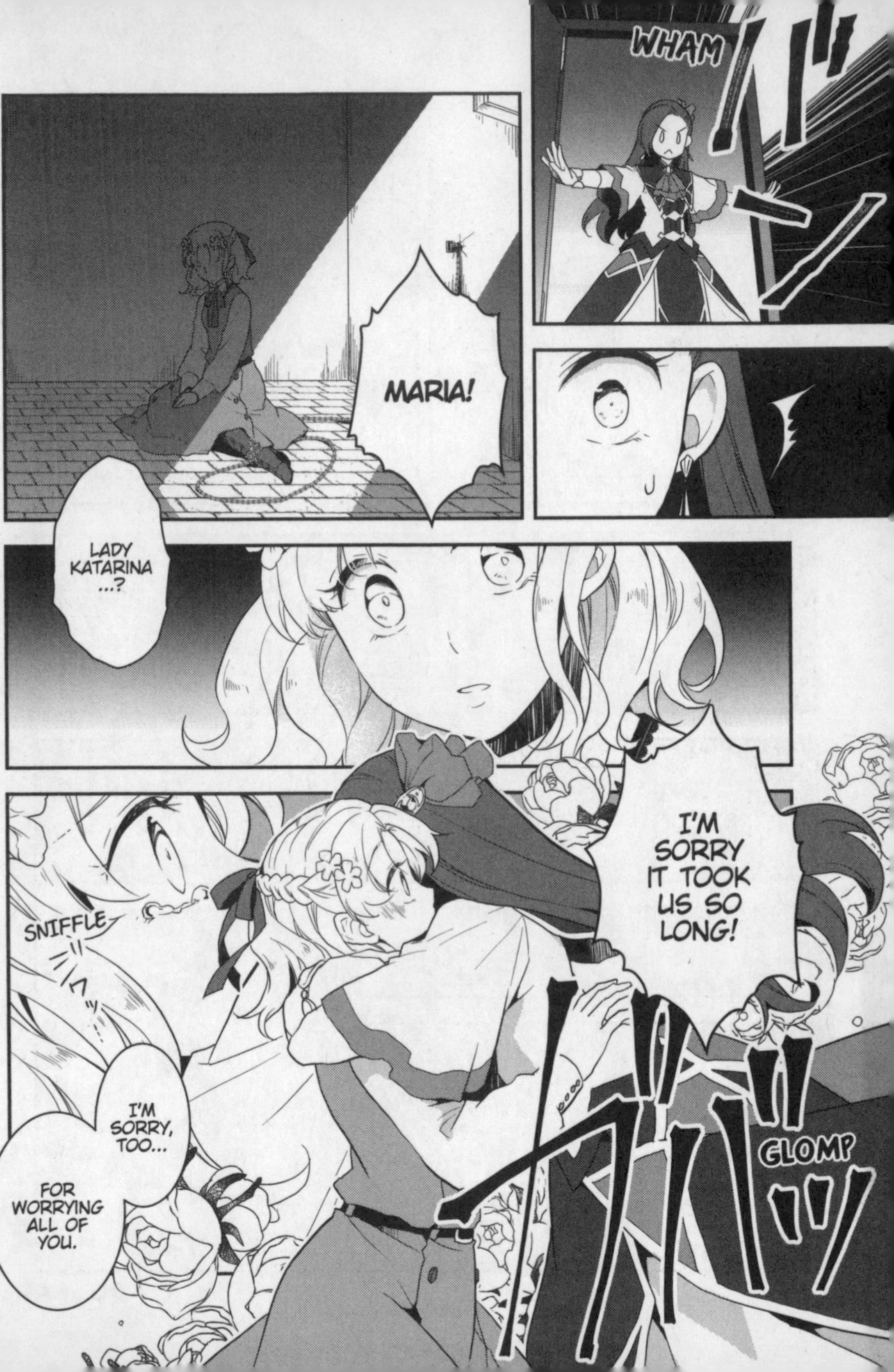
WHAM
MARIA!
LADY KATARINA ...?
I'M SORRY IT TOOK US SO LONG!
GLOMP
SNIFFLE
I'M SORRY, TOO...
FOR WORRYING ALL OF YOU.

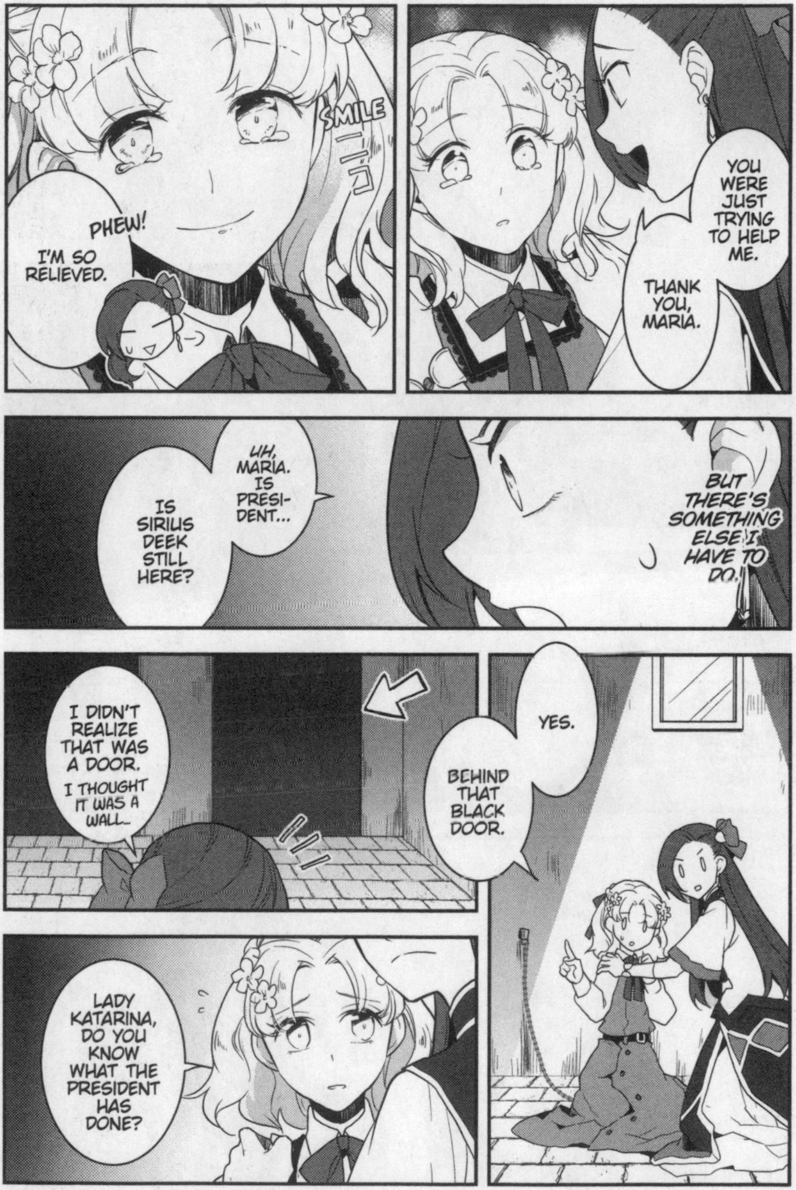
YOU WERE JUST TRYING TO HELP ME.
THANK YOU, MARIA.
SMILE
PHEW!
I'M SO RELIEVED.
BUT THERE'S SOMETHING ELSE I HAVE TO DO.
UH, MARIA. IS PRESIDENT...
IS SIRIUS DEEK STILL HERE?
YES.
BEHIND THAT BLACK DOOR.
I DIDN'T REALIZE THAT WAS A DOOR.
I THOUGHT IT WAS A WALL...
LADY KATARINA, DO YOU KNOW WHAT THE PRESIDENT HAS DONE?

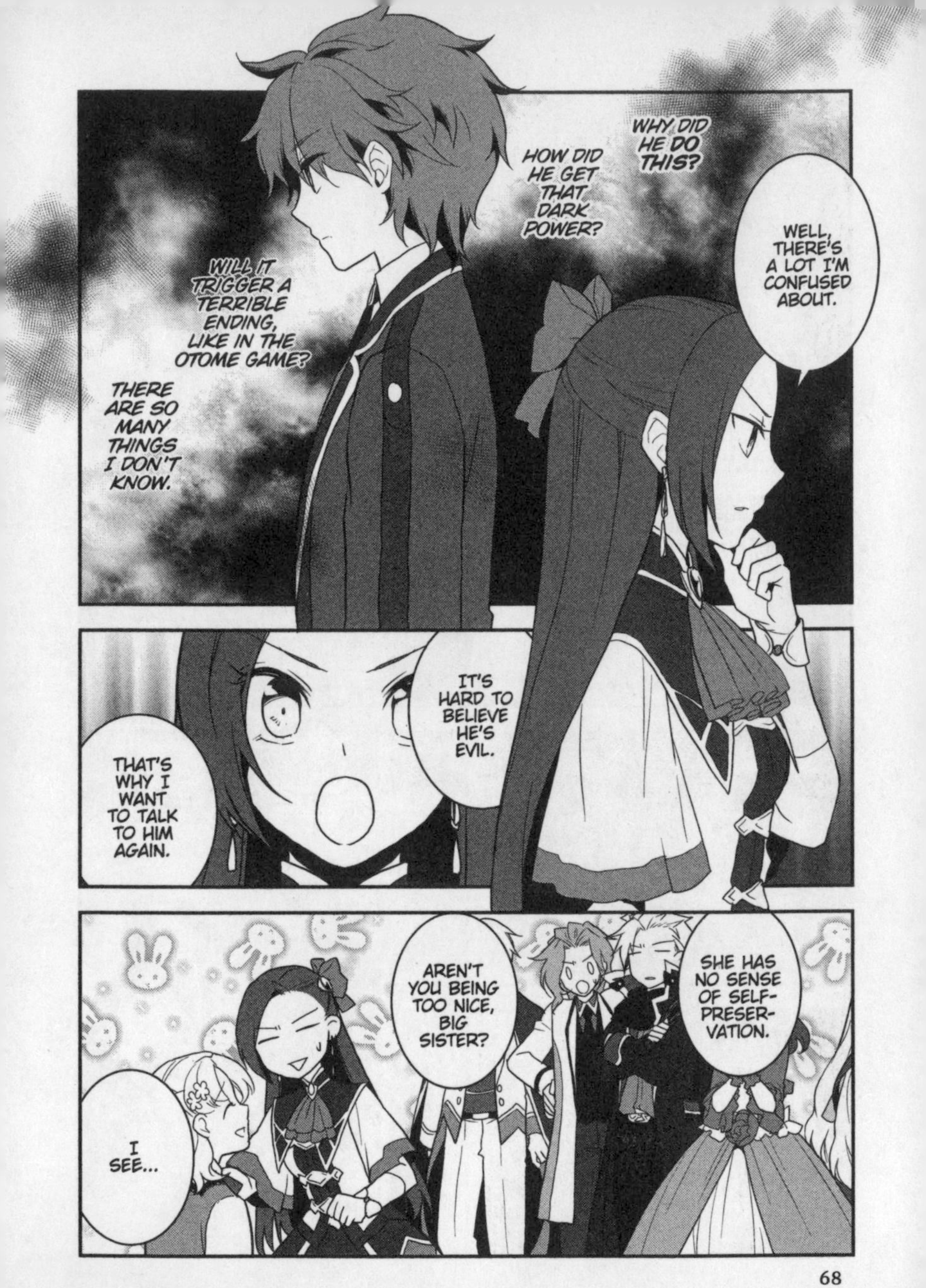
WHY DID HE DO THIS?
HOW DID HE GET THAT DARK POWER?
WELL, THERE'S A LOT I'M CONFUSED ABOUT.
WILL IT TRIGGER A TERRIBLE ENDING, LIKE IN THE OTOME GAME?
THERE ARE SO MANY THINGS I DON'T KNOW.
IT'S HARD TO BELIEVE HE'S EVIL.
THAT'S WHY I WANT TO TALK TO HIM AGAIN.
SHE HAS NO SENSE OF SELF-PRESER-VATION.
AREN'T YOU BEING TOO NICE, BIG SISTER?
I SEE...

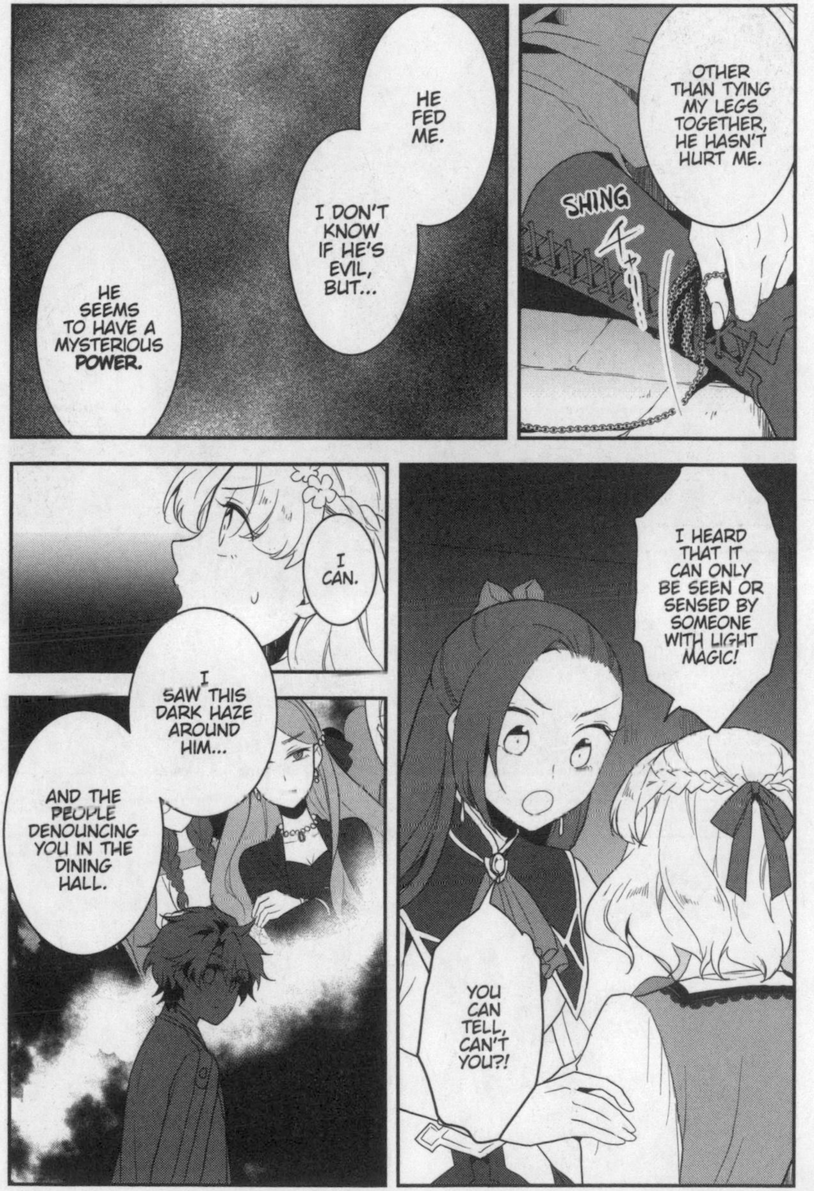
OTHER THAN TYING MY LEGS TOGETHER, HE HASN'T HURT ME.
SHING
HE FED ME.
I DON'T KNOW IF HE'S EVIL, BUT...
HE SEEMS TO HAVE A MYSTERIOUS POWER.
I HEARD THAT IT CAN ONLY BE SEEN OR SENSED BY SOMEONE WITH LIGHT MAGIC!
YOU CAN TELL, CAN'T YOU?!
I CAN.
I SAW THIS DARK HAZE AROUND HIM...
AND THE PEOPLE DENOUNCING YOU IN THE DINING HALL.

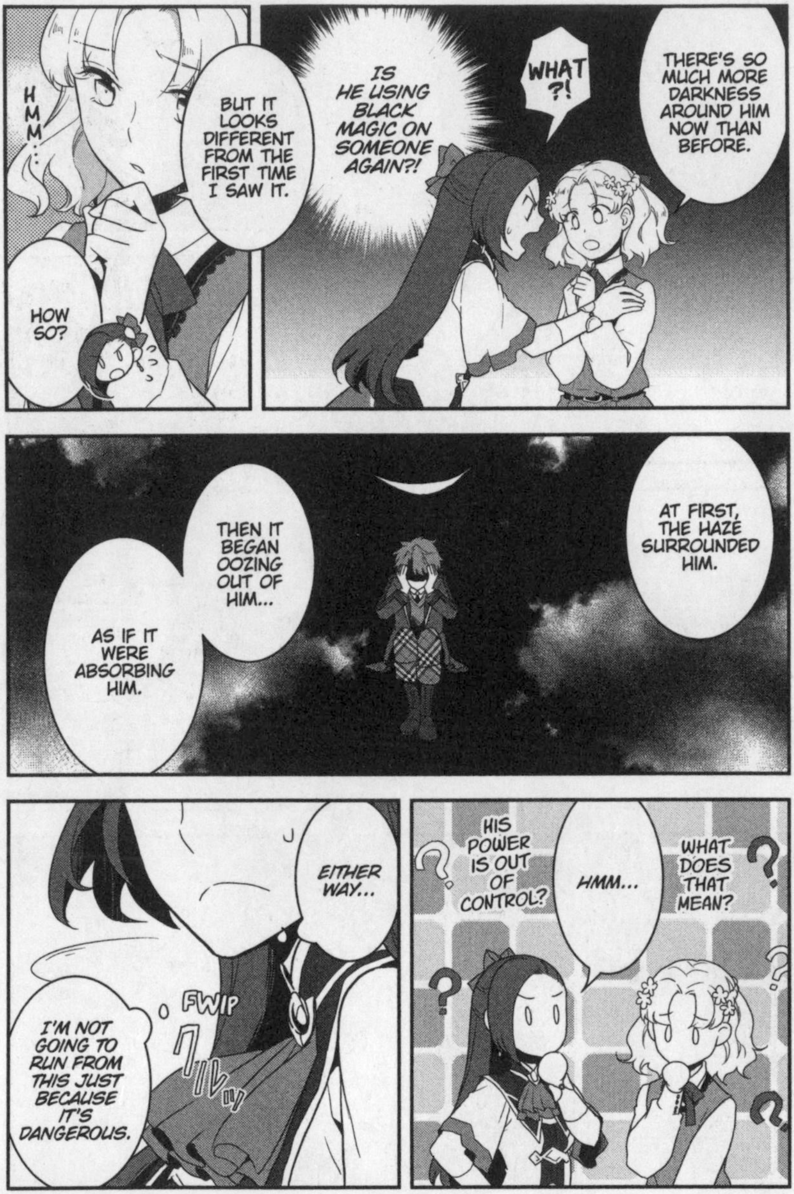
THERE'S SO MUCH MORE DARKNESS AROUND HIM NOW THAN BEFORE.
WHAT?!
IS HE USING BLACK MAGIC ON SOMEONE AGAIN?!
BUT IT LOOKS DIFFERENT FROM THE FIRST TIME I SAW IT.
HMM...
HOW SO?
AT FIRST, THE HAZE SURROUNDED HIM.
THEN IT BEGAN OOZING OUT OF HIM...
AS IF IT WERE ABSORBING HIM.
WHAT DOES THAT MEAN?
HMM...
HIS POWER IS OUT OF CONTROL?
EITHER WAY...
FWIP
I'M NOT GOING TO RUN FROM THIS JUST BECAUSE IT'S DANGEROUS.

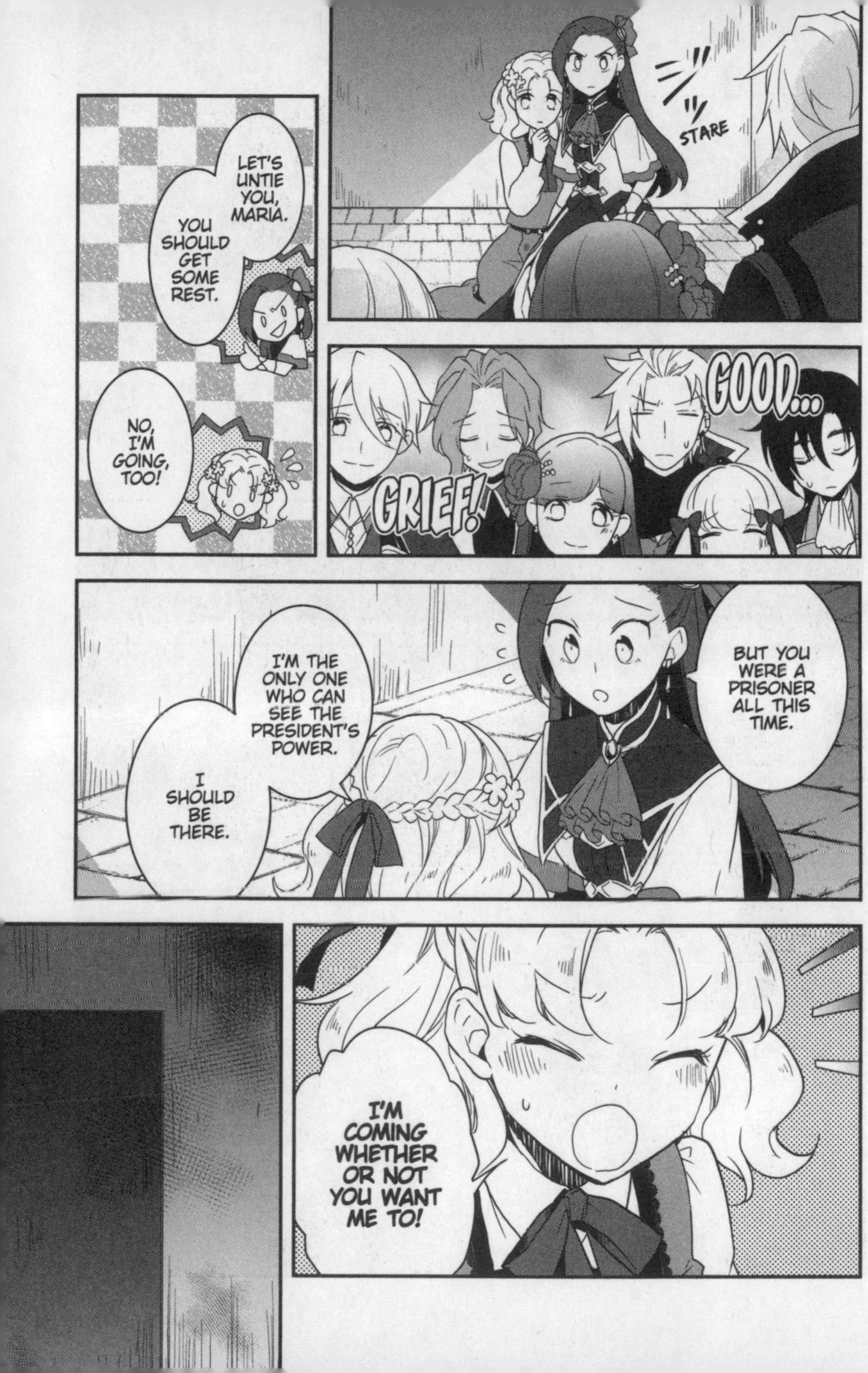
STARE
GOOD...
GRIEF!
LET'S UNTIE YOU, MARIA.
YOU SHOULD GET SOME REST.
NO, I'M GOING, TOO!
BUT YOU WERE A PRISONER ALL THIS TIME.
I'M THE ONLY ONE WHO CAN SEE THE PRESIDENT'S POWER.
I SHOULD BE THERE.
I'M COMING WHETHER OR NOT YOU WANT ME TO!

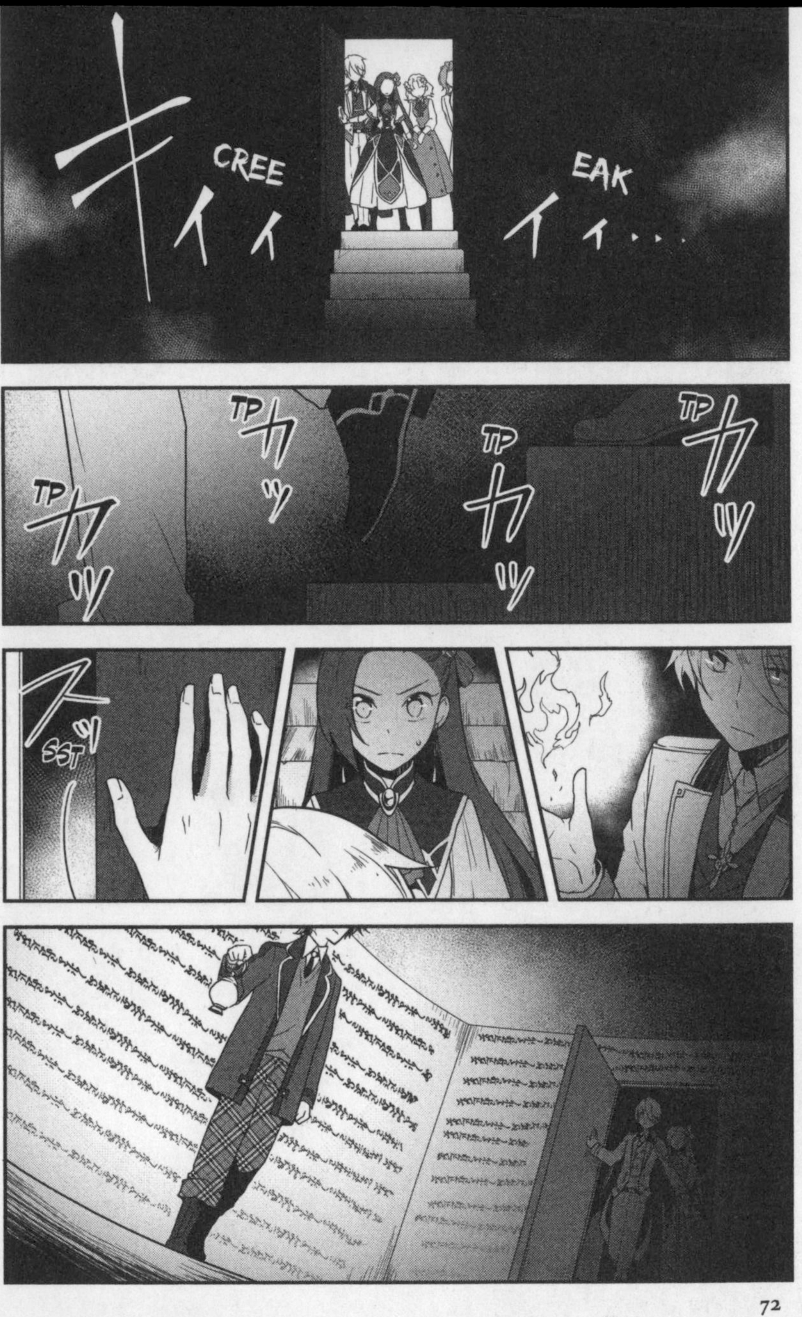
キイイ
CREE
EAK
イイ...
TP
カッ
TP
カッ
TP
カッ
TP
カッ
スッ
SST

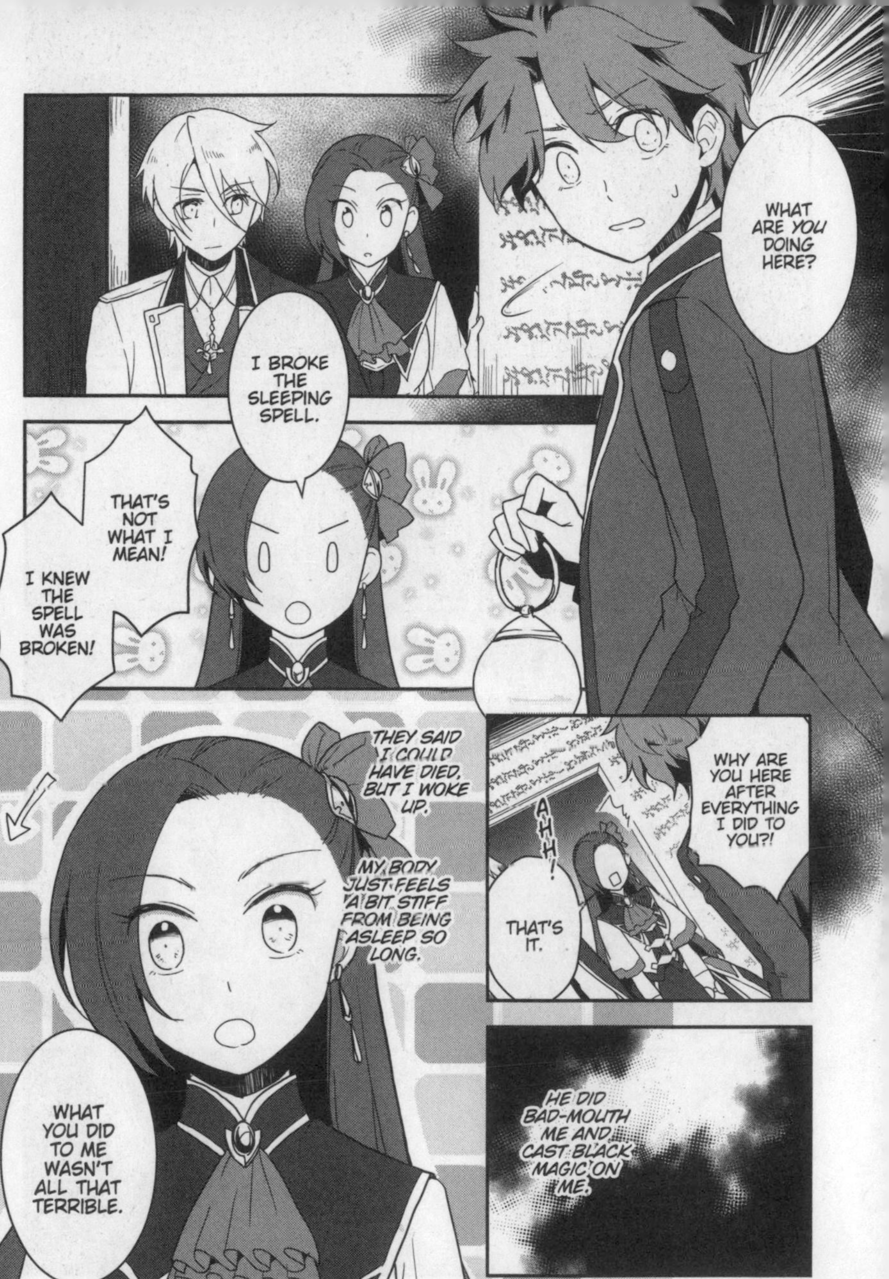
WHAT ARE YOU DOING HERE?
I BROKE THE SLEEPING SPELL.
THAT'S NOT WHAT I MEAN!
I KNEW THE SPELL WAS BROKEN!
WHY ARE YOU HERE AFTER EVERYTHING I DID TO YOU?!
AHH!
THAT'S IT.
HE DID BAD-MOUTH ME AND CAST BLACK MAGIC ON ME.
THEY SAID I COULD HAVE DIED, BUT I WOKE UP.
MY BODY JUST FEELS A BIT STIFF FROM BEING ASLEEP SO LONG.
WHAT YOU DID TO ME WASN'T ALL THAT TERRIBLE.

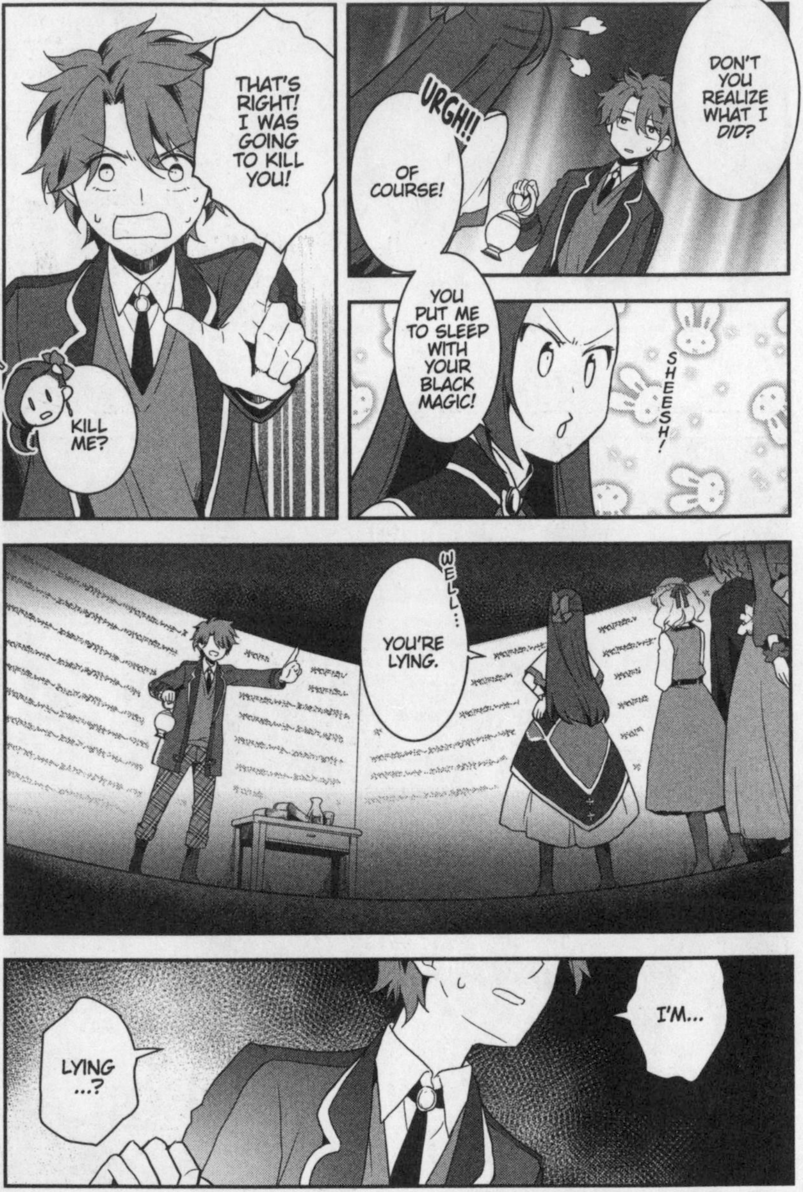
DON'T YOU REALIZE WHAT I DID?
URGH!!
OF COURSE!
YOU PUT ME TO SLEEP WITH YOUR BLACK MAGIC!
SHEESH!
THAT'S RIGHT! I WAS GOING TO KILL YOU!
KILL ME?
WELL...
YOU'RE LYING.
I'M...
LYING ...?

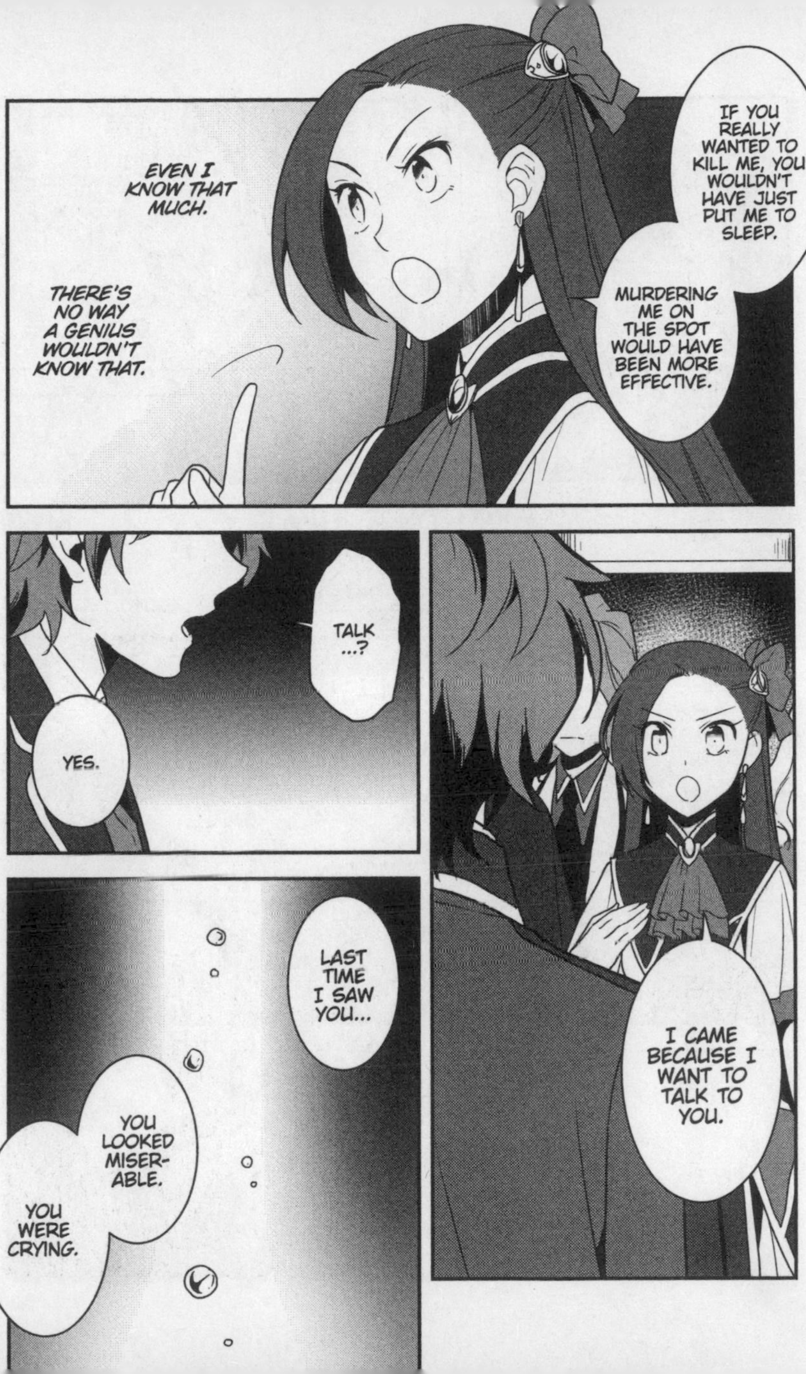
IF YOU REALLY WANTED TO KILL ME, YOU WOULDN'T HAVE JUST PUT ME TO SLEEP.
MURDERING ME ON THE SPOT WOULD HAVE BEEN MORE EFFECTIVE.
EVEN I KNOW THAT MUCH.
THERE'S NO WAY A GENIUS WOULDN'T KNOW THAT.
I CAME BECAUSE I WANT TO TALK TO YOU.
TALK ...?
YES.
LAST TIME I SAW YOU...
YOU LOOKED MISER-ABLE.
YOU WERE CRYING.

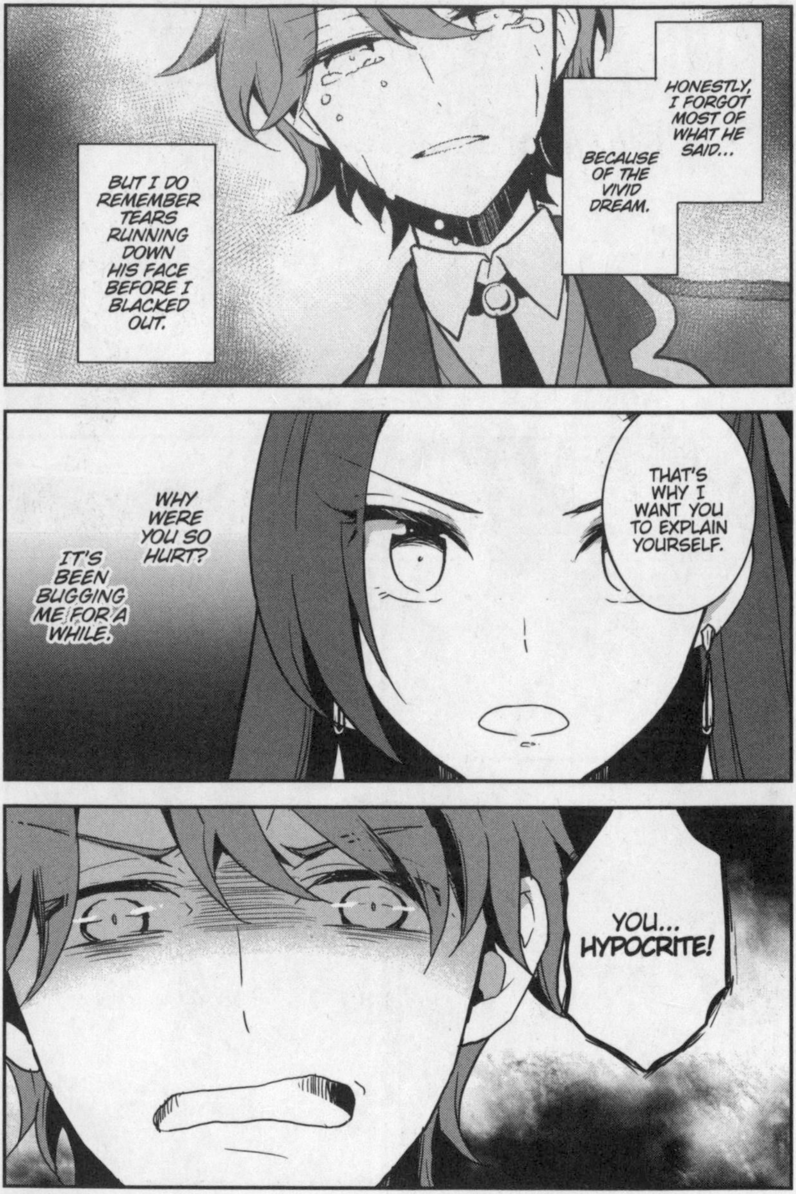
HONESTLY, I FORGOT MOST OF WHAT HE SAID...
BECAUSE OF THE VIVID DREAM.
BUT I DO REMEMBER TEARS RUNNING DOWN HIS FACE BEFORE I BLACKED OUT.
THAT'S WHY I WANT YOU TO EXPLAIN YOURSELF.
WHY WERE YOU SO HURT?
IT'S BEEN BUGGING ME FOR A WHILE.
YOU... HYPOCRITE!

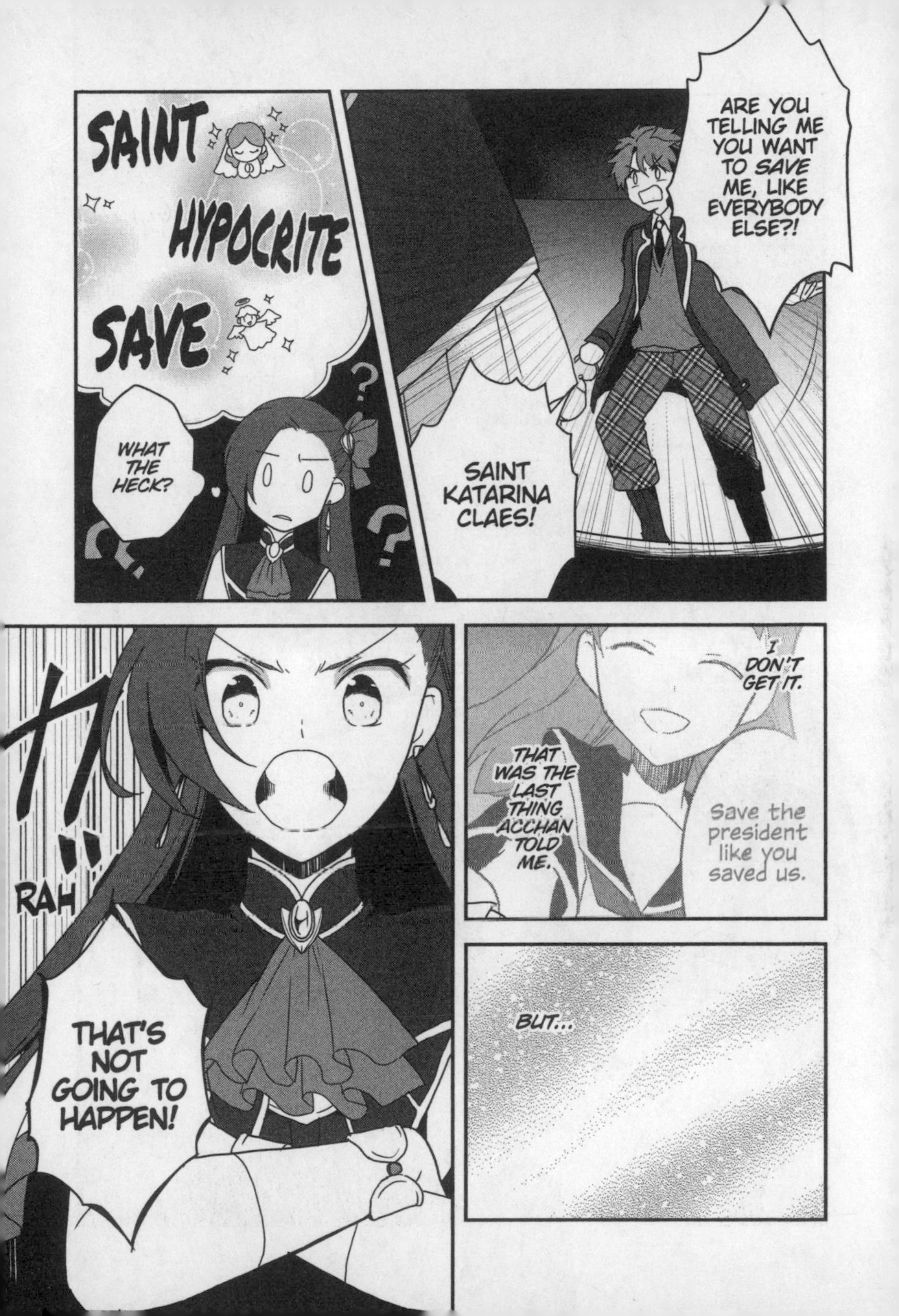
ARE YOU TELLING ME YOU WANT TO SAVE ME, LIKE EVERYBODY ELSE?!
SAINT KATARINA CLAES!
SAINT
HYPOCRITE
SAVE
WHAT THE HECK?
I DON'T GET IT.
THAT WAS THE LAST THING ACCHAN TOLD ME.
Save the president like you saved us.
BUT...
RAH
THAT'S NOT GOING TO HAPPEN!

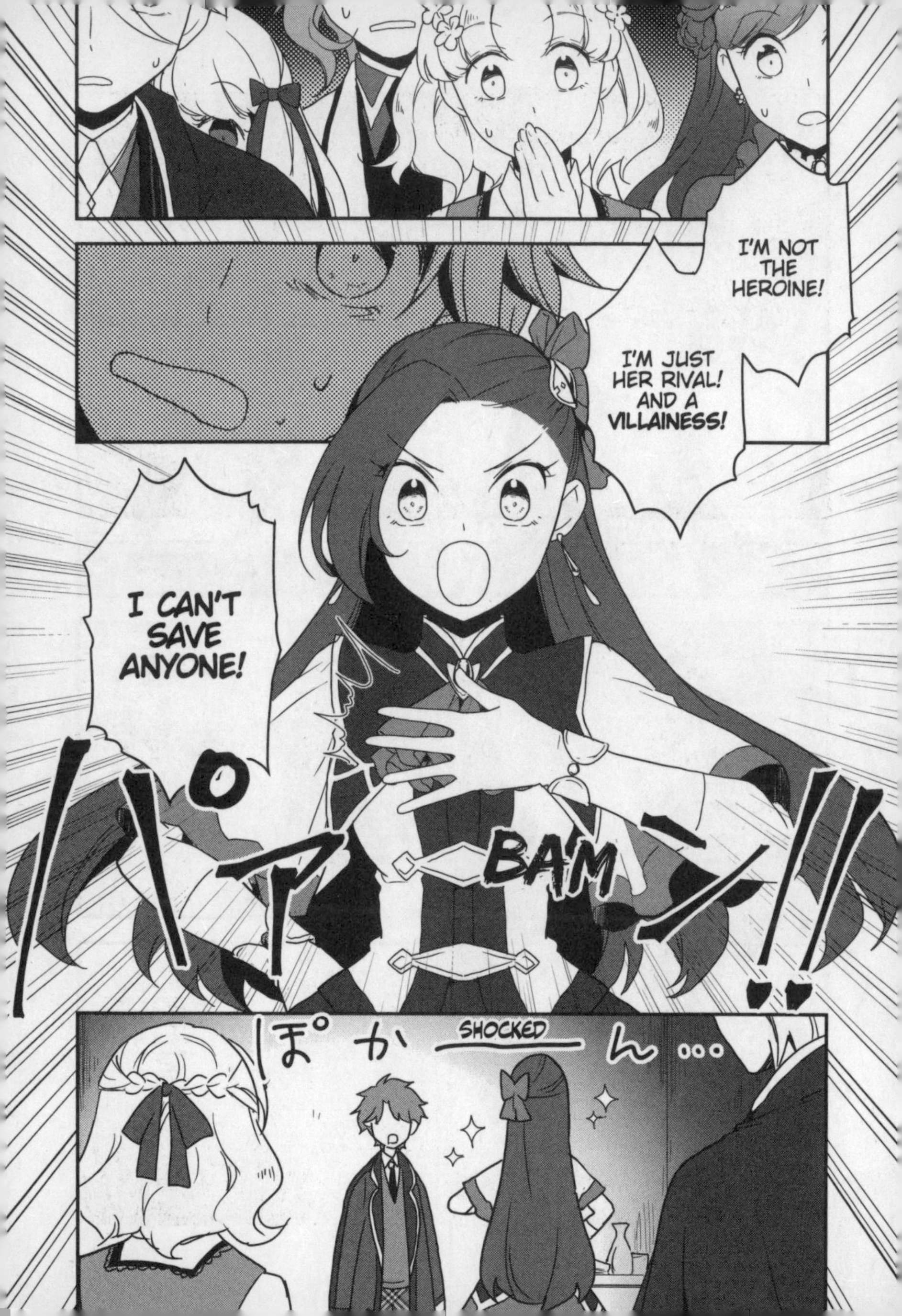
I'M NOT THE HEROINE!
I'M JUST HER RIVAL! AND A VILLAINESS!
I CAN'T SAVE ANYONE!
パァン!!
BAM
ぽか――ん…
SHOCKED

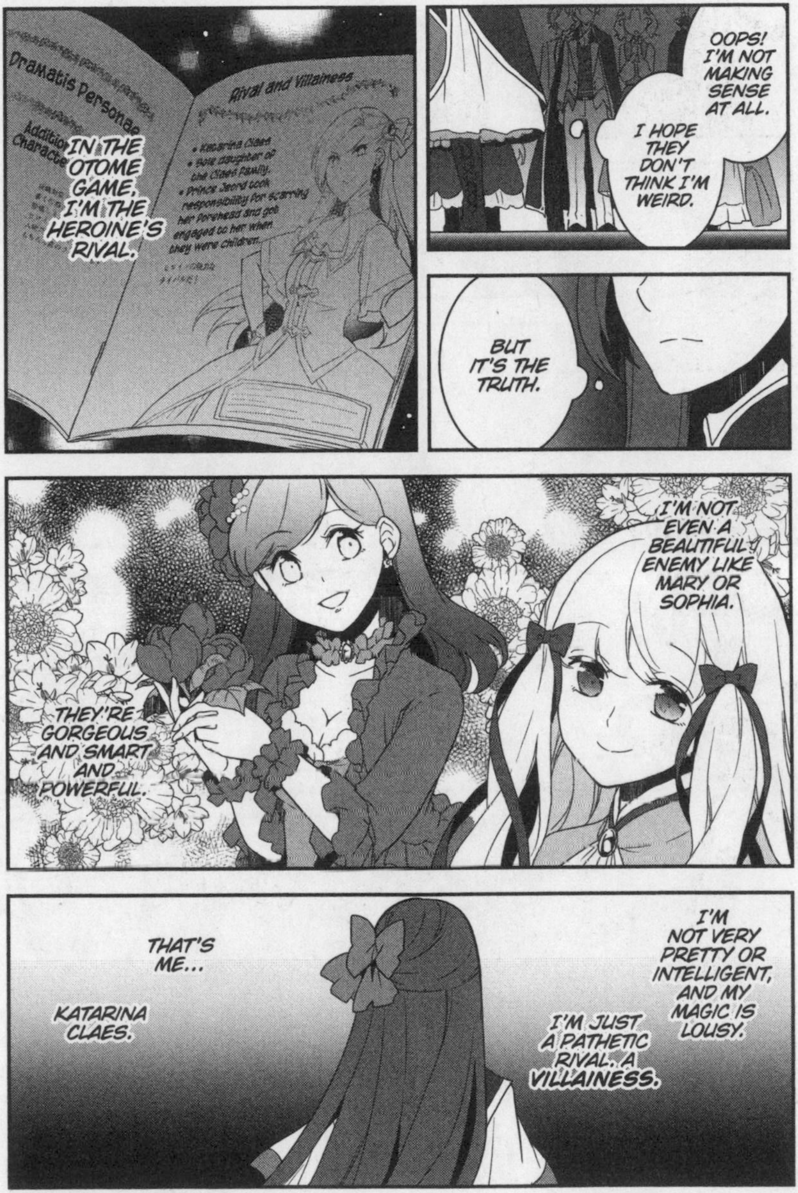
OOPS! I'M NOT MAKING SENSE AT ALL.
I HOPE THEY DON'T THINK I'M WEIRD.
BUT IT'S THE TRUTH.
Dramatis Personae
Rival and Villainess
• Katarina Claes
• Sole daughter of the Claes Family.
• Prince Jeord took responsibility for scarring her forehead and got engaged to her when they were children.
IN THE OTOME GAME, I'M THE HEROINE'S RIVAL.
I'M NOT EVEN A BEAUTIFUL ENEMY LIKE MARY OR SOPHIA.
THEY'RE GORGEOUS AND SMART AND POWERFUL.
I'M NOT VERY PRETTY OR INTELLIGENT, AND MY MAGIC IS LOUSY.
I'M JUST A PATHETIC RIVAL. A VILLAINESS.
THAT'S ME...
KATARINA CLAES.

BUT IF THERE'S ONE THING I CAN DO...

I CAN'T SAVE YOU...

FROM SUFFERING.

UNLIKE THE HEROINE...

I CAN'T HELP ANYONE OVERCOME TRAUMA... OR MEND BROKEN HEARTS.

BUT I CAN BE BY YOUR SIDE.

WHEN-EVER YOU'RE HAVING A HARD TIME, I'LL LISTEN TO YOU...

AND STAY UNTIL YOU CHEER UP.

I'VE RECOVERED MY MEMORY FROM MY PREVIOUS LIFE.

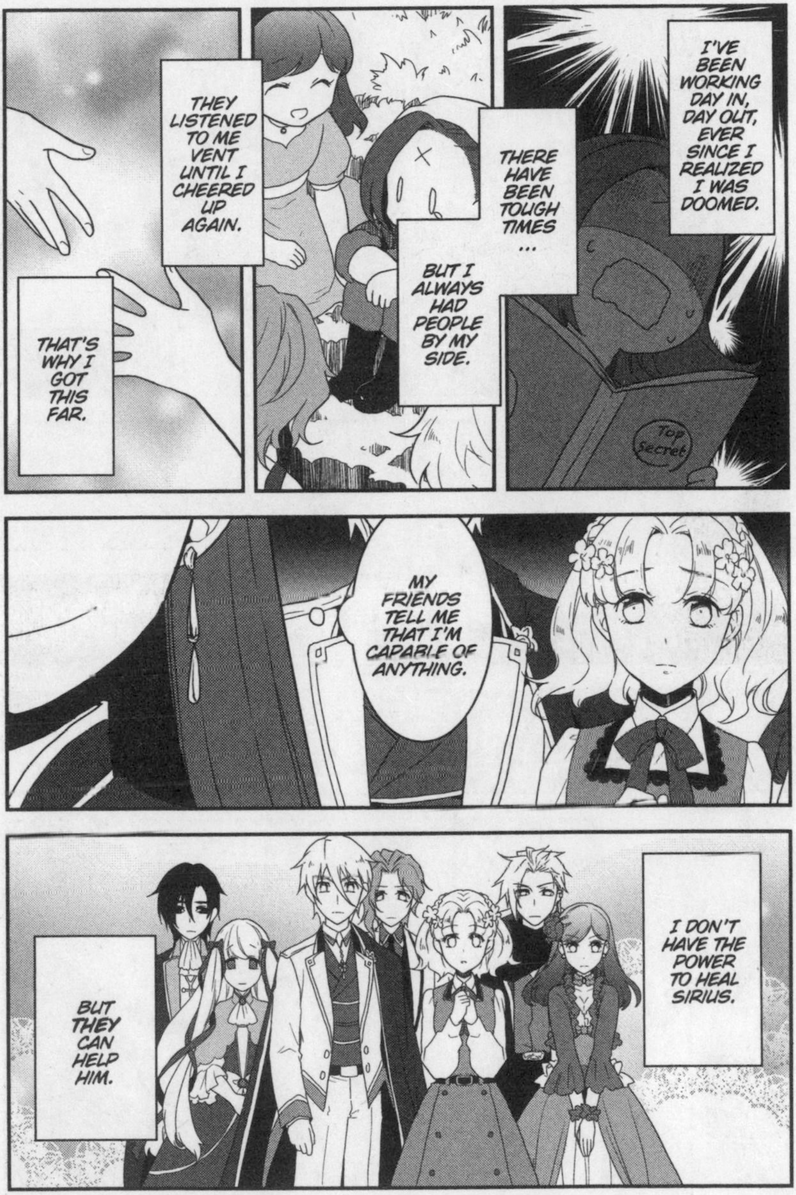
I'VE BEEN WORKING DAY IN, DAY OUT, EVER SINCE I REALIZED I WAS DOOMED.
Top Secret
THERE HAVE BEEN TOUGH TIMES ...
BUT I ALWAYS HAD PEOPLE BY MY SIDE.
THEY LISTENED TO ME VENT UNTIL I CHEERED UP AGAIN.
THAT'S WHY I GOT THIS FAR.
MY FRIENDS TELL ME THAT I'M CAPABLE OF ANYTHING.
I DON'T HAVE THE POWER TO HEAL SIRIUS.
BUT THEY CAN HELP HIM.

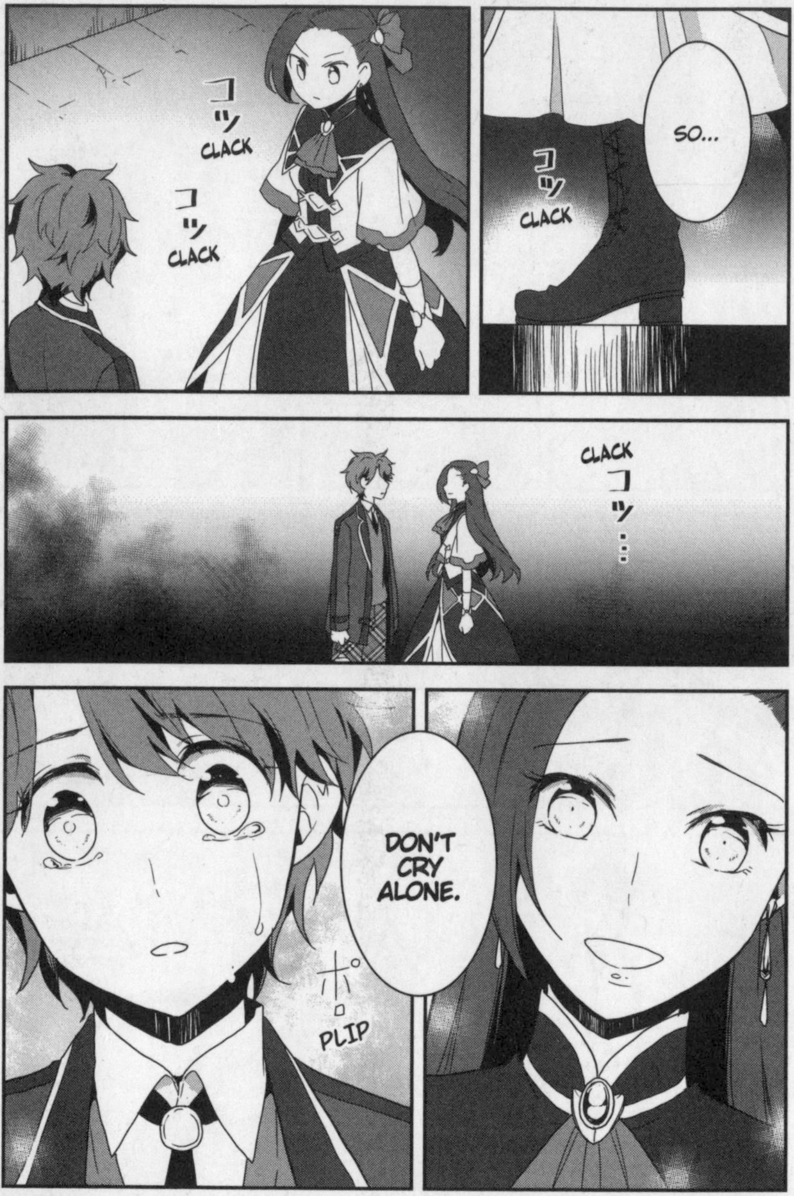
SO...
コッ
CLACK
コッ
CLACK
コッ
CLACK
CLACK
コッ...
DON'T CRY ALONE.
ポロ
PLIP

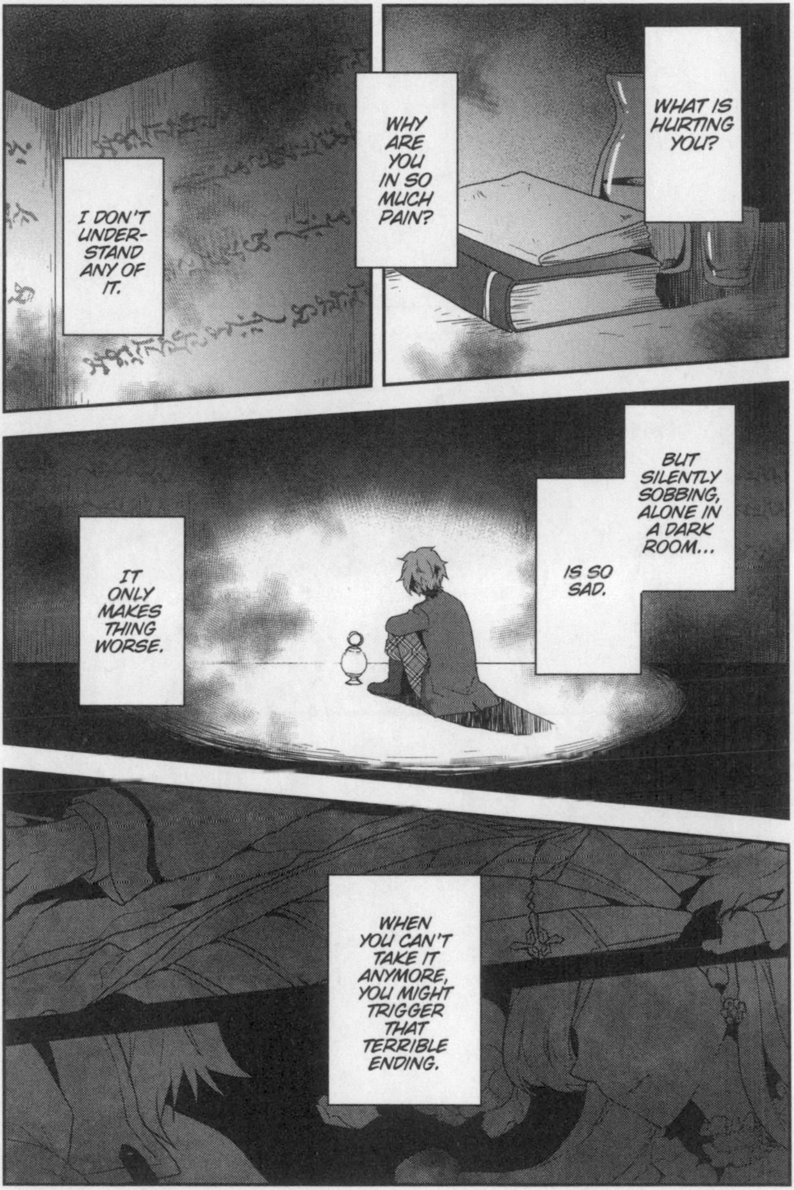
WHAT IS HURTING YOU?
WHY ARE YOU IN SO MUCH PAIN?
I DON'T UNDER-STAND ANY OF IT.
BUT SILENTLY SOBBING, ALONE IN A DARK ROOM...
IS SO SAD.
IT ONLY MAKES THING WORSE.
WHEN YOU CAN'T TAKE IT ANYMORE, YOU MIGHT TRIGGER THAT TERRIBLE ENDING.

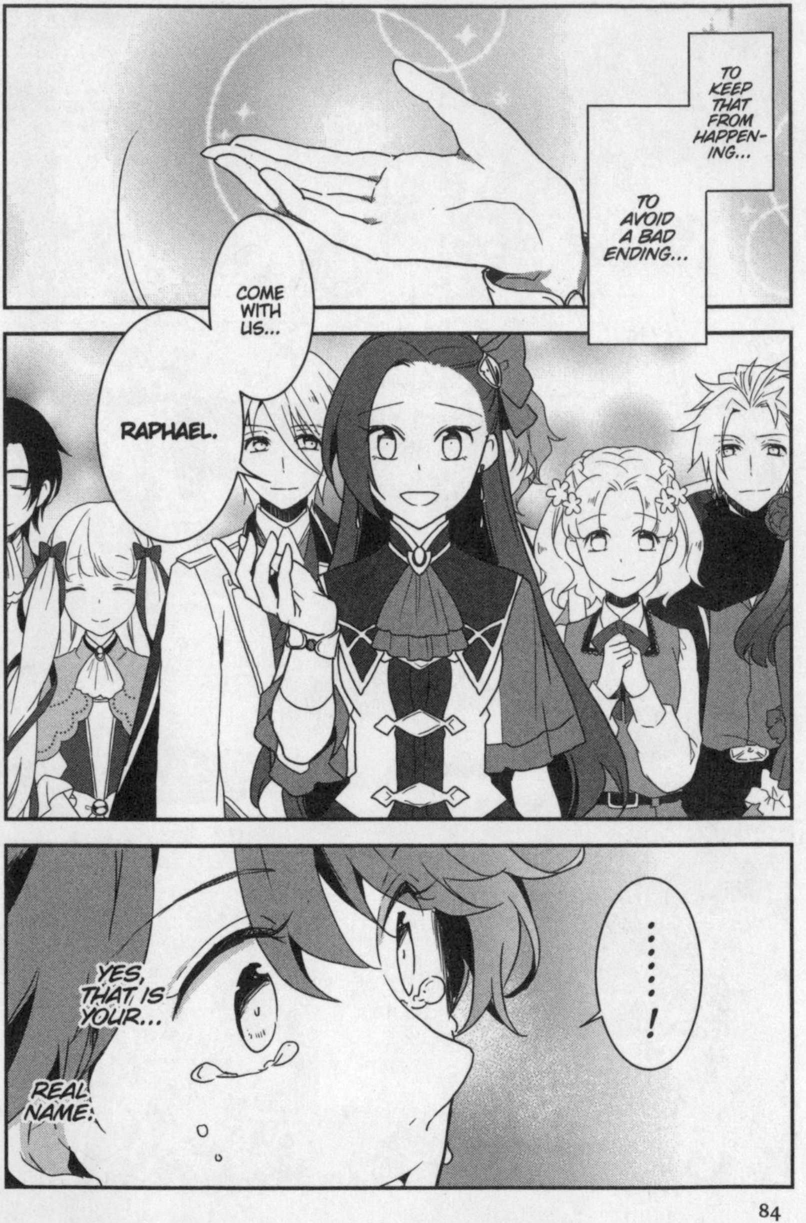
TO KEEP THAT FROM HAPPEN-ING...
TO AVOID A BAD ENDING...
COME WITH US...
RAPHAEL.
......!
YES, THAT IS YOUR...
REAL NAME.

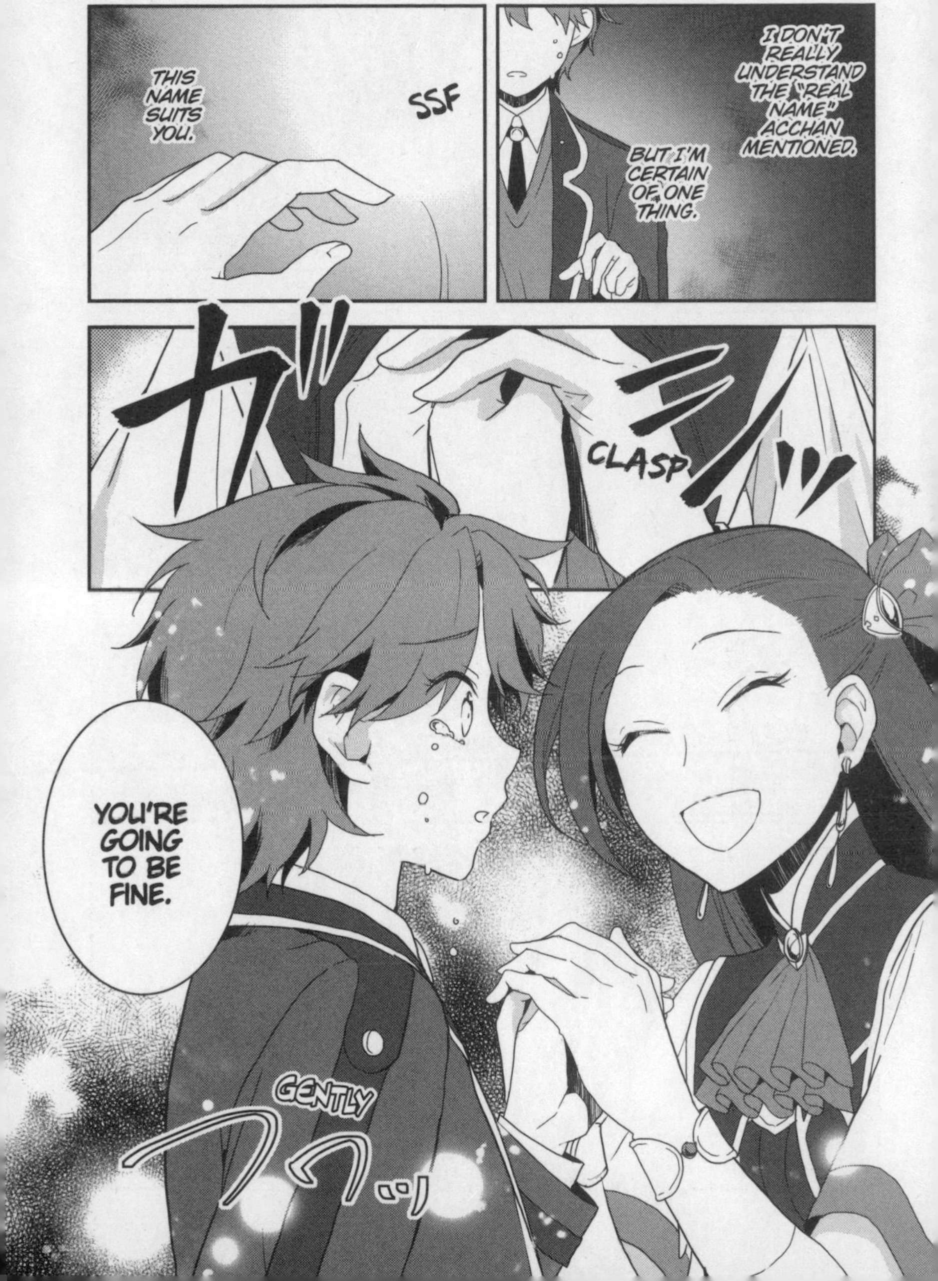
I DON'T REALLY UNDERSTAND THE "REAL NAME" ACCHAN MENTIONED.
BUT I'M CERTAIN OF ONE THING.
THIS NAME SUITS YOU.
SSF
CLASP
YOU'RE GOING TO BE FINE.
GENTLY

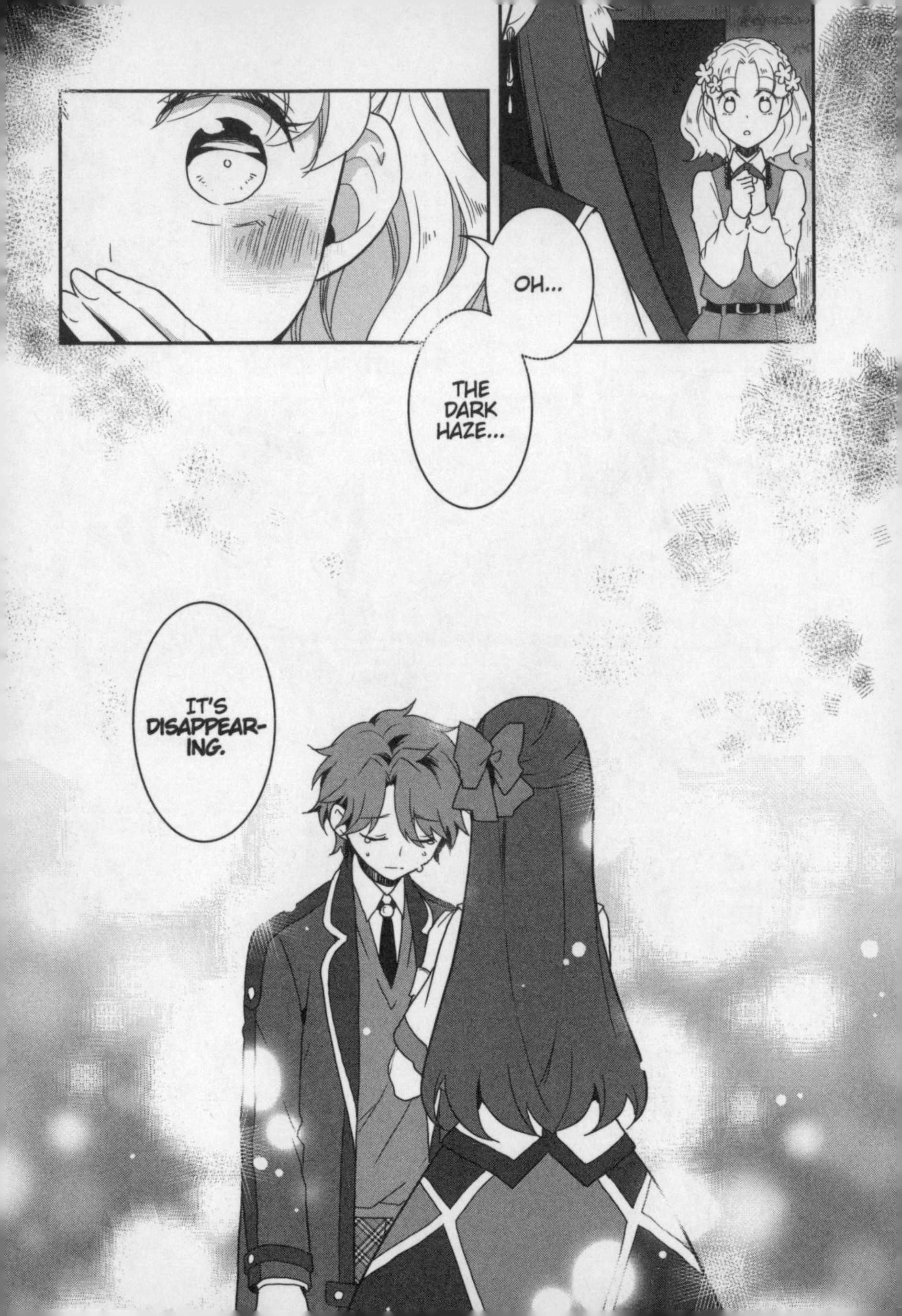
OH...
THE DARK HAZE...
IT'S DISAPPEAR-ING.

BAD

ENDING

My Next Life
as a VILLAINESS:
ALL ROUTES
LEAD
TO DOOM!

Chapter 21: The Approaching Footsteps of Doom (Part 9)

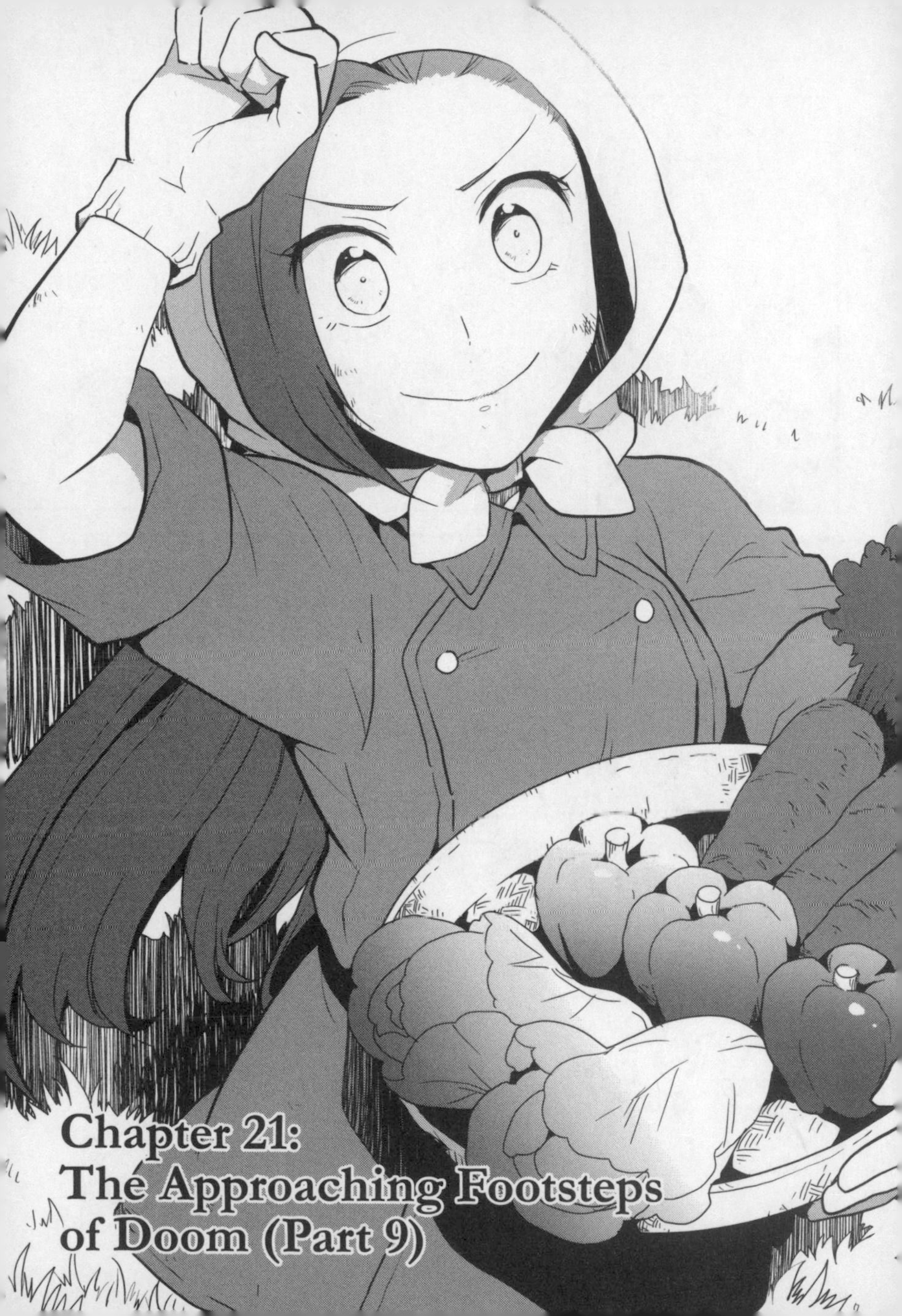

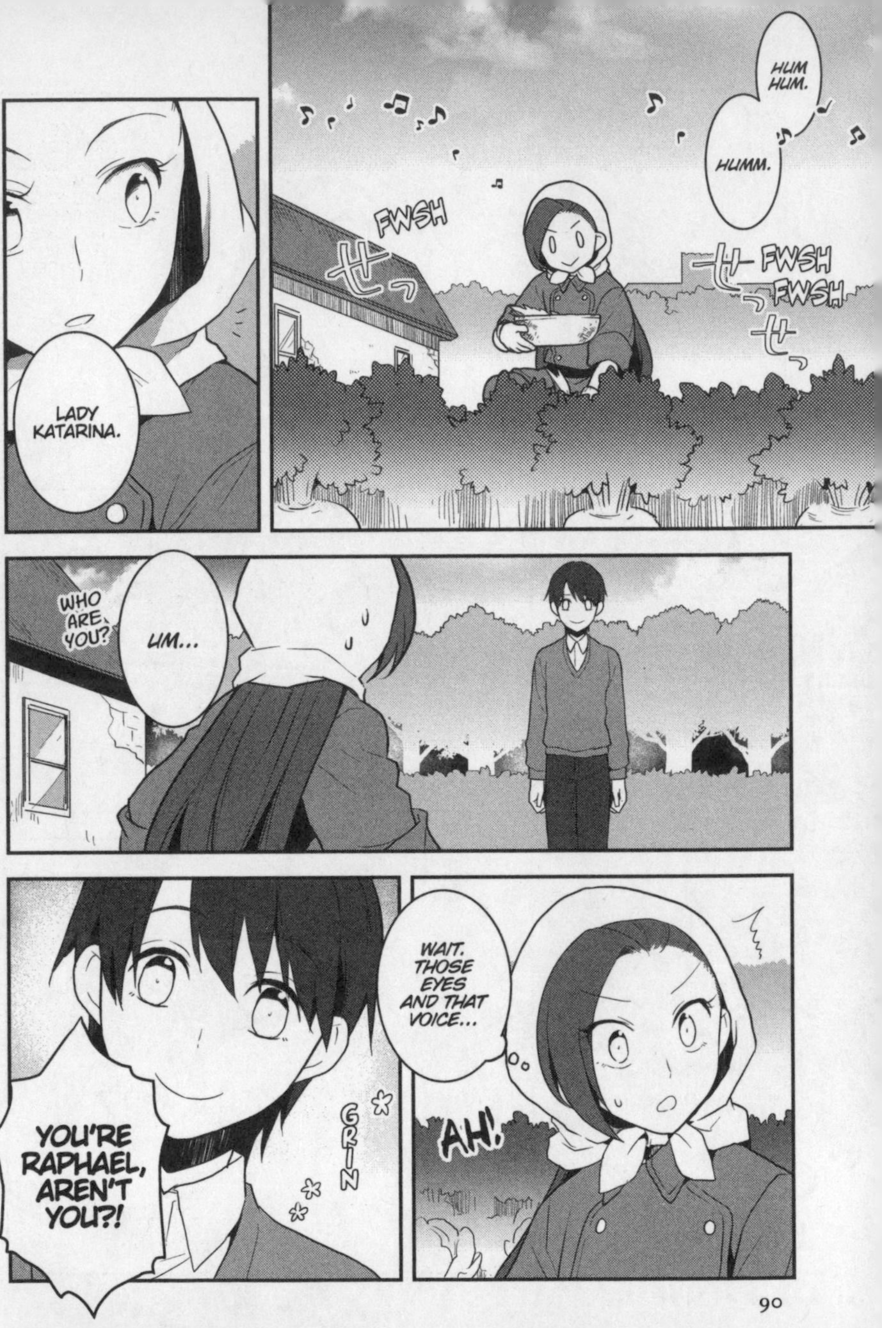
HUM HUM.
HUMM.
FWSH
FWSH
FWSH
FWSH
LADY KATARINA.
UM...
WHO ARE YOU?
WAIT. THOSE EYES AND THAT VOICE...
AH!
GRIN
YOU'RE RAPHAEL, AREN'T YOU?!

I WAS WORRIED! I HADN'T HEARD FROM YOU SINCE YOU CONFESSED YOUR CRIMES TO THE AUTHORITIES!

WHY DO YOU LOOK SO DIFFERENT?

I'LL EXPLAIN LATER.

I'M SORRY. I'VE BEEN BUSY.

LADY KATARINA, CAN YOU TALK FOR A MOMENT?

TALK? SURE!

BOXES

TWEET TWEET TWEET

CHIRP CHIRP CHIRP CHIRP

OH!

HERE, HAVE A SEAT.

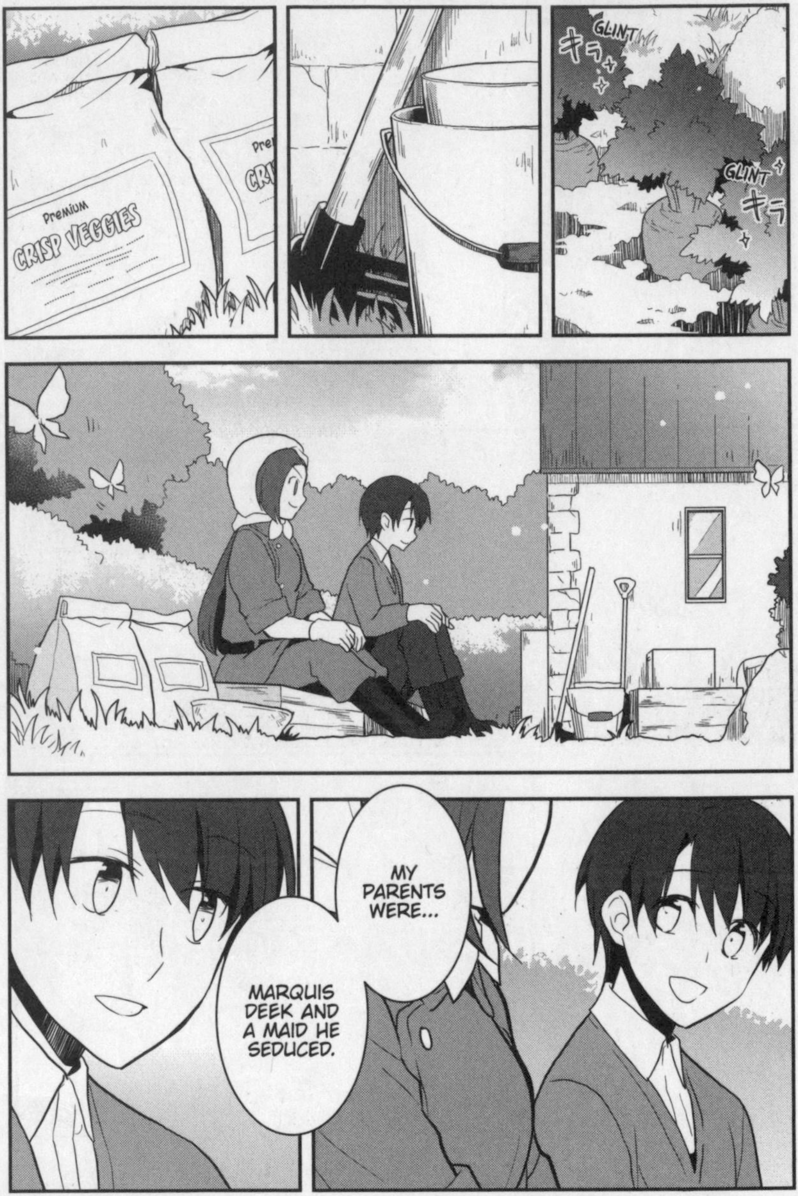
GLINT
キラ
GLINT
キラ
Premium
CRISP VEGGIES
MY PARENTS WERE...
MARQUIS DEEK AND A MAID HE SEDUCED.

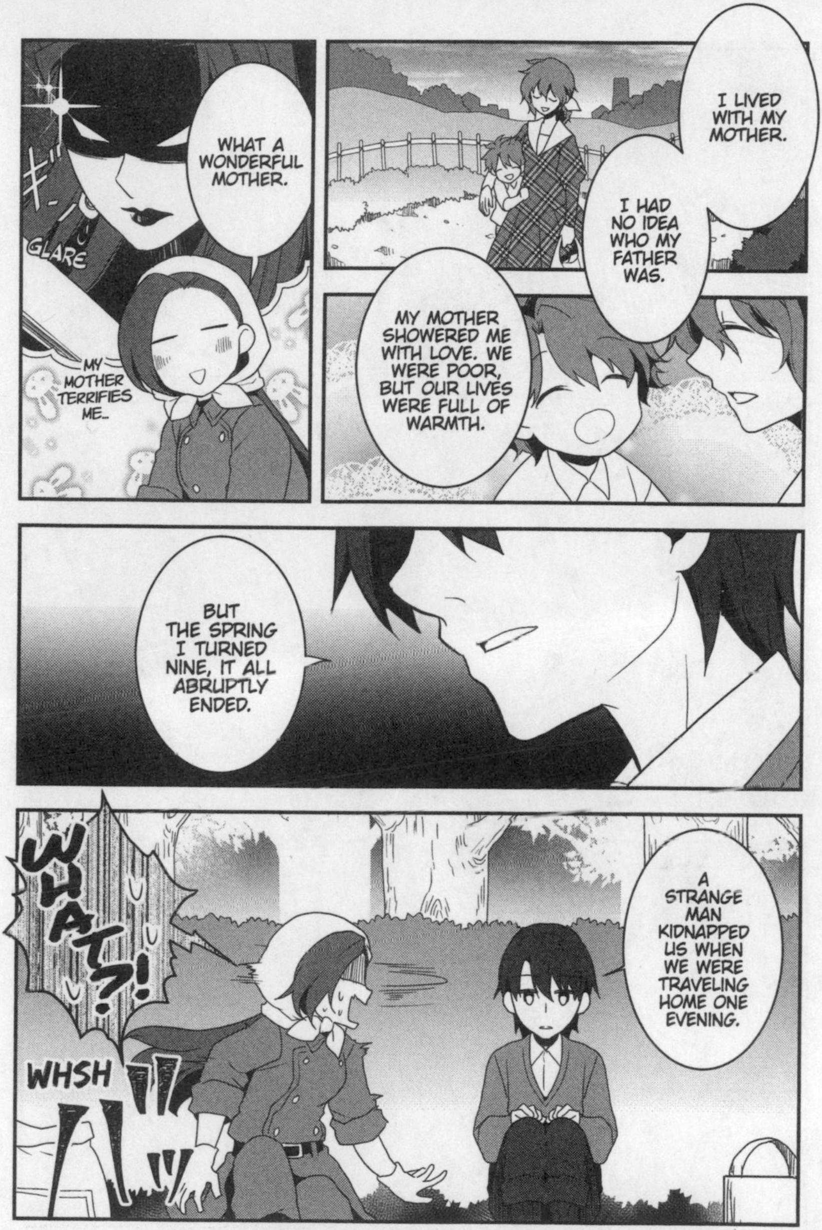
I LIVED WITH MY MOTHER.
I HAD NO IDEA WHO MY FATHER WAS.
MY MOTHER SHOWERED ME WITH LOVE. WE WERE POOR, BUT OUR LIVES WERE FULL OF WARMTH.
WHAT A WONDERFUL MOTHER.
GLARE
MY MOTHER TERRIFIES ME..
BUT THE SPRING I TURNED NINE, IT ALL ABRUPTLY ENDED.
A STRANGE MAN KIDNAPPED US WHEN WE WERE TRAVELING HOME ONE EVENING.
WHAT?!
WHSH

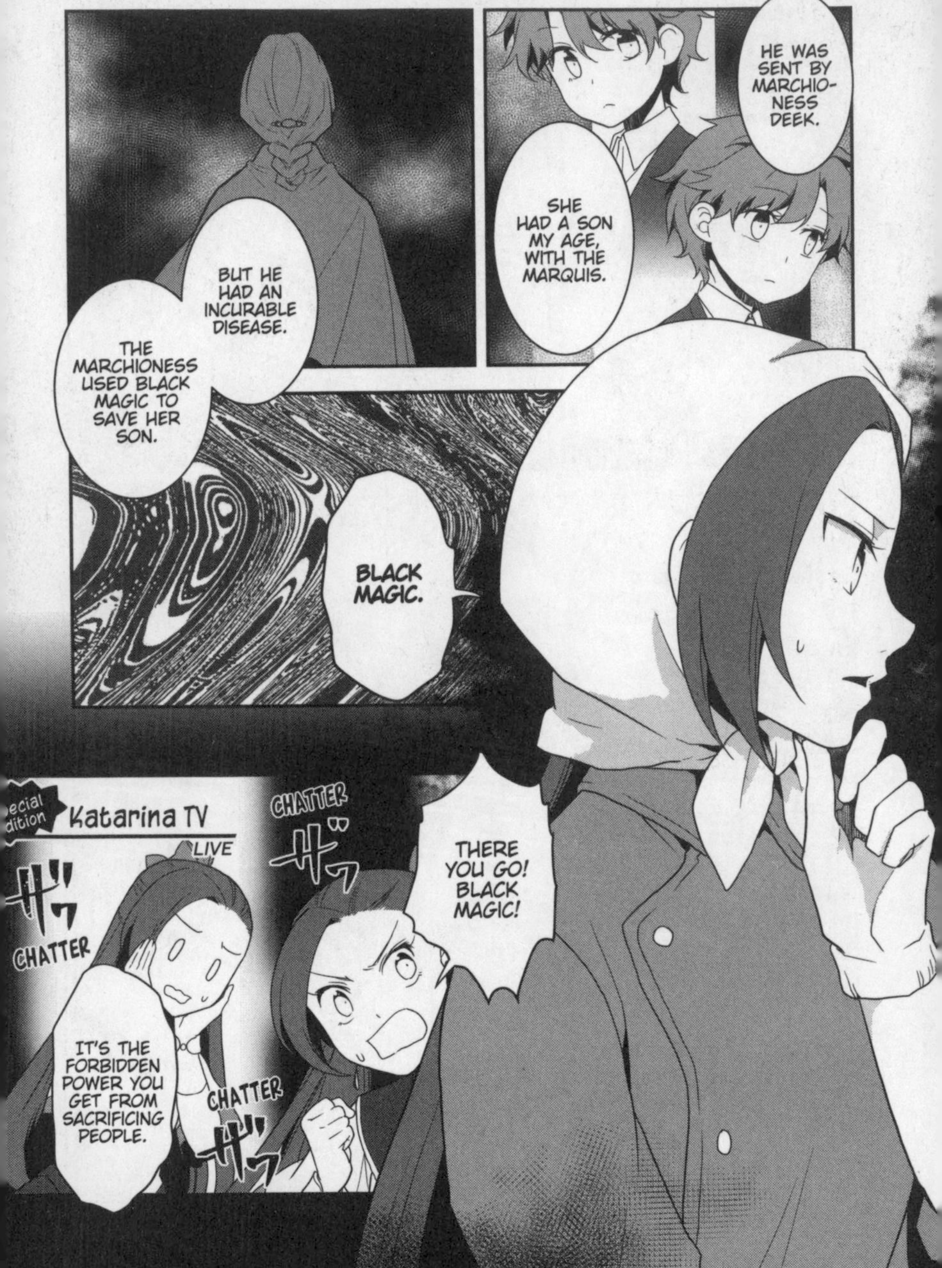
HE WAS SENT BY MARCHIONESS DEEK.
SHE HAD A SON MY AGE, WITH THE MARQUIS.
BUT HE HAD AN INCURABLE DISEASE.
THE MARCHIONESS USED BLACK MAGIC TO SAVE HER SON.
BLACK MAGIC.
Katarina TV
LIVE
CHATTER
THERE YOU GO! BLACK MAGIC!
CHATTER
CHATTER
IT'S THE FORBIDDEN POWER YOU GET FROM SACRIFICING PEOPLE.

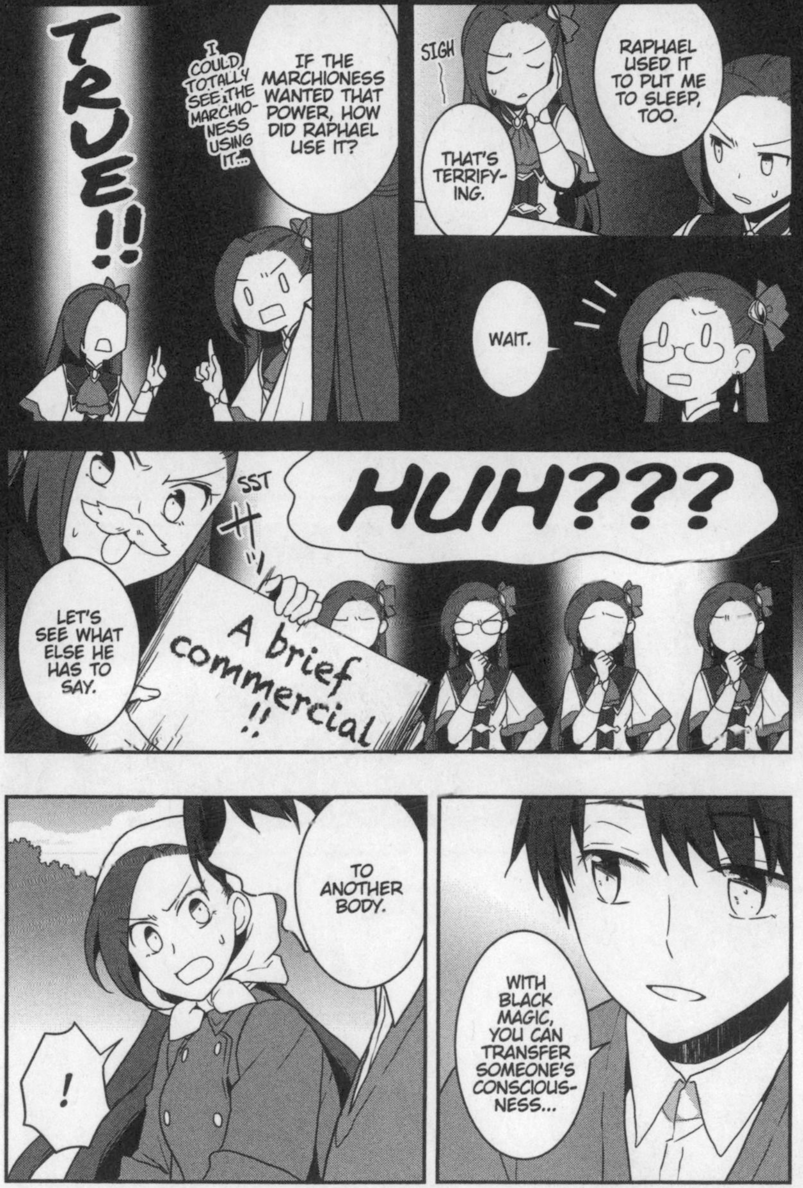
RAPHAEL USED IT TO PUT ME TO SLEEP, TOO.
SIGH
THAT'S TERRIFYING.
WAIT.
IF THE MARCHIONESS WANTED THAT POWER, HOW DID RAPHAEL USE IT?
I COULD TOTALLY SEE THE MARCHIONESS USING IT...
TRUE!!
HUH???
SST
A brief commercial!!
LET'S SEE WHAT ELSE HE HAS TO SAY.
WITH BLACK MAGIC, YOU CAN TRANSFER SOMEONE'S CONSCIOUSNESS...
TO ANOTHER BODY.
!

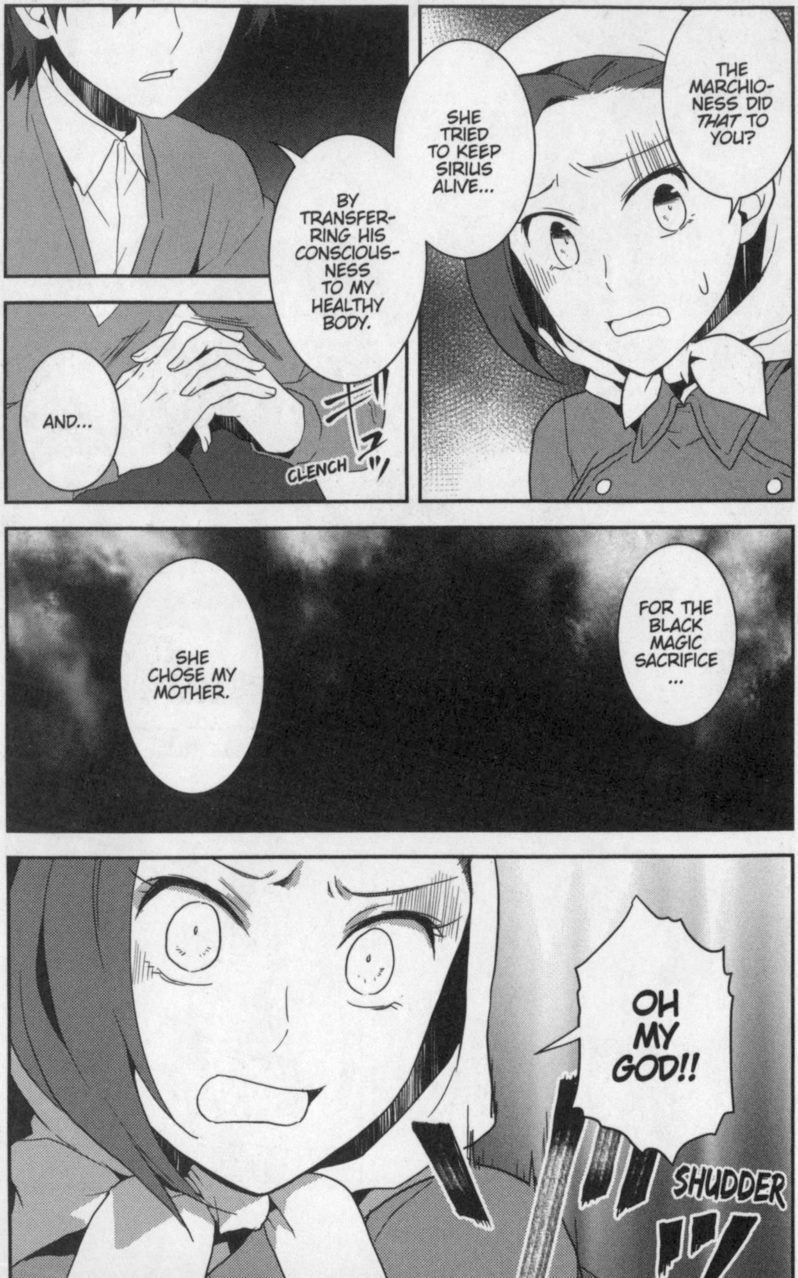
THE MARCHIONESS DID *THAT* TO YOU?
SHE TRIED TO KEEP SIRIUS ALIVE...
BY TRANSFERRING HIS CONSCIOUSNESS TO MY HEALTHY BODY.
AND...
CLENCH
FOR THE BLACK MAGIC SACRIFICE ...
SHE CHOSE MY MOTHER.
OH MY GOD!!
SHUDDER

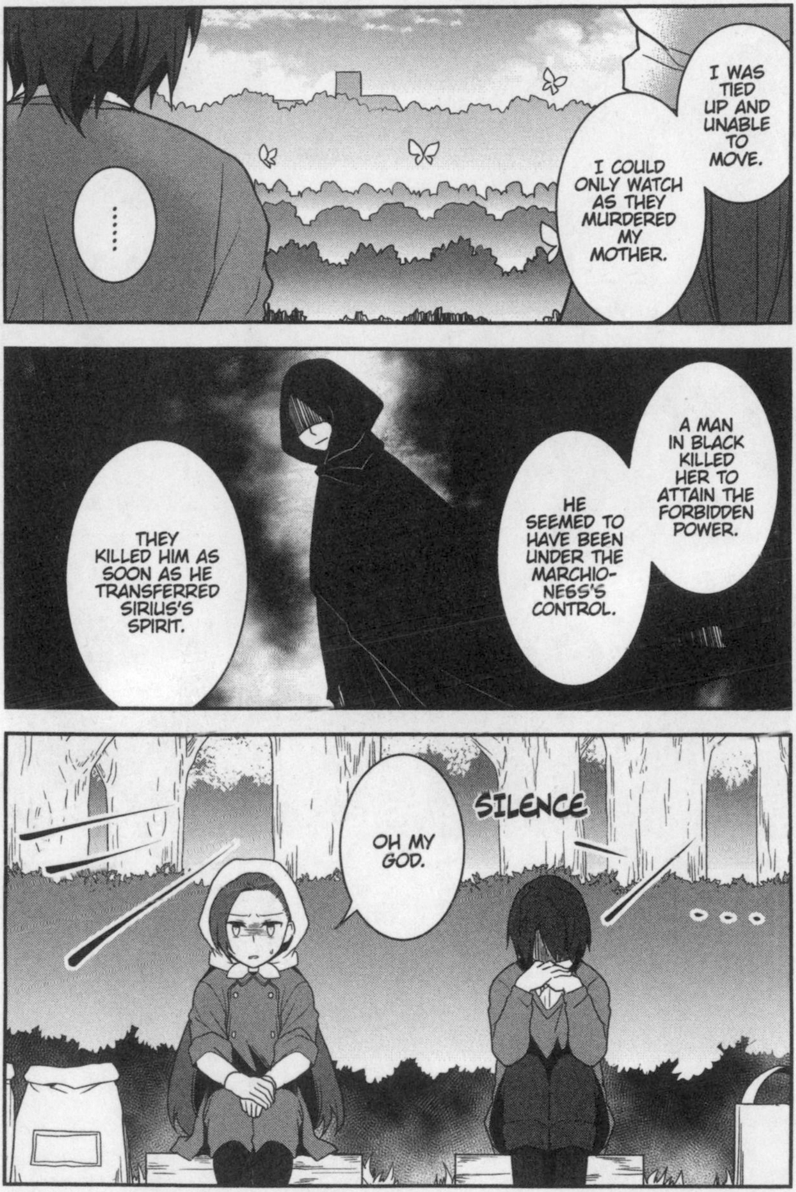
I WAS TIED UP AND UNABLE TO MOVE.
I COULD ONLY WATCH AS THEY MURDERED MY MOTHER.
......
A MAN IN BLACK KILLED HER TO ATTAIN THE FORBIDDEN POWER.
HE SEEMED TO HAVE BEEN UNDER THE MARCHIONESS'S CONTROL.
THEY KILLED HIM AS SOON AS HE TRANSFERRED SIRIUS'S SPIRIT.
SILENCE
OH MY GOD.

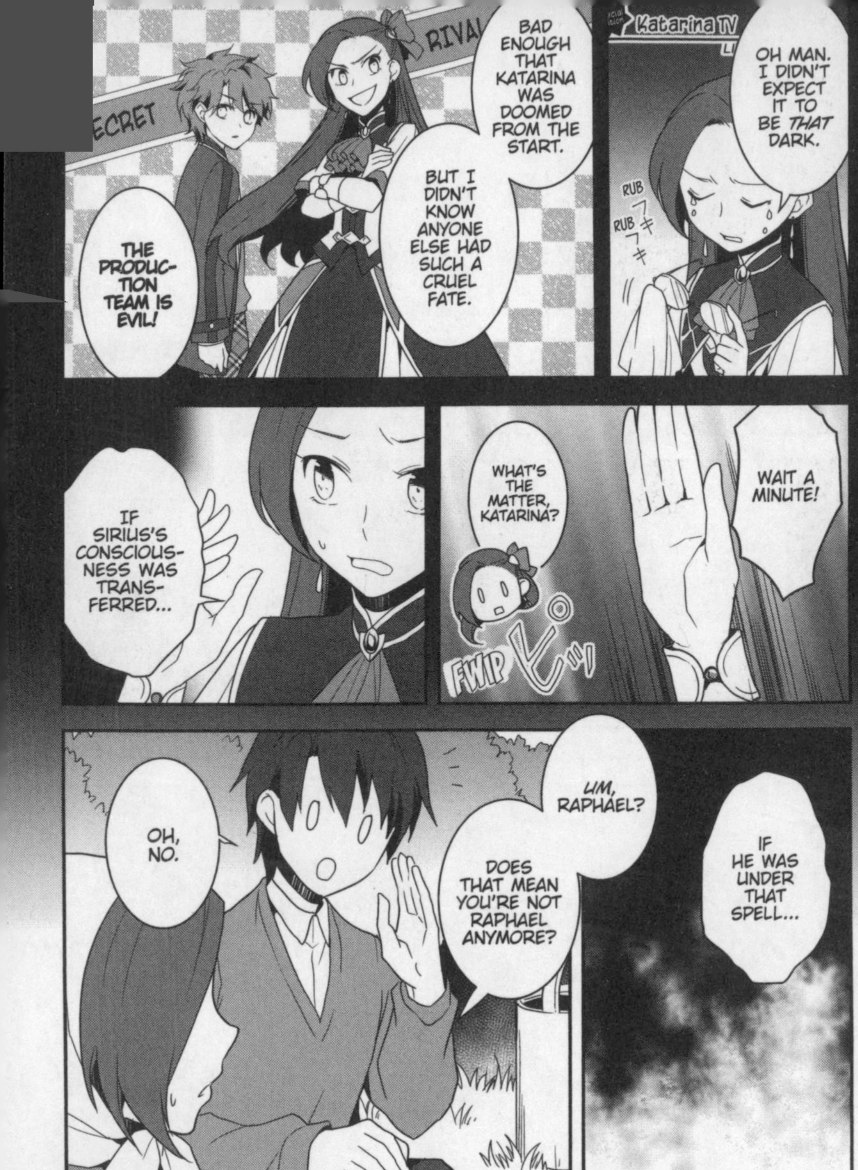
Katarina TV
OH MAN. I DIDN'T EXPECT IT TO BE *THAT* DARK.
RUB RUB
BAD ENOUGH THAT KATARINA WAS DOOMED FROM THE START.
BUT I DIDN'T KNOW ANYONE ELSE HAD SUCH A CRUEL FATE.
THE PRODUCTION TEAM IS EVIL!
WAIT A MINUTE!
WHAT'S THE MATTER, KATARINA?
FWIP
IF SIRIUS'S CONSCIOUSNESS WAS TRANSFERRED...
IF HE WAS UNDER THAT SPELL...
UM, RAPHAEL?
DOES THAT MEAN YOU'RE NOT RAPHAEL ANYMORE?
OH, NO.

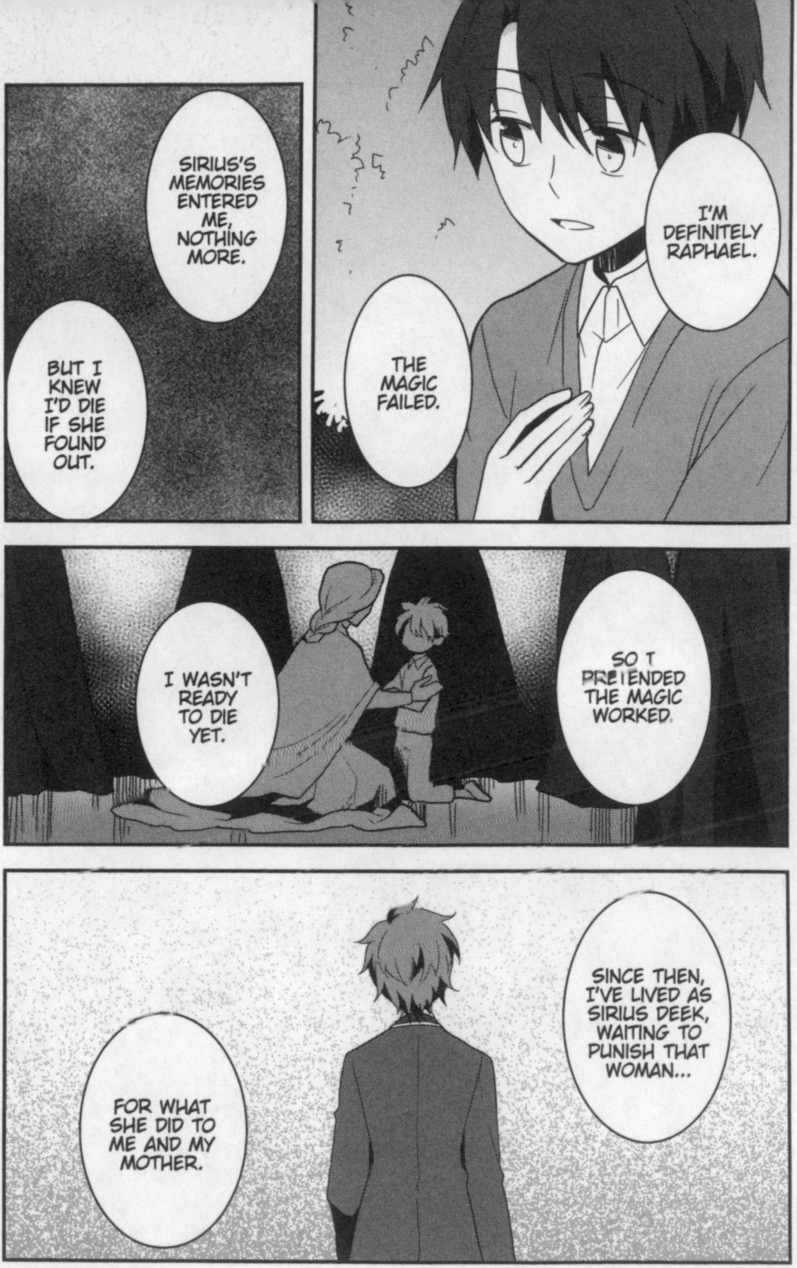
I'M DEFINITELY RAPHAEL.
THE MAGIC FAILED.
SIRIUS'S MEMORIES ENTERED ME, NOTHING MORE.
BUT I KNEW I'D DIE IF SHE FOUND OUT.
SO I PRETENDED THE MAGIC WORKED.
I WASN'T READY TO DIE YET.
SINCE THEN, I'VE LIVED AS SIRIUS DEEK, WAITING TO PUNISH THAT WOMAN...
FOR WHAT SHE DID TO ME AND MY MOTHER.

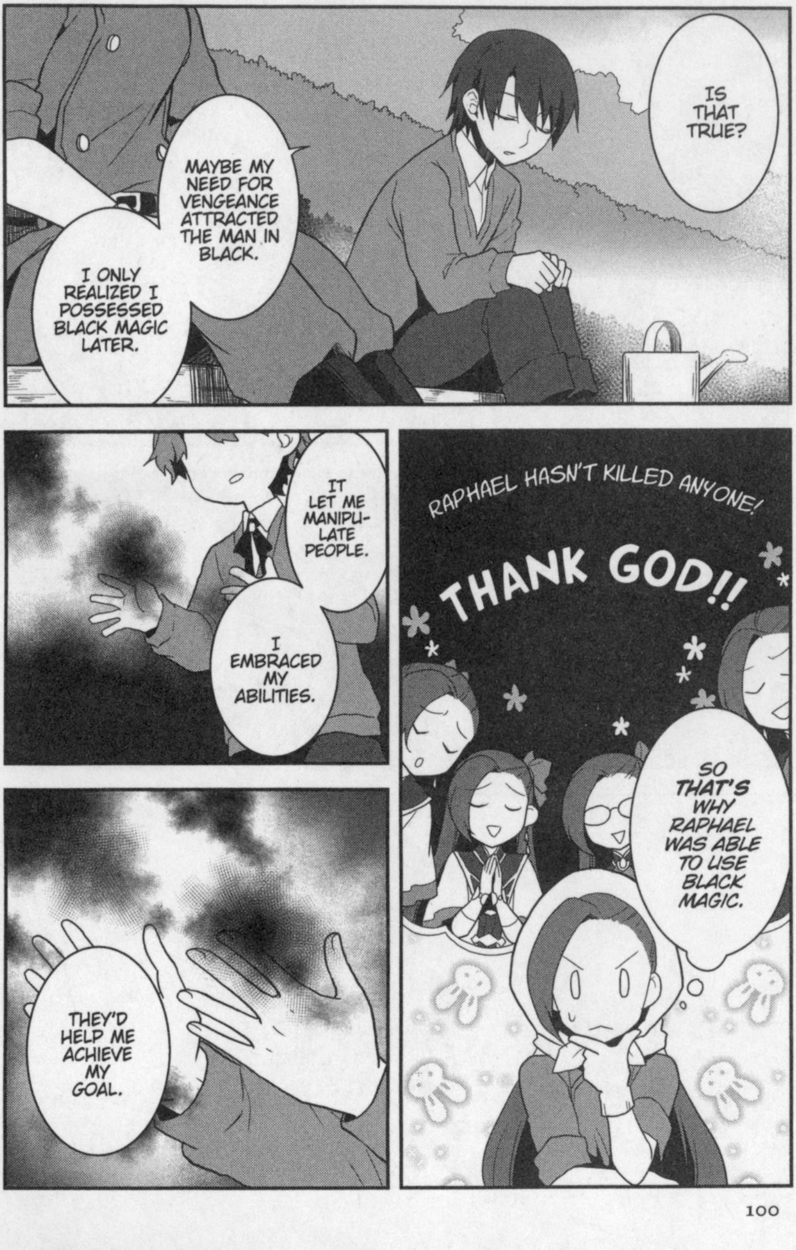
IS THAT TRUE?
MAYBE MY NEED FOR VENGEANCE ATTRACTED THE MAN IN BLACK.
I ONLY REALIZED I POSSESSED BLACK MAGIC LATER.
RAPHAEL HASN'T KILLED ANYONE!
THANK GOD!!
SO THAT'S WHY RAPHAEL WAS ABLE TO USE BLACK MAGIC.
IT LET ME MANIPU-LATE PEOPLE.
I EMBRACED MY ABILITIES.
THEY'D HELP ME ACHIEVE MY GOAL.

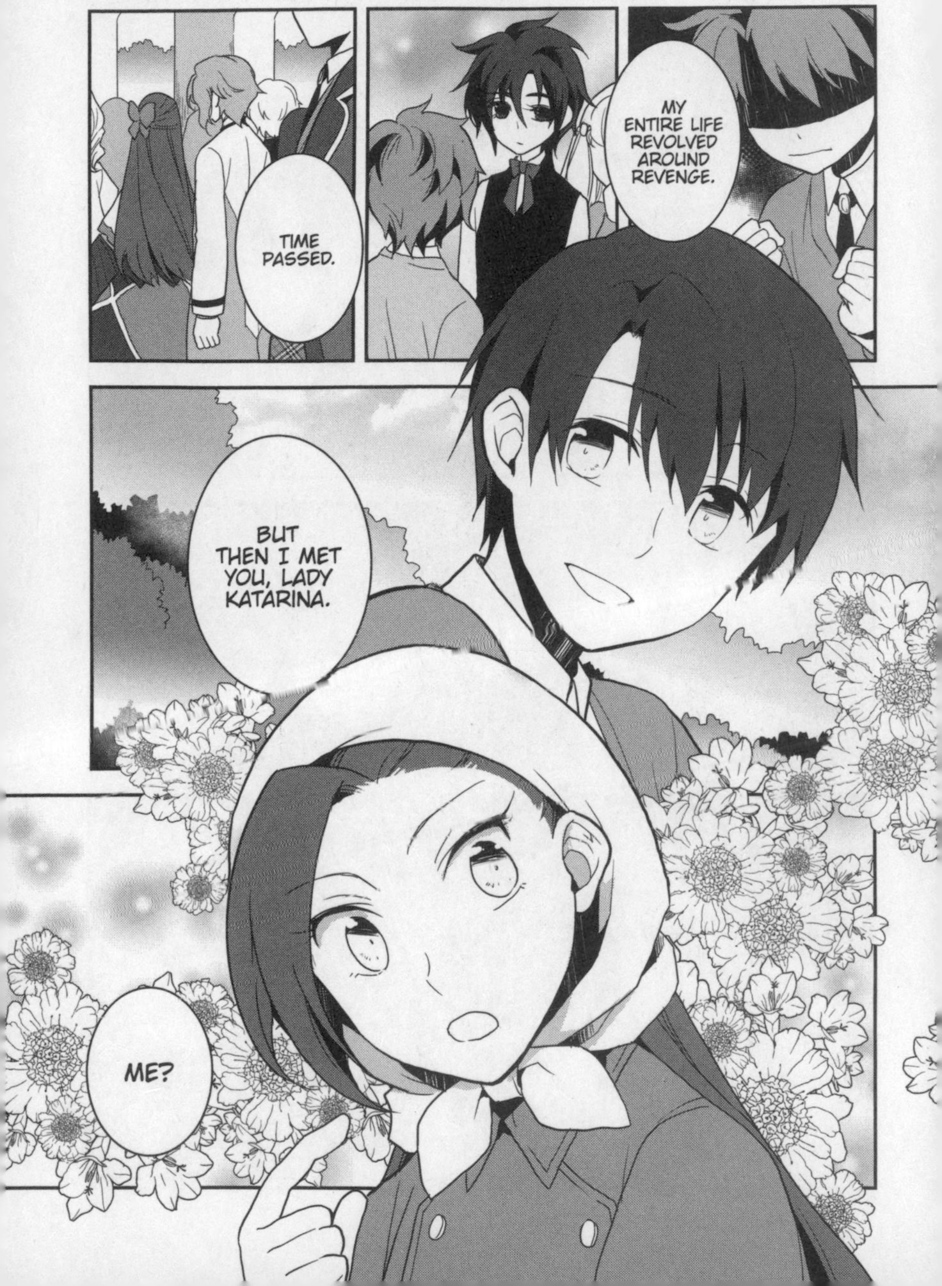
MY ENTIRE LIFE REVOLVED AROUND REVENGE.
TIME PASSED.
BUT THEN I MET YOU, LADY KATARINA.
ME?

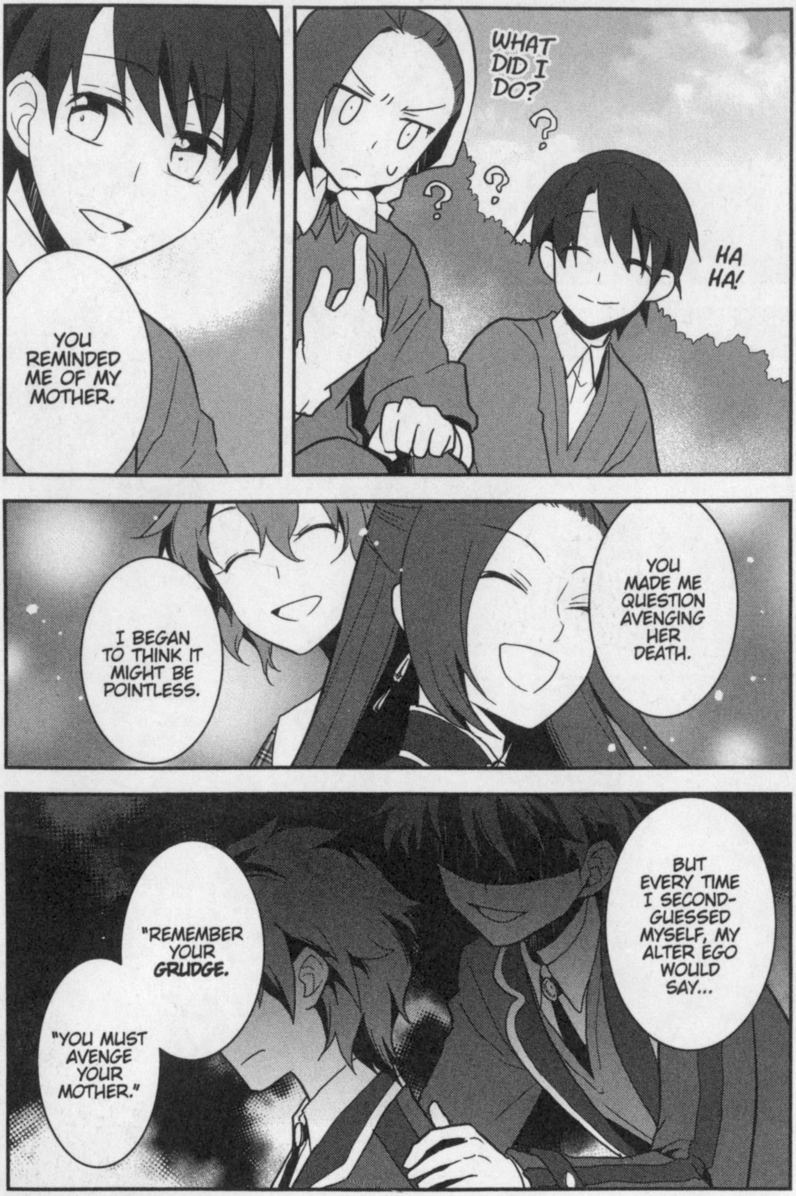
WHAT DID I DO?
HA HA!
YOU REMINDED ME OF MY MOTHER.
YOU MADE ME QUESTION AVENGING HER DEATH.
I BEGAN TO THINK IT MIGHT BE POINTLESS.
BUT EVERY TIME I SECOND-GUESSED MYSELF, MY ALTER EGO WOULD SAY...
"REMEMBER YOUR GRUDGE.
"YOU MUST AVENGE YOUR MOTHER."

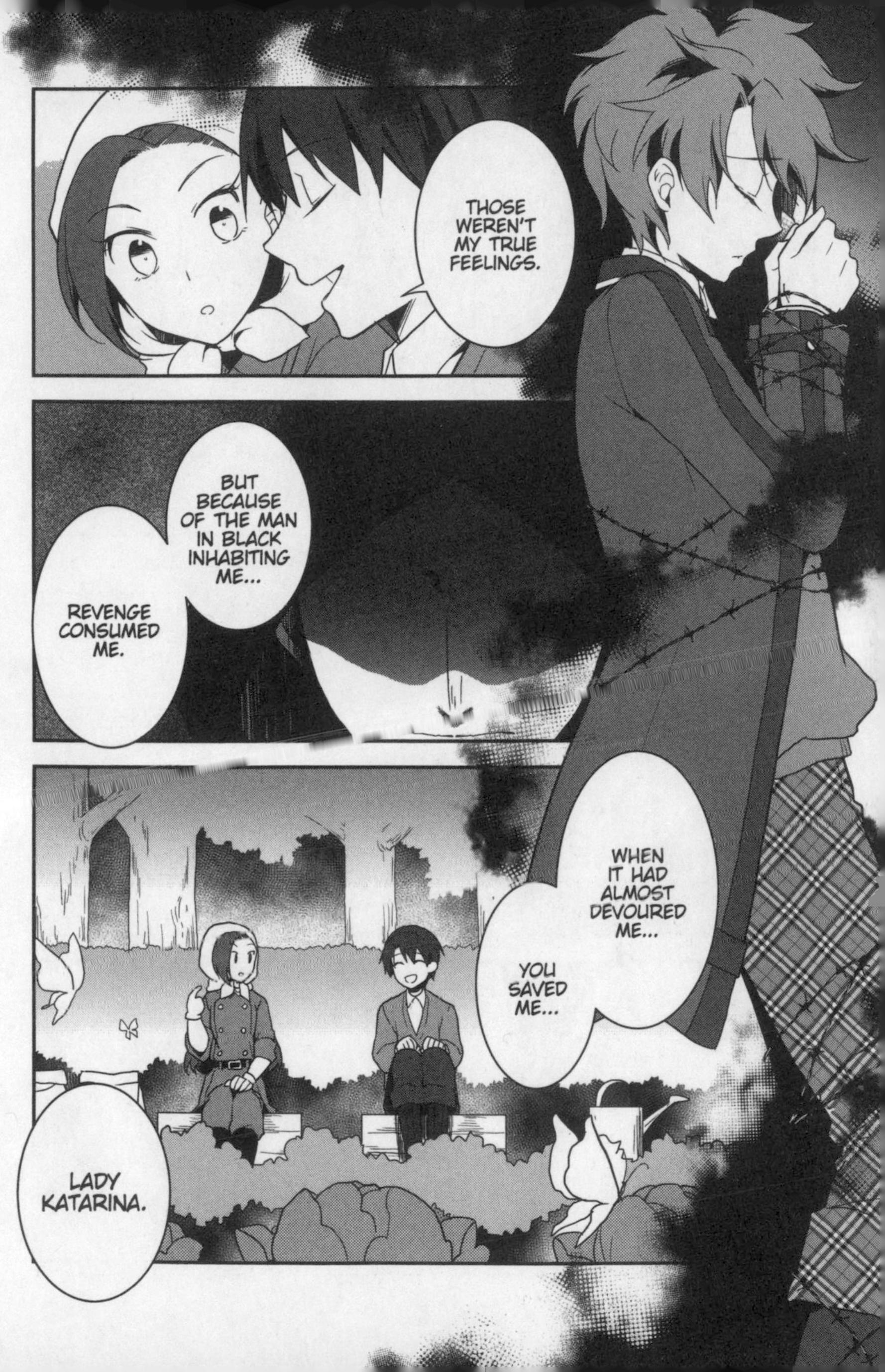
THOSE WEREN'T MY TRUE FEELINGS.
BUT BECAUSE OF THE MAN IN BLACK INHABITING ME...
REVENGE CONSUMED ME.
WHEN IT HAD ALMOST DEVOURED ME...
YOU SAVED ME...
LADY KATARINA.

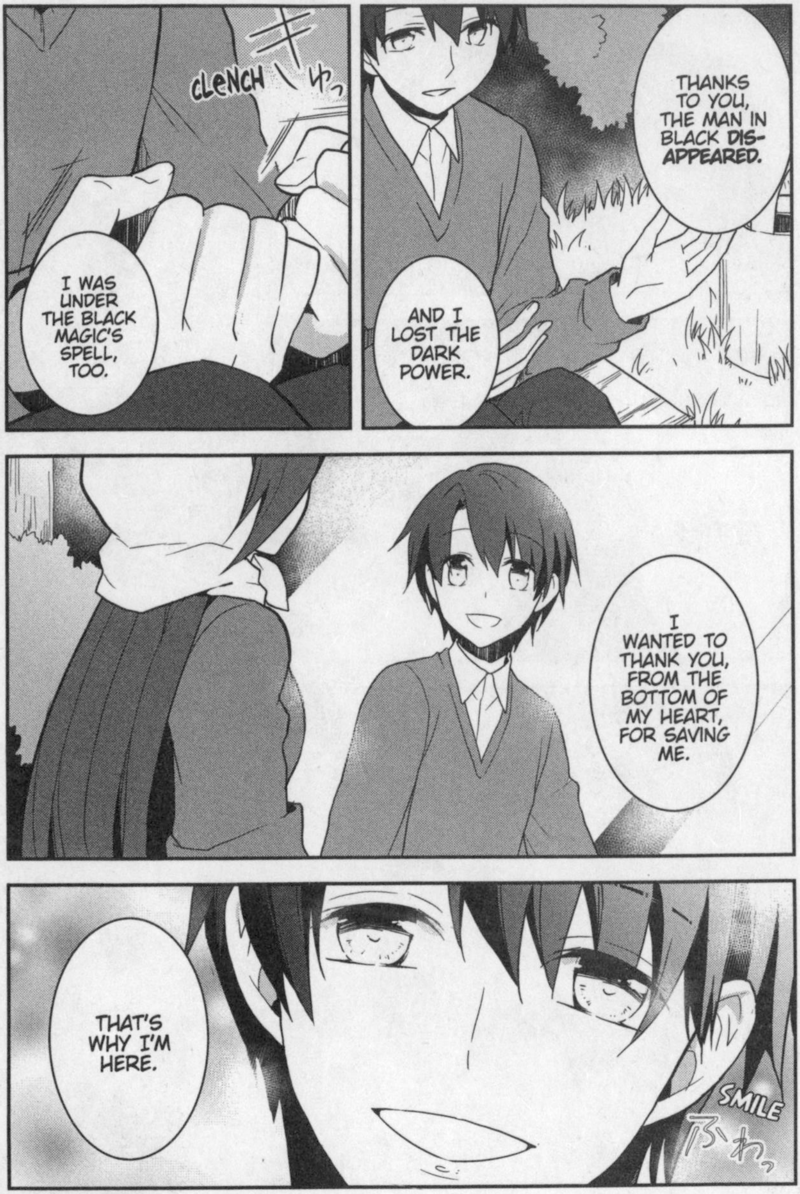
THANKS TO YOU, THE MAN IN BLACK **DISAPPEARED.**
AND I LOST THE DARK POWER.
CLENCH
I WAS UNDER THE BLACK MAGIC'S SPELL, TOO.
I WANTED TO THANK YOU, FROM THE BOTTOM OF MY HEART, FOR SAVING ME.
THAT'S WHY I'M HERE.
SMILE

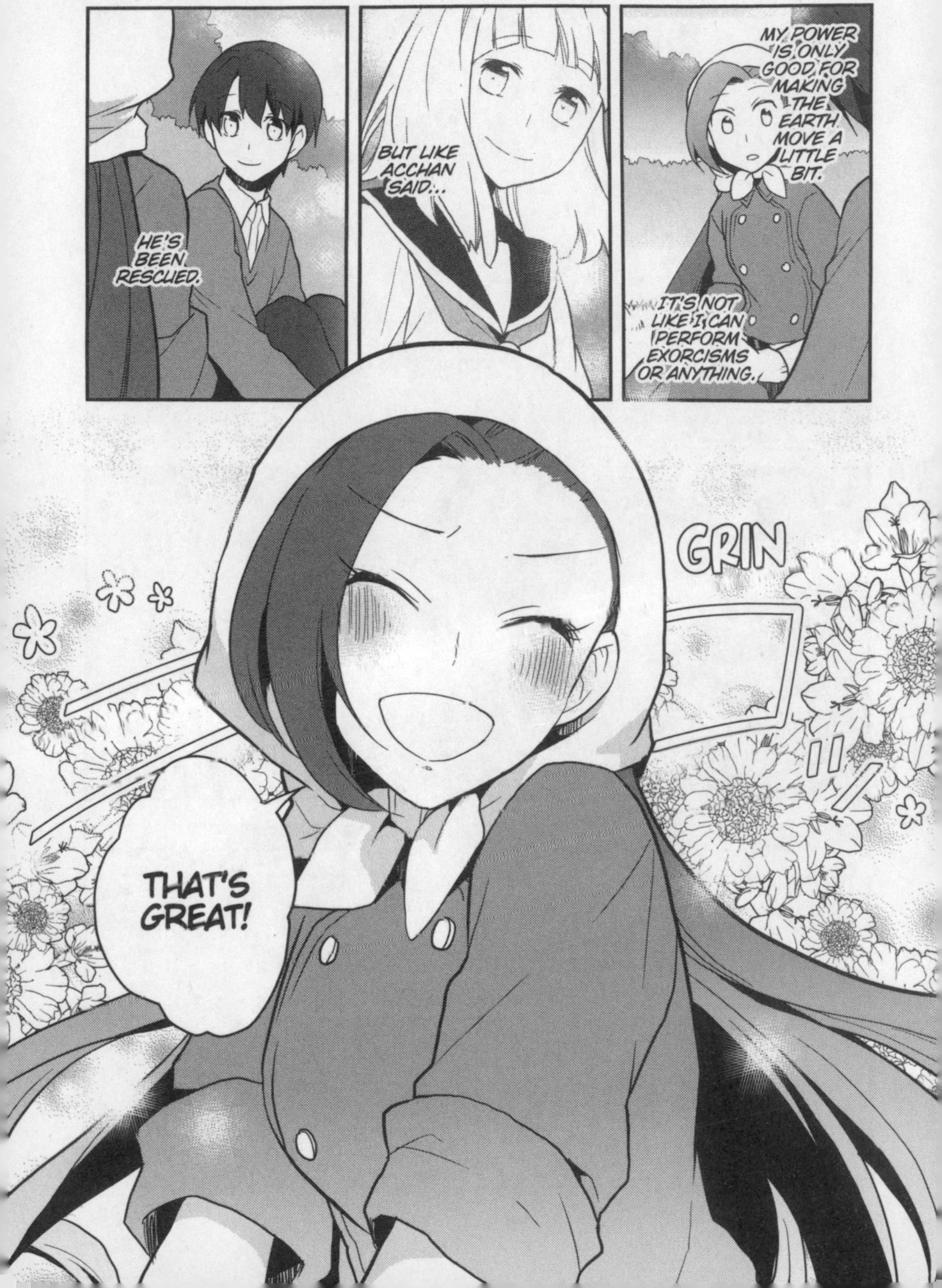
MY POWER IS ONLY GOOD FOR MAKING THE EARTH MOVE A LITTLE BIT.
IT'S NOT LIKE I CAN PERFORM EXORCISMS OR ANYTHING.
BUT LIKE ACCHAN SAID...
HE'S BEEN RESCUED.
GRIN
THAT'S GREAT!

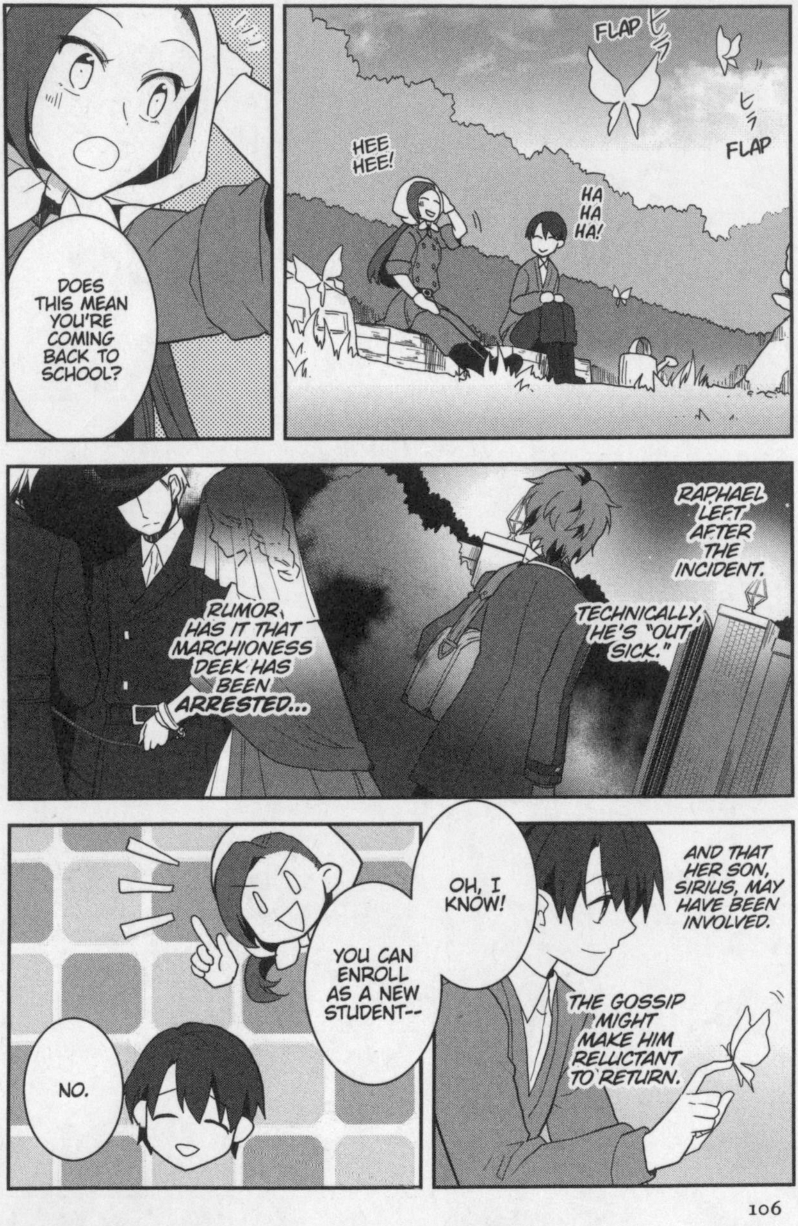

FLAP ヒラ
ヒラ FLAP
HEE HEE!
HA HA HA!
DOES THIS MEAN YOU'RE COMING BACK TO SCHOOL?
RAPHAEL LEFT AFTER THE INCIDENT.
TECHNICALLY, HE'S "OUT SICK."
RUMOR HAS IT THAT MARCHIONESS DEEK HAS BEEN ARRESTED...
AND THAT HER SON, SIRIUS, MAY HAVE BEEN INVOLVED.
THE GOSSIP MIGHT MAKE HIM RELUCTANT TO RETURN.
OH, I KNOW!
YOU CAN ENROLL AS A NEW STUDENT--
NO.

EVEN THOUGH I WAS MANIPULATED, WHAT I DID WAS UNFORGIVABLE.

I WISH I COULD'VE GRADUATED THOUGH.

. . . . .

I'M NOT GOING BACK TO SCHOOL.

I SEE...

DOES THIS MEAN I WON'T SEE YOU ANYMORE?

SST

NO.

I HAD THE MASTER OF DISGUISE FROM MY NEW HOME CREATE THIS LOOK FOR ME.

GRIN

MASTER ....?

BUT I'M NOT COMFORTABLE GOING TO SCHOOL LIKE THIS.

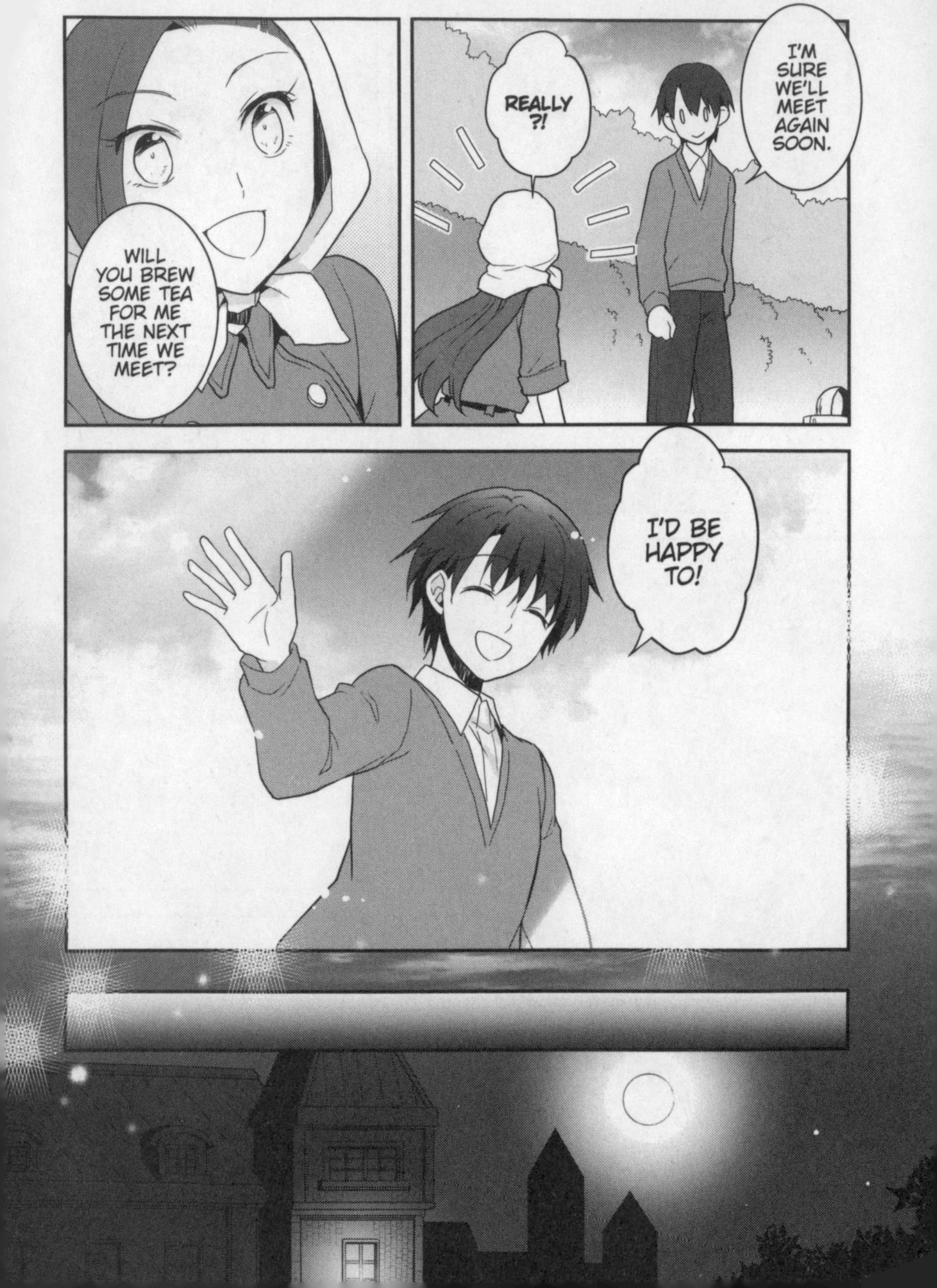
I'M SURE WE'LL MEET AGAIN SOON.
REALLY ?!
WILL YOU BREW SOME TEA FOR ME THE NEXT TIME WE MEET?
I'D BE HAPPY TO!

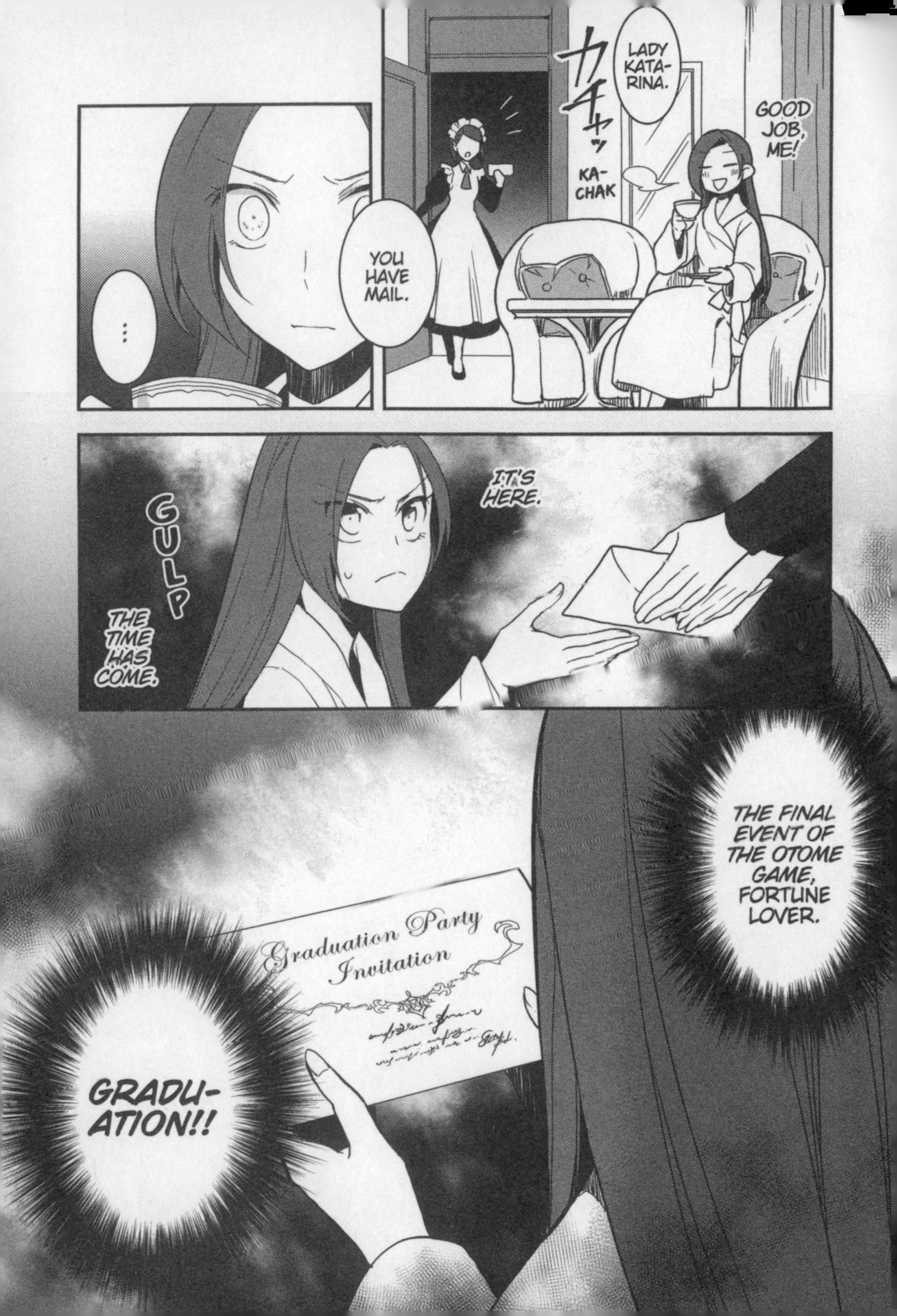
GOOD JOB, ME!
LADY KATA-RINA.
カチャッ
KA-CHAK
YOU HAVE MAIL.
…
IT'S HERE.
GULP
THE TIME HAS COME.
THE FINAL EVENT OF THE OTOME GAME, FORTUNE LOVER.
Graduation Party Invitation
GRADU-ATION!!

My Next Life
as a VILLAINESS:
ALL ROUTES
LEAD TO DOOM!

Chapter 22

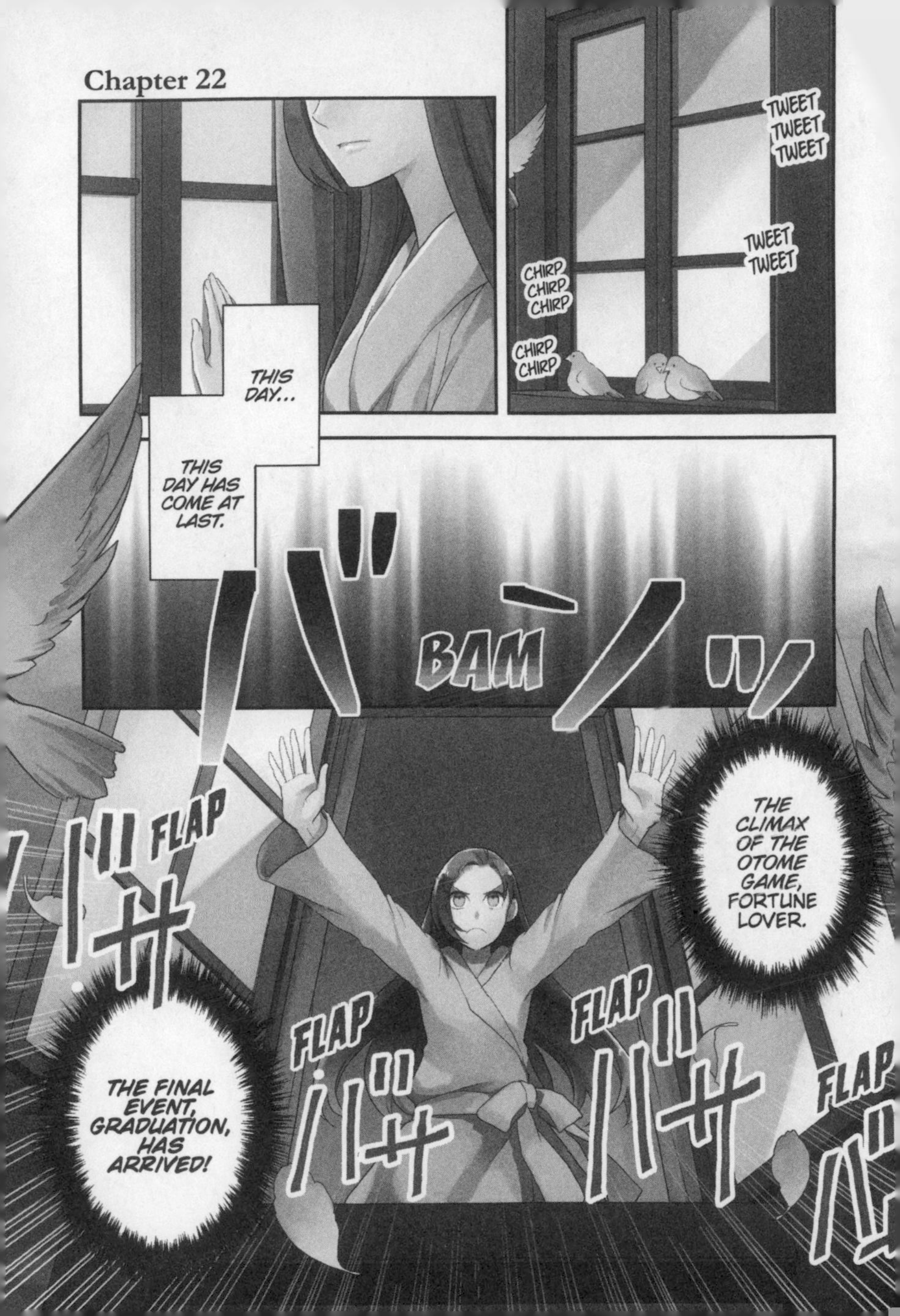
TWEET TWEET TWEET
TWEET TWEET
CHIRP CHIRP CHIRP
CHIRP CHIRP
THIS DAY...
THIS DAY HAS COME AT LAST.
BAM
FLAP
THE CLIMAX OF THE OTOME GAME, FORTUNE LOVER.
FLAP
FLAP
FLAP
THE FINAL EVENT, GRADUATION, HAS ARRIVED!

Chapter 22: The Final Event

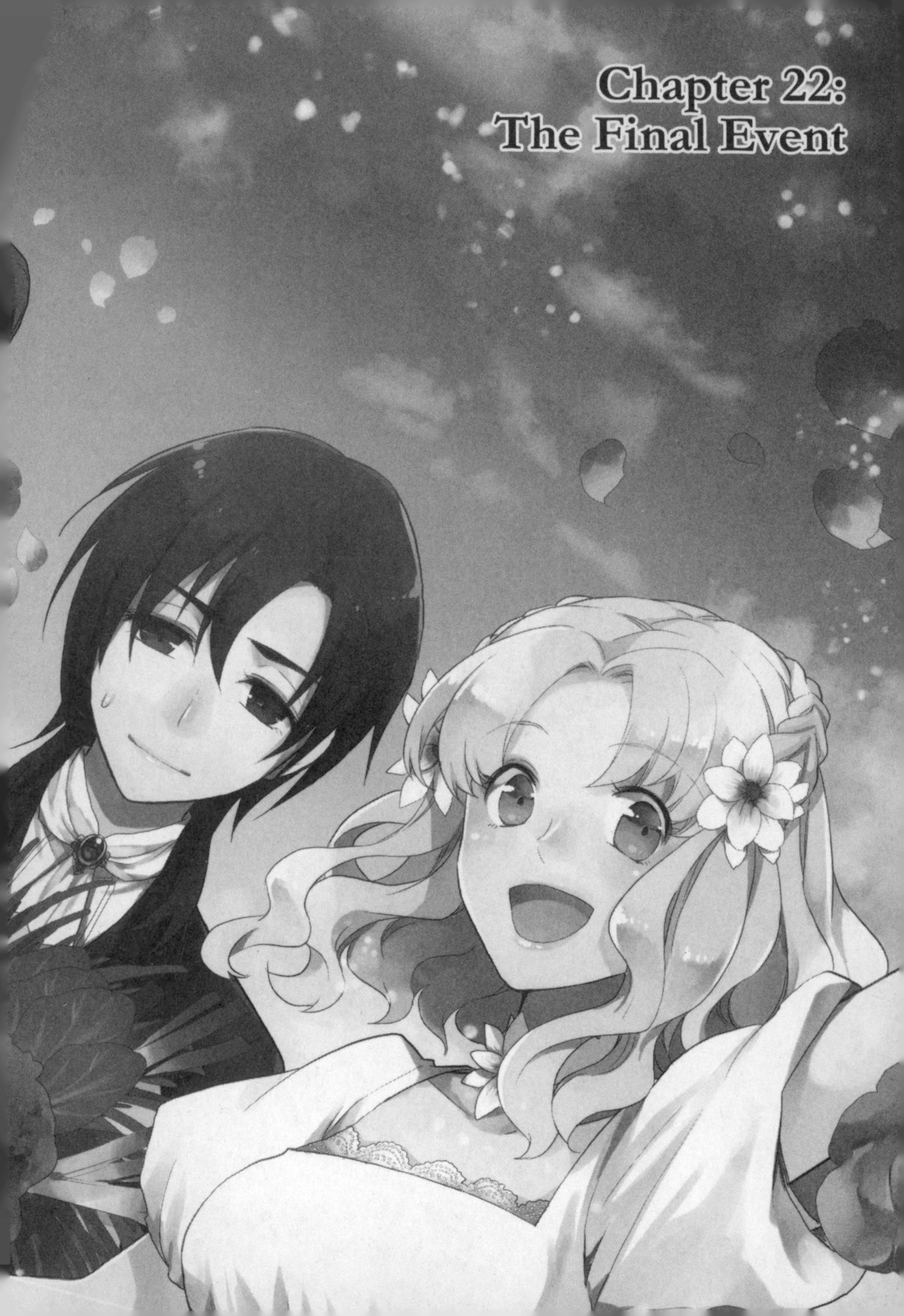

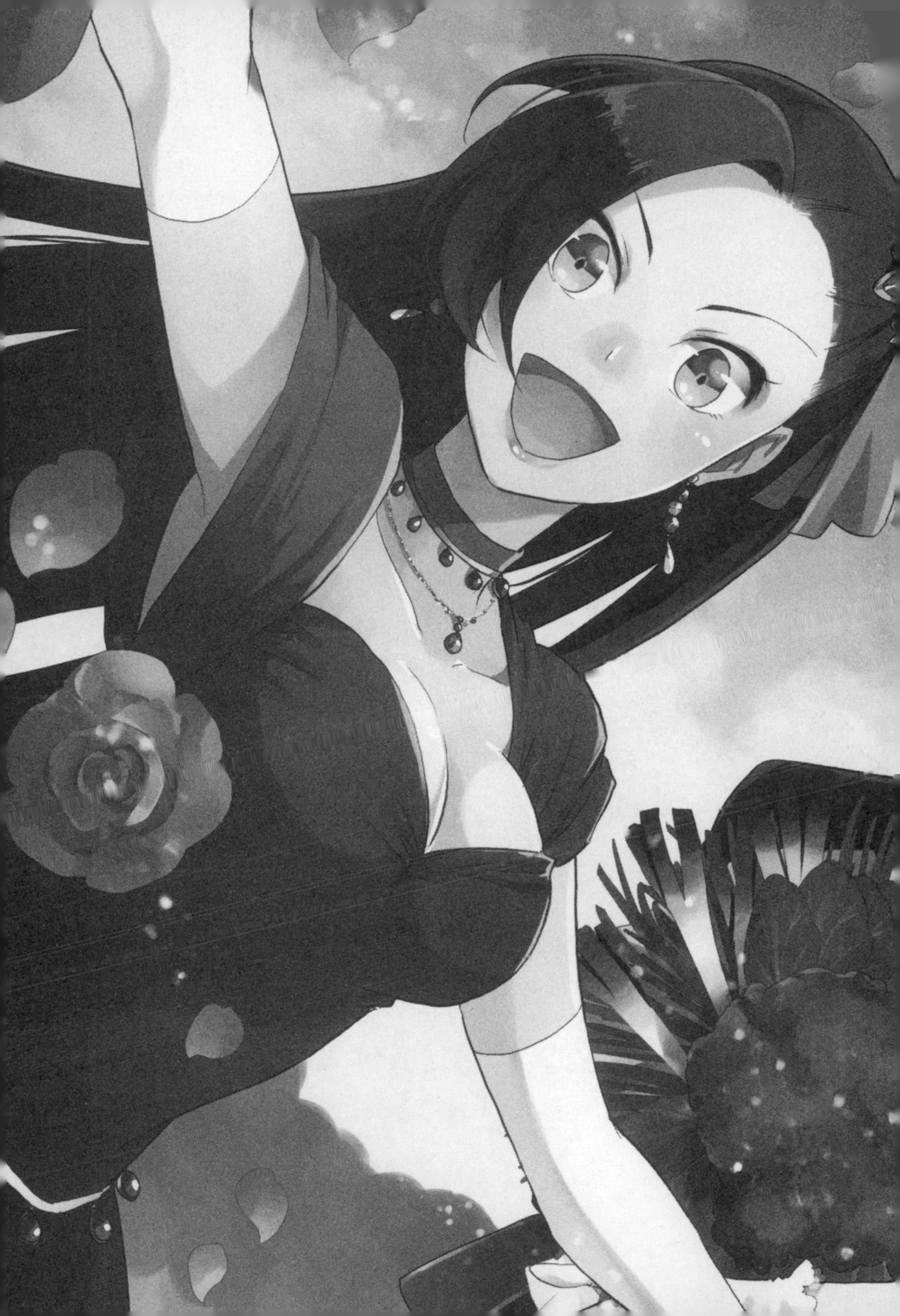

My Next Life
as a VILLAINESS:
ALL ROUTES
LEAD TO DOOM!

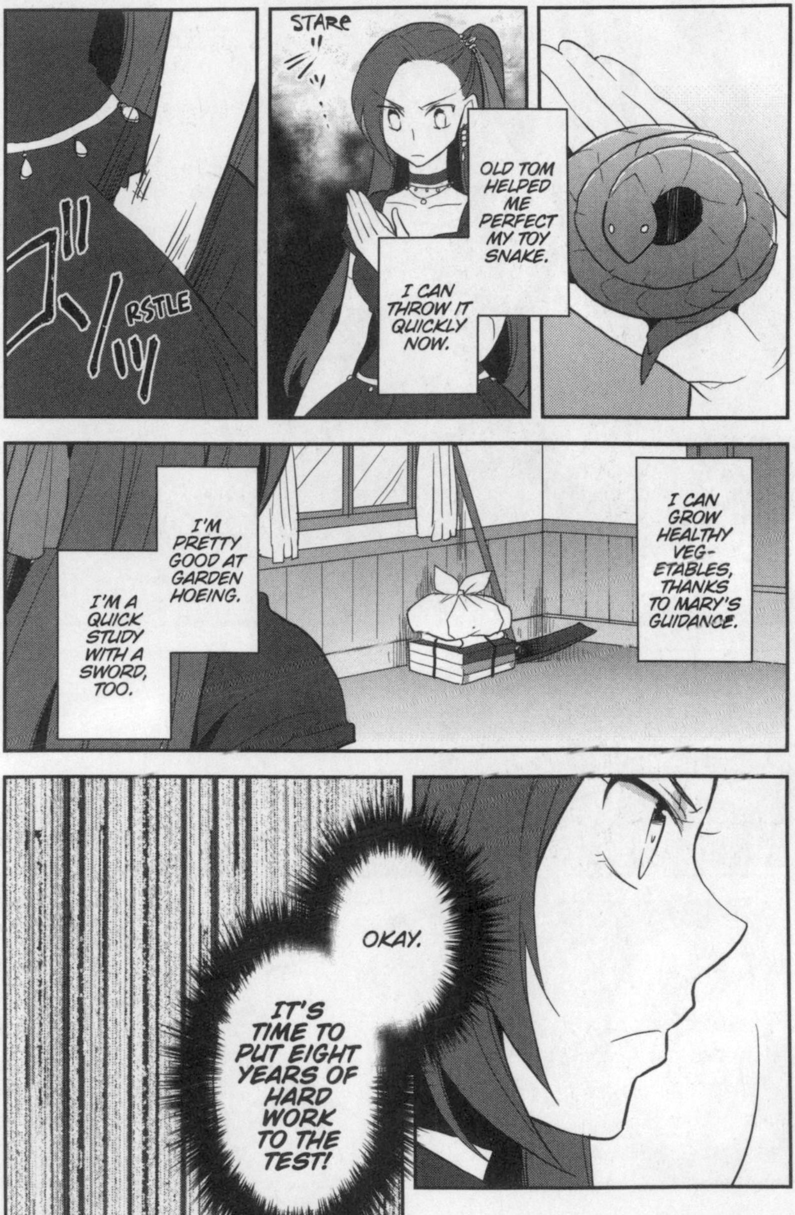
STARE
OLD TOM HELPED ME PERFECT MY TOY SNAKE.
I CAN THROW IT QUICKLY NOW.
RSTLE
I CAN GROW HEALTHY VEG-ETABLES, THANKS TO MARY'S GUIDANCE.
I'M PRETTY GOOD AT GARDEN HOEING.
I'M A QUICK STUDY WITH A SWORD, TOO.
OKAY.
IT'S TIME TO PUT EIGHT YEARS OF HARD WORK TO THE TEST!

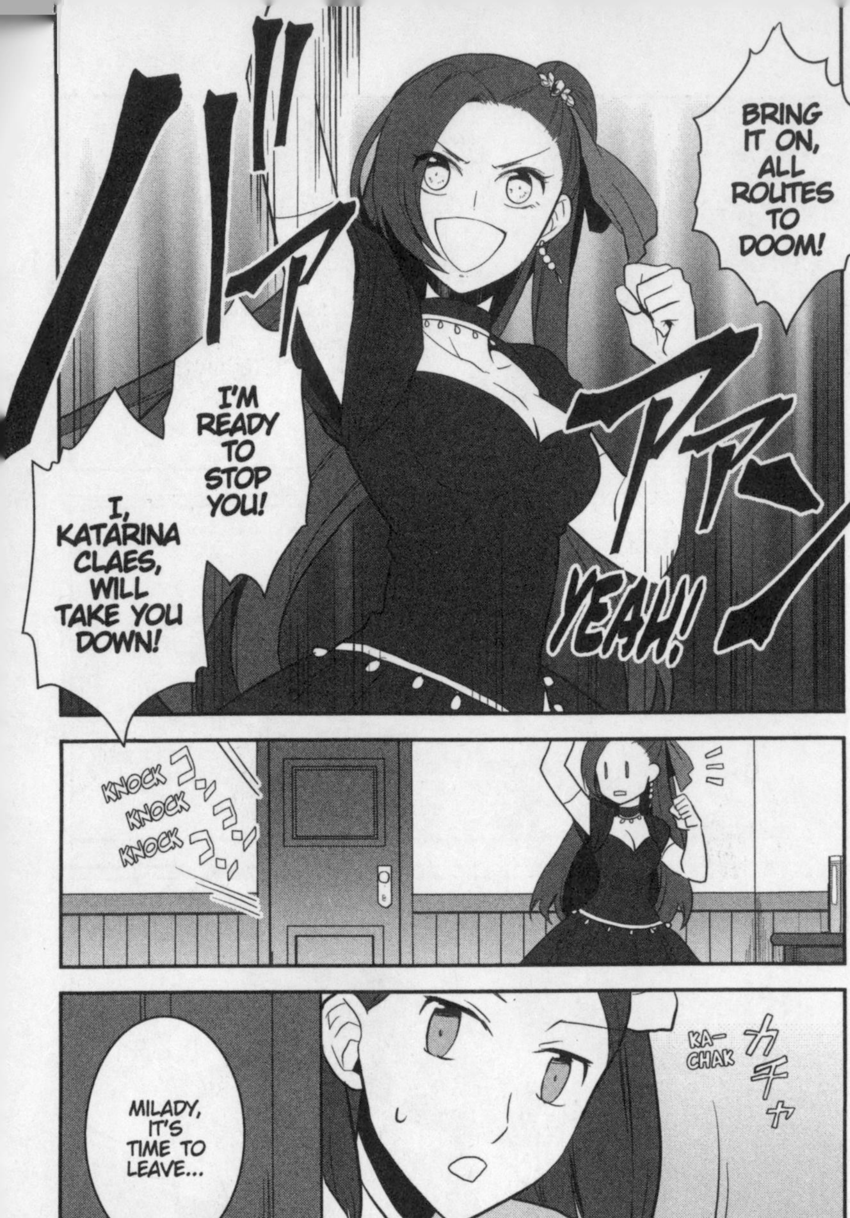
BRING IT ON, ALL ROUTES TO DOOM!
YEAH!
I'M READY TO STOP YOU!
I, KATARINA CLAES, WILL TAKE YOU DOWN!
KNOCK KNOCK KNOCK
KA-CHAK
MILADY, IT'S TIME TO LEAVE...

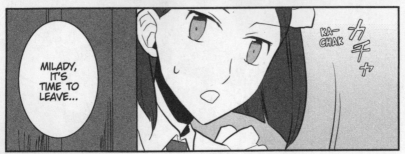

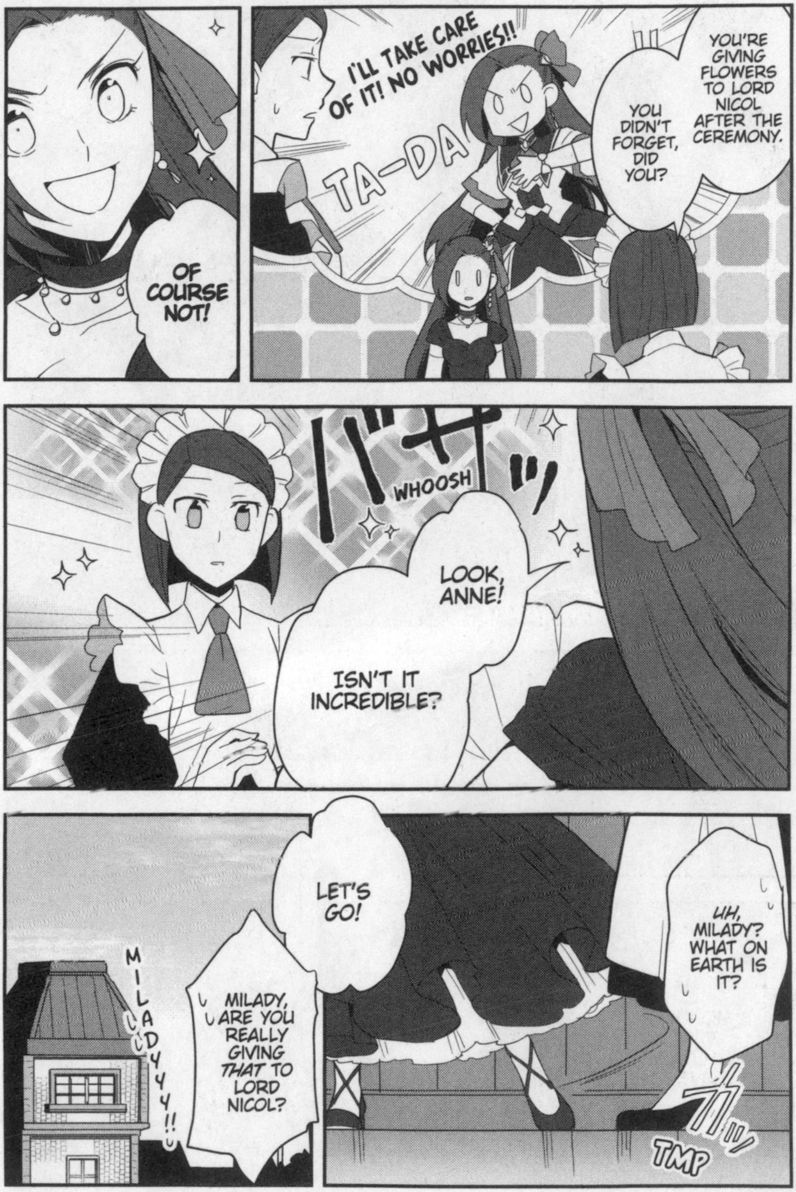
YOU'RE GIVING FLOWERS TO LORD NICOL AFTER THE CEREMONY.
YOU DIDN'T FORGET, DID YOU?
I'LL TAKE CARE OF IT! NO WORRIES!!
TA-DA
OF COURSE NOT!
バサッ
WHOOSH
LOOK, ANNE!
ISN'T IT INCREDIBLE?
UH, MILADY? WHAT ON EARTH IS IT?
LET'S GO!
TMP
MILADY, ARE YOU REALLY GIVING *THAT* TO LORD NICOL?
MILADYYY!!

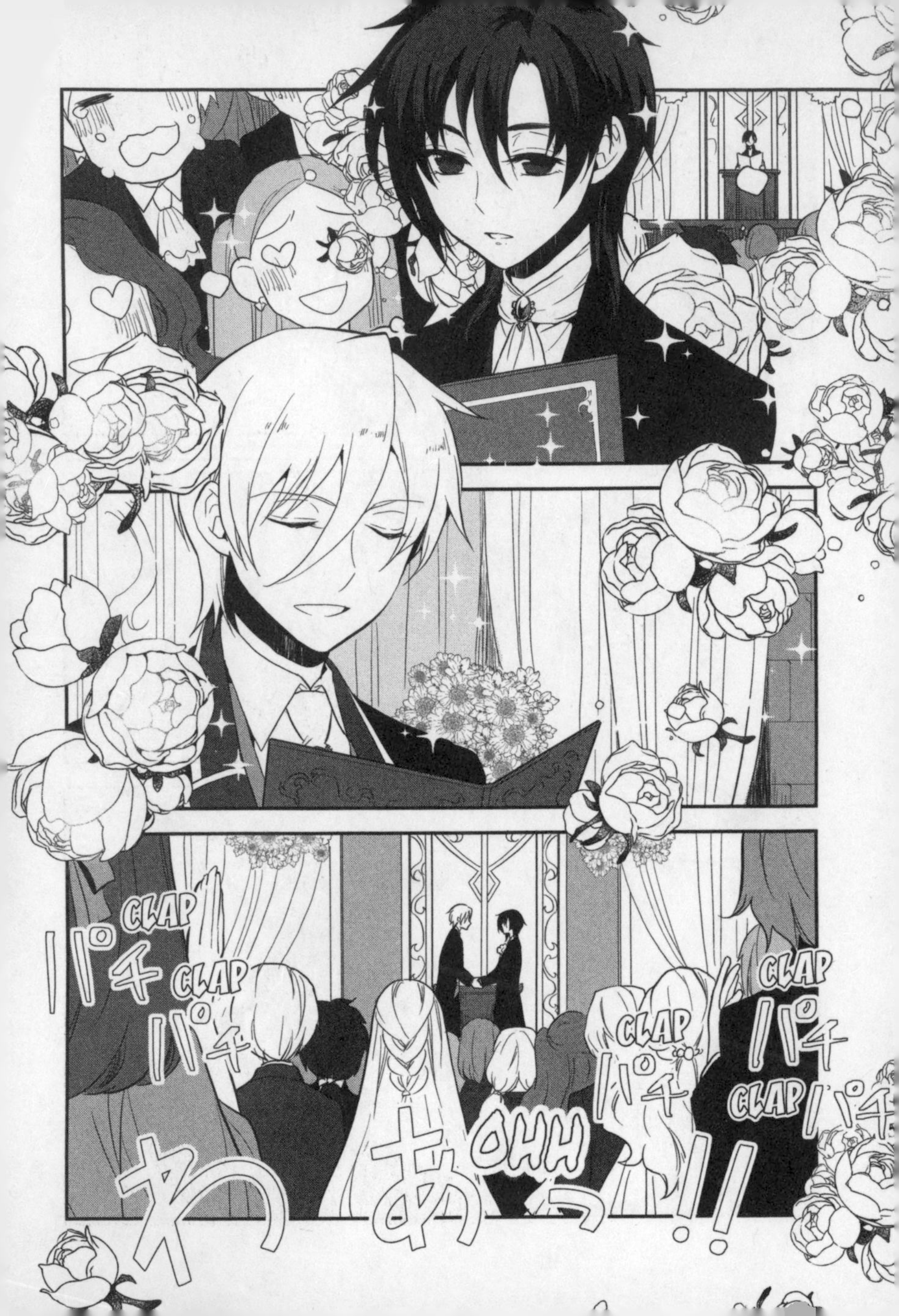
CLAP
パチ
CLAP
パチ
CLAP
パチ
CLAP
パチ
CLAP
パチ
わあっ!!
OHH

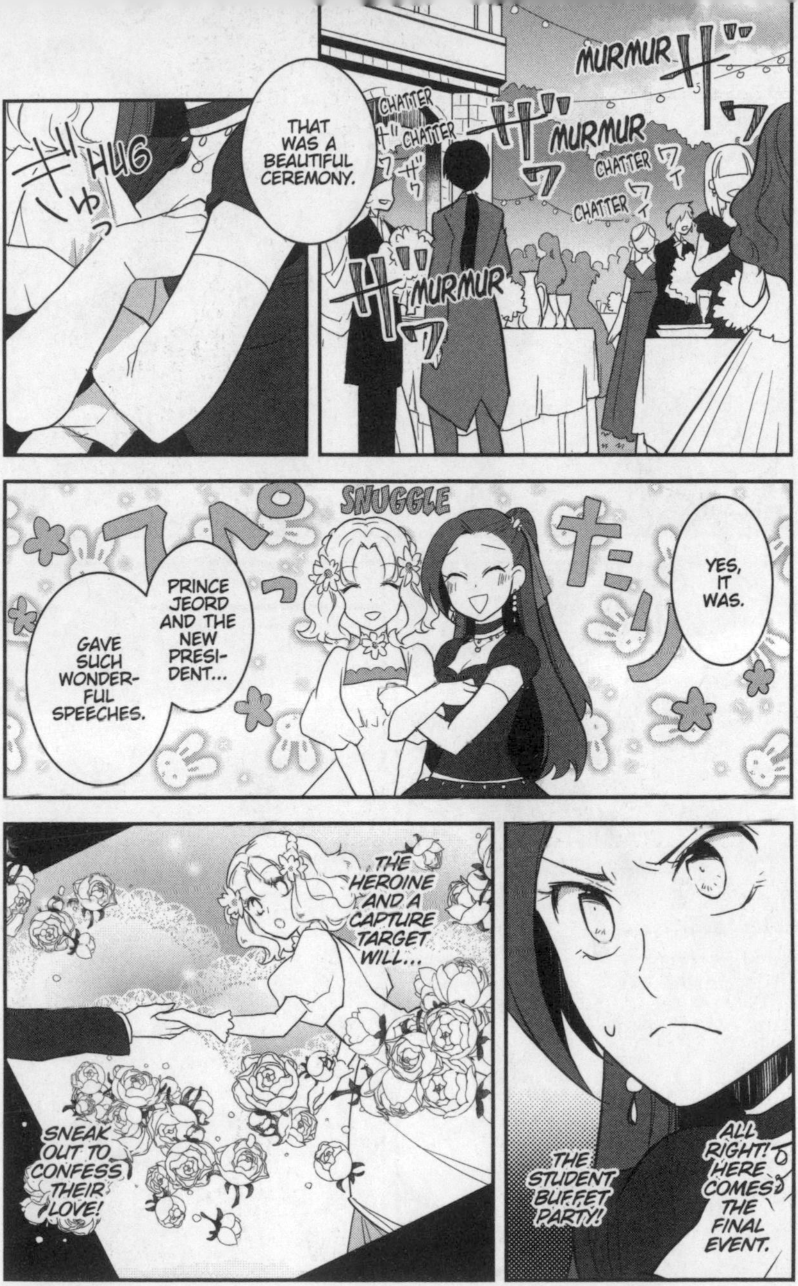
MURMUR
CHATTER
CHATTER
MURMUR
CHATTER
CHATTER
MURMUR
THAT WAS A BEAUTIFUL CEREMONY.
HUG
SNUGGLE
YES, IT WAS.
PRINCE JEORD AND THE NEW PRESIDENT...
GAVE SUCH WONDERFUL SPEECHES.
ALL RIGHT! HERE COMES THE FINAL EVENT.
THE STUDENT BUFFET PARTY!
THE HEROINE AND A CAPTURE TARGET WILL...
SNEAK OUT TO CONFESS THEIR LOVE!

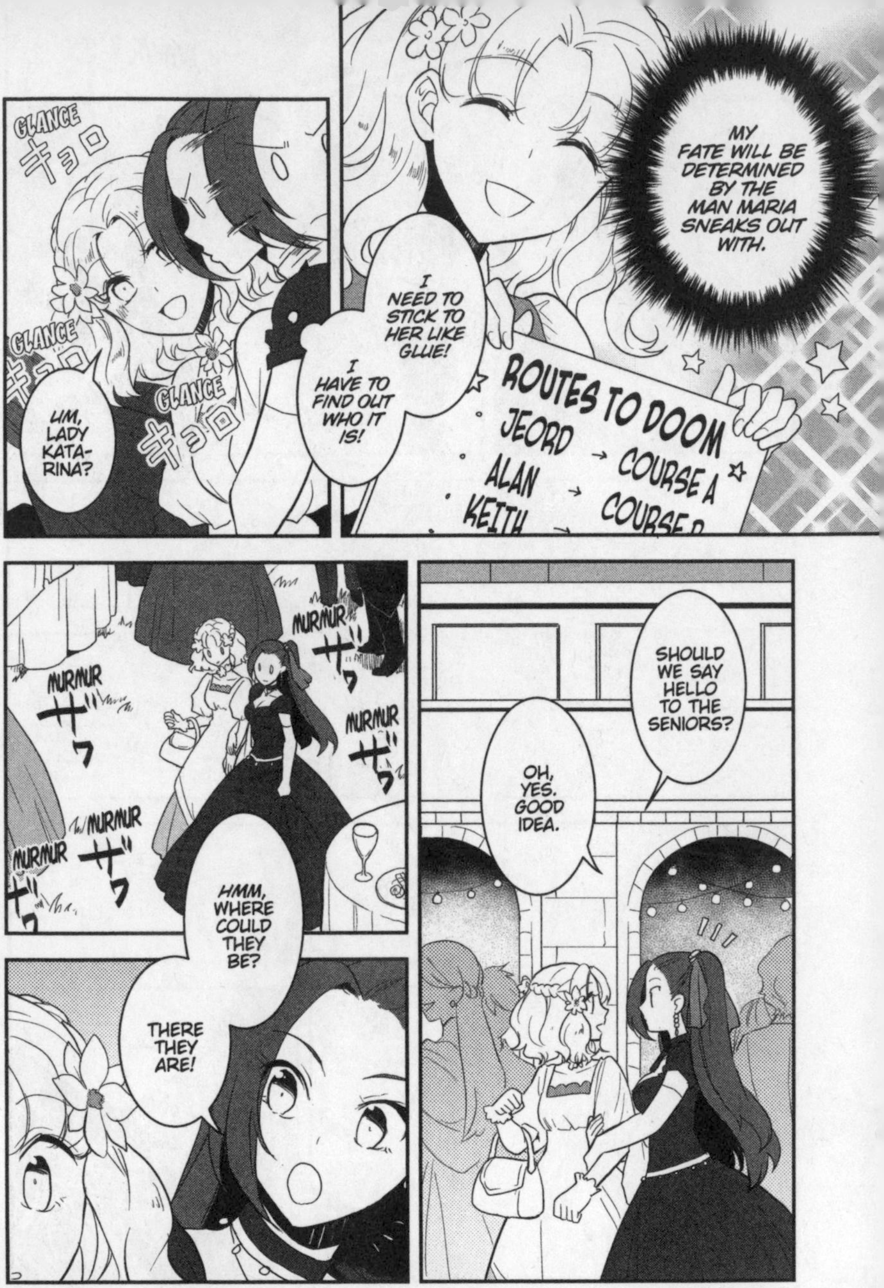
MY FATE WILL BE DETERMINED BY THE MAN MARIA SNEAKS OUT WITH.
ROUTES TO DOOM
JEORD → COURSE A
ALAN → COURSE
KEITH →
I NEED TO STICK TO HER LIKE GLUE!
I HAVE TO FIND OUT WHO IT IS!
GLANCE キョロ
GLANCE キョロ
GLANCE キョロ
UM, LADY KATARINA?
SHOULD WE SAY HELLO TO THE SENIORS?
OH, YES. GOOD IDEA.
MURMUR ザワ
MURMUR ザワ
MURMUR ザワ
MURMUR ザワ
MURMUR ザワ
HMM, WHERE COULD THEY BE?
THERE THEY ARE!

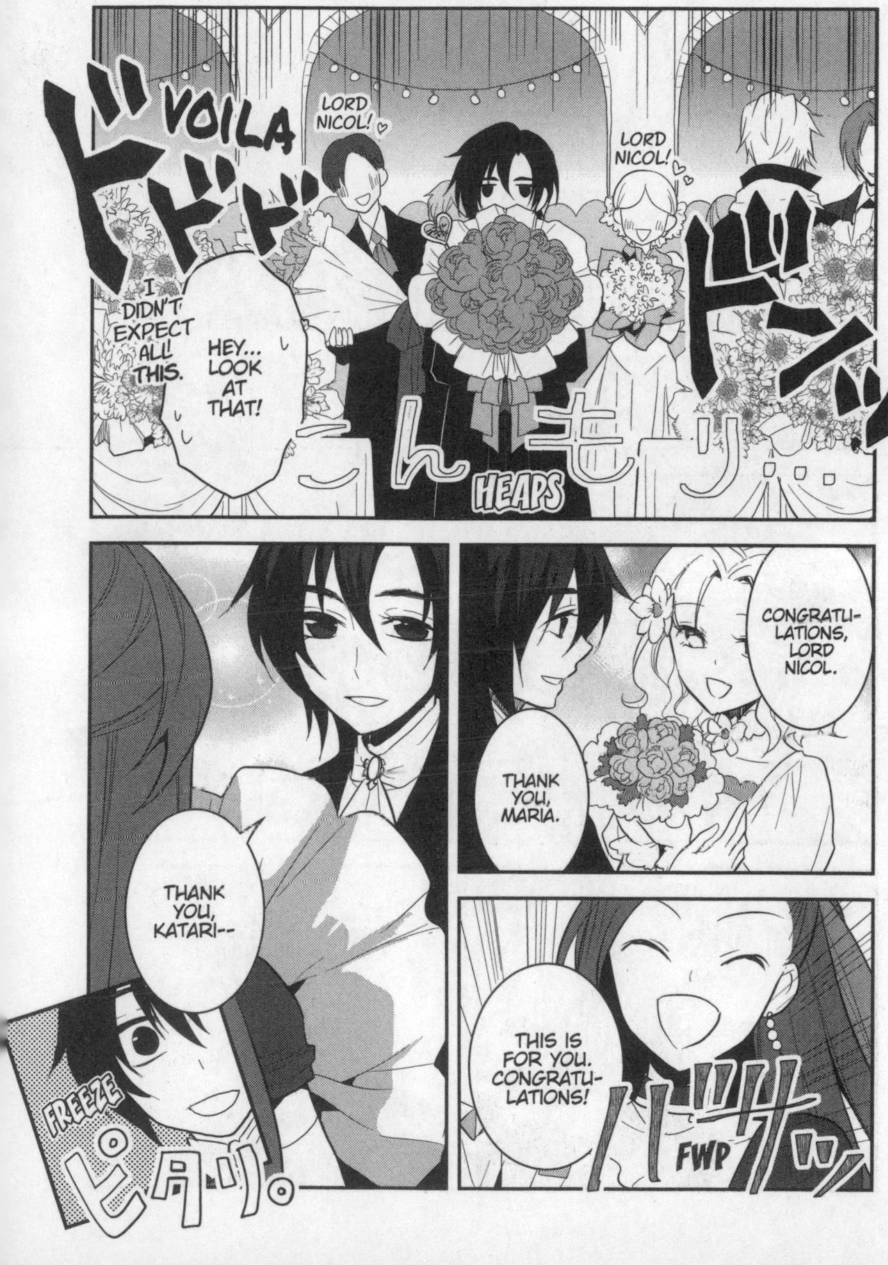
LORD NICOL!
LORD NICOL!
VOILA
HEY... LOOK AT THAT!
I DIDN'T EXPECT ALL THIS.
HEAPS
CONGRATULATIONS, LORD NICOL.
THANK YOU, MARIA.
THIS IS FOR YOU. CONGRATULATIONS!
FWP
THANK YOU, KATARI--
FREEZE

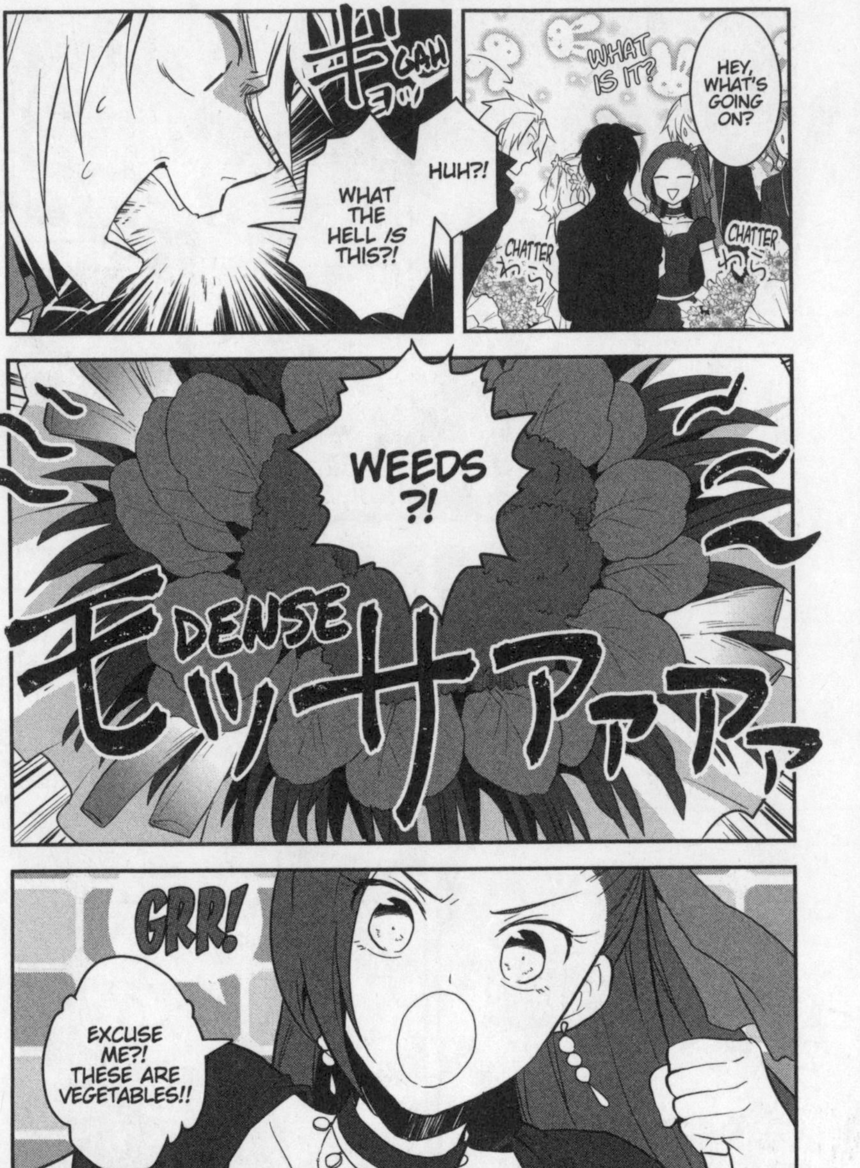
HEY, WHAT'S GOING ON?
WHAT IS IT?
CHATTER
わら
CHATTER
わら
GAH
HUH?!
WHAT THE HELL IS THIS?!
WEEDS ?!
DENSE
GRR!
EXCUSE ME?! THESE ARE VEGETABLES!!

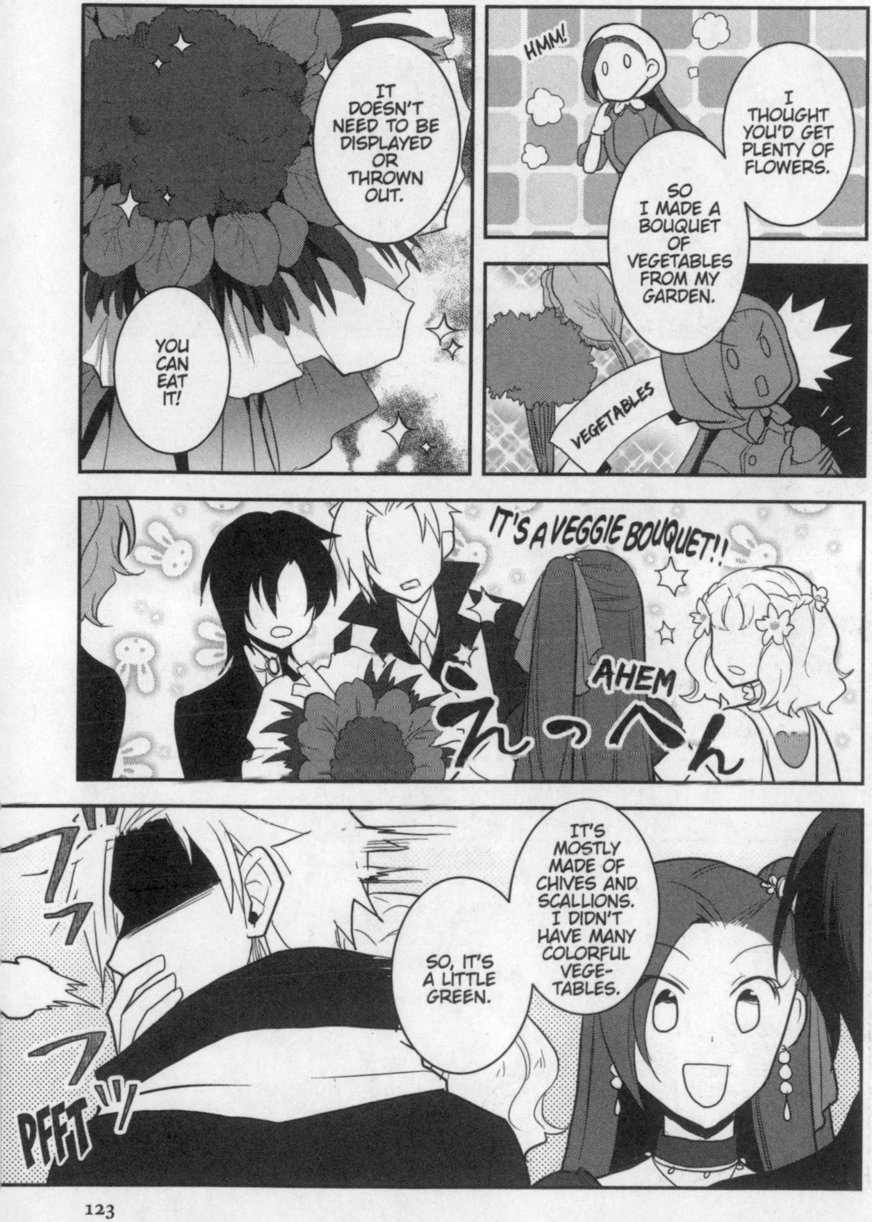
HMM!
I THOUGHT YOU'D GET PLENTY OF FLOWERS.
SO I MADE A BOUQUET OF VEGETABLES FROM MY GARDEN.
VEGETABLES
IT DOESN'T NEED TO BE DISPLAYED OR THROWN OUT.
YOU CAN EAT IT!
IT'S A VEGGIE BOUQUET!!
AHEM
えっへん
IT'S MOSTLY MADE OF CHIVES AND SCALLIONS. I DIDN'T HAVE MANY COLORFUL VEGE-TABLES.
SO, IT'S A LITTLE GREEN.
PFFT

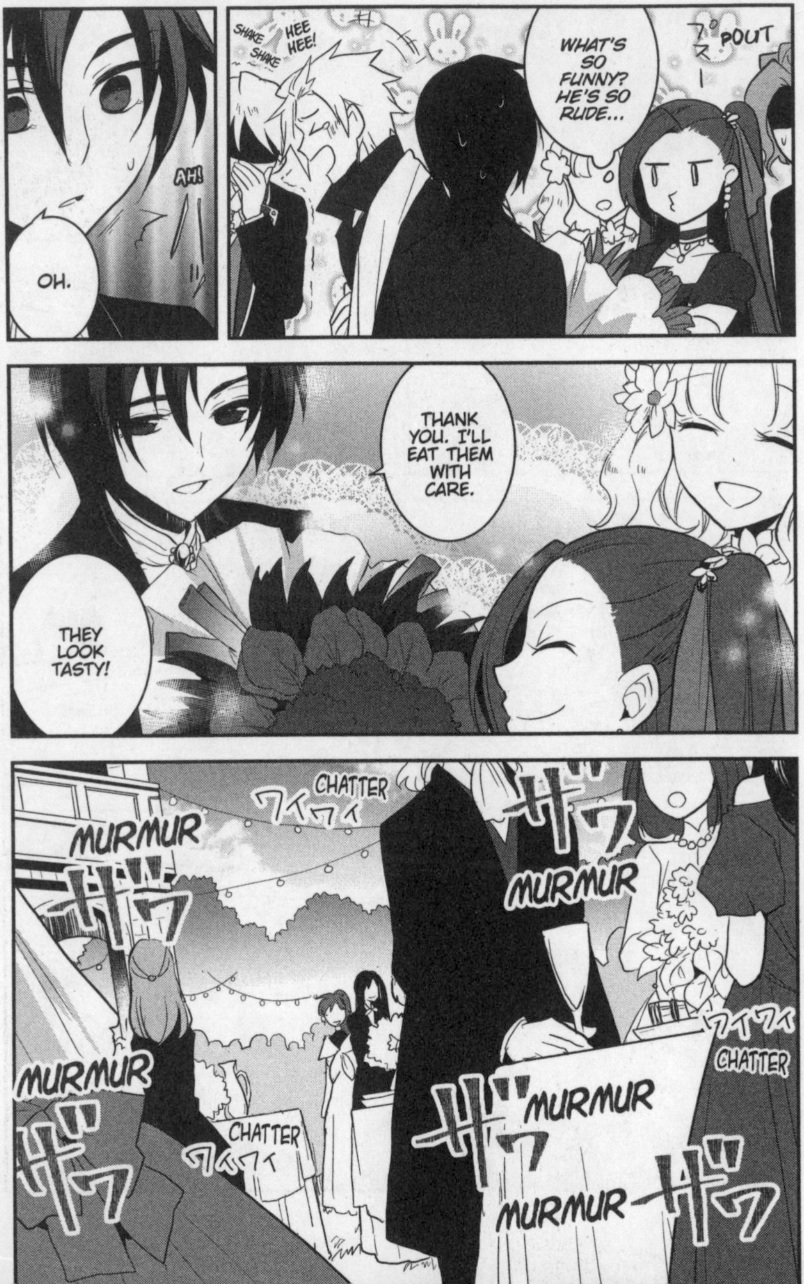
POUT
WHAT'S SO FUNNY? HE'S SO RUDE...
HEE HEE!
SHAKE SHAKE
AH!
OH.
THANK YOU. I'LL EAT THEM WITH CARE.
THEY LOOK TASTY!
ザワ
MURMUR
CHATTER
ワイワイ
MURMUR
ワイワイ
CHATTER
MURMUR
CHATTER
MURMUR
MURMUR
MURMUR

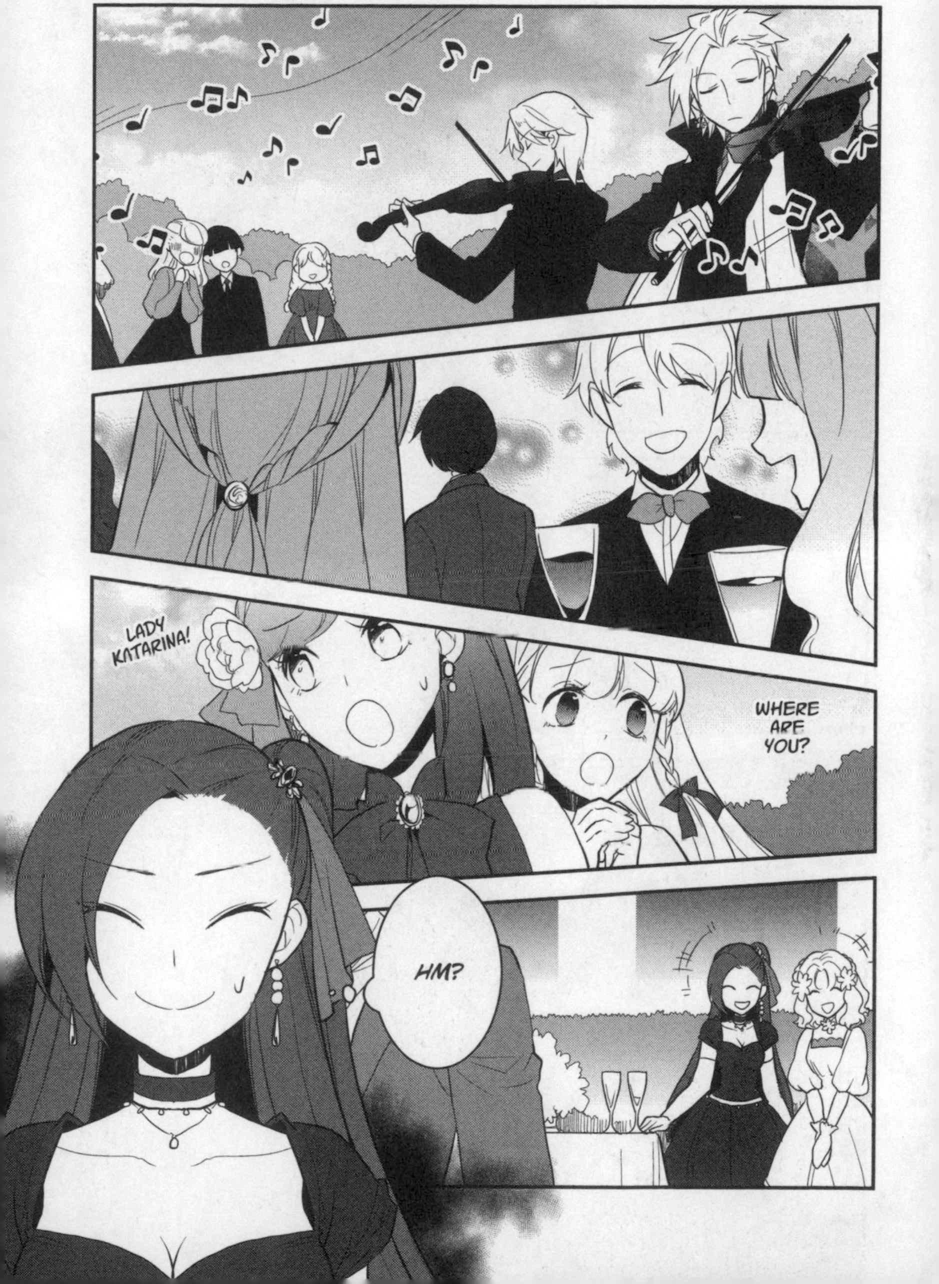
LADY KATARINA!
WHERE ARE YOU?
HM?

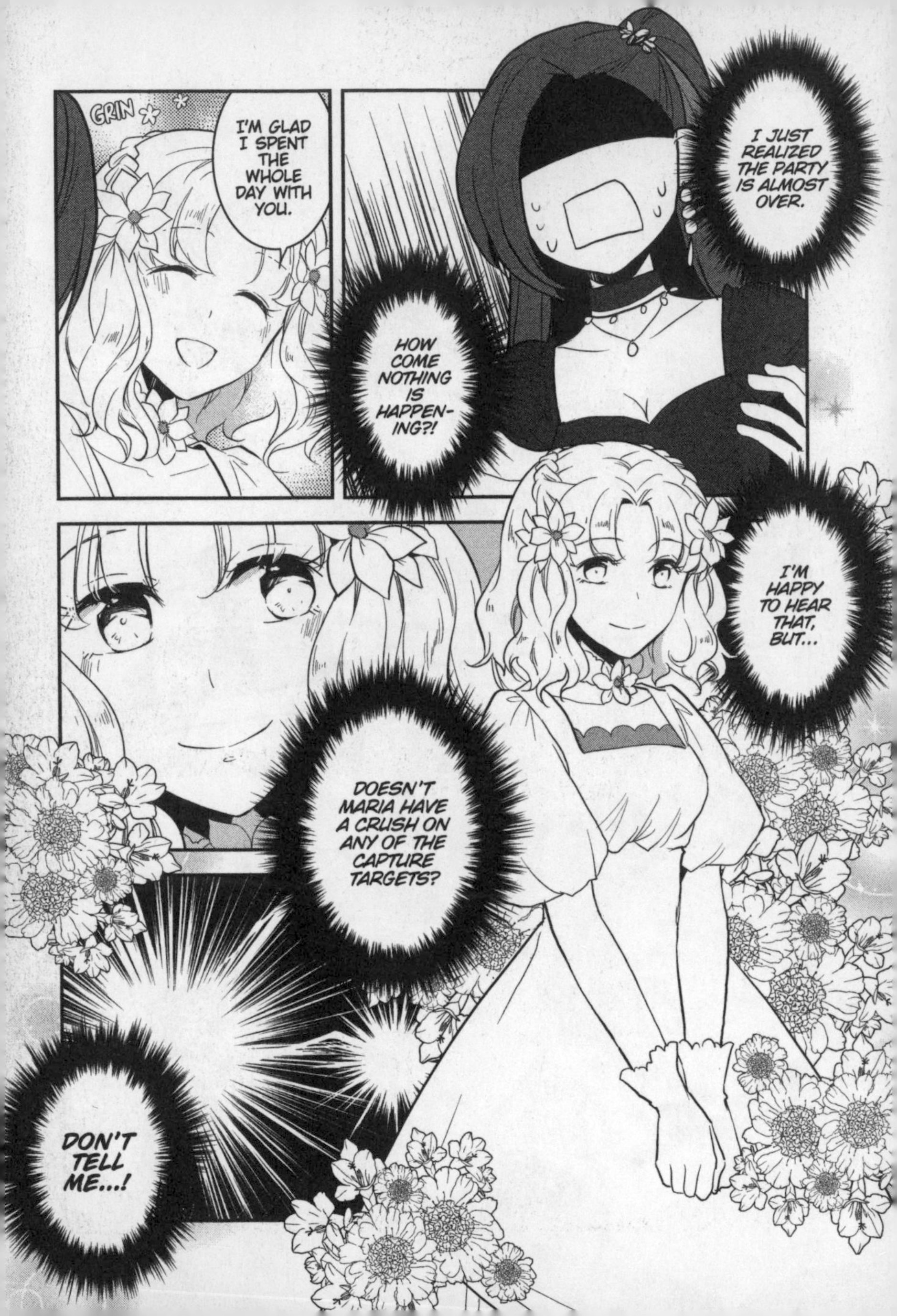
I JUST REALIZED THE PARTY IS ALMOST OVER.
HOW COME NOTHING IS HAPPENING?!
GRIN
I'M GLAD I SPENT THE WHOLE DAY WITH YOU.
I'M HAPPY TO HEAR THAT, BUT...
DOESN'T MARIA HAVE A CRUSH ON ANY OF THE CAPTURE TARGETS?
DON'T TELL ME...!

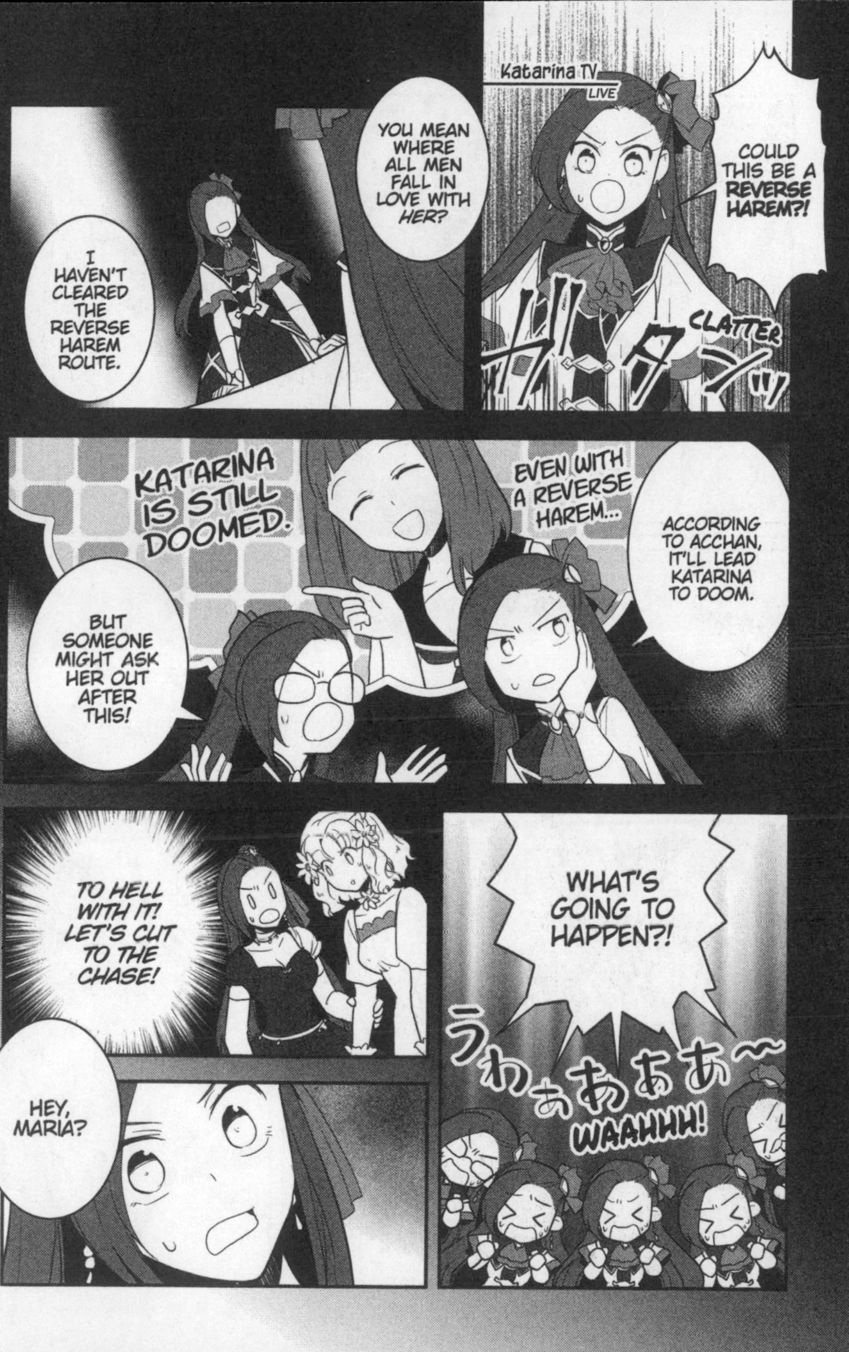
Katarina TV
LIVE
COULD THIS BE A REVERSE HAREM?!
CLATTER
YOU MEAN WHERE ALL MEN FALL IN LOVE WITH HER?
I HAVEN'T CLEARED THE REVERSE HAREM ROUTE.
ACCORDING TO ACCHAN, IT'LL LEAD KATARINA TO DOOM.
EVEN WITH A REVERSE HAREM...
KATARINA IS STILL DOOMED.
BUT SOMEONE MIGHT ASK HER OUT AFTER THIS!
WHAT'S GOING TO HAPPEN?!
うわぁあああ～
WAAHHH!
TO HELL WITH IT! LET'S CUT TO THE CHASE!
HEY, MARIA?

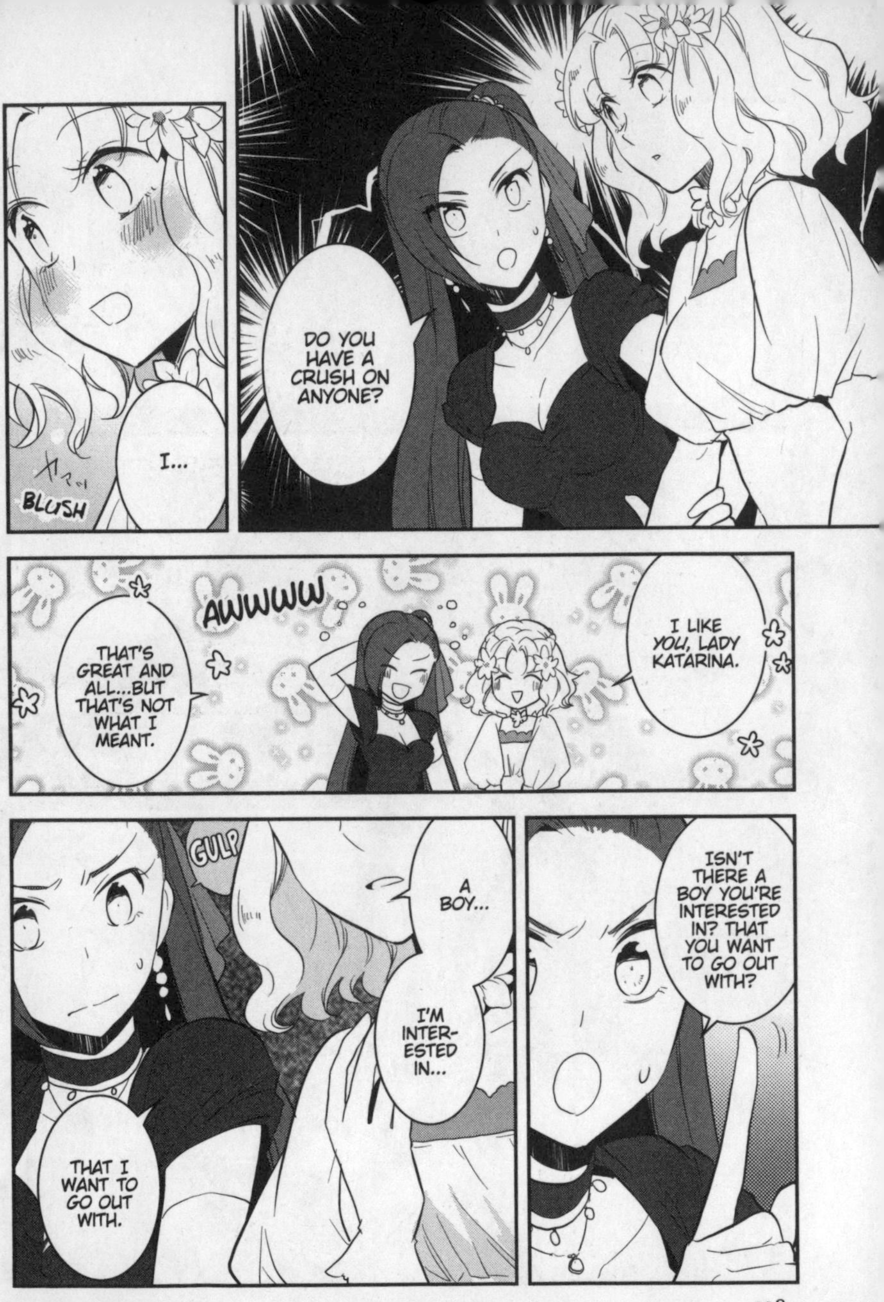

DO YOU HAVE A CRUSH ON ANYONE?
I...
BLUSH
I LIKE YOU, LADY KATARINA.
AWWWW
THAT'S GREAT AND ALL...BUT THAT'S NOT WHAT I MEANT.
ISN'T THERE A BOY YOU'RE INTERESTED IN? THAT YOU WANT TO GO OUT WITH?
A BOY...
GULP
I'M INTERESTED IN...
THAT I WANT TO GO OUT WITH.

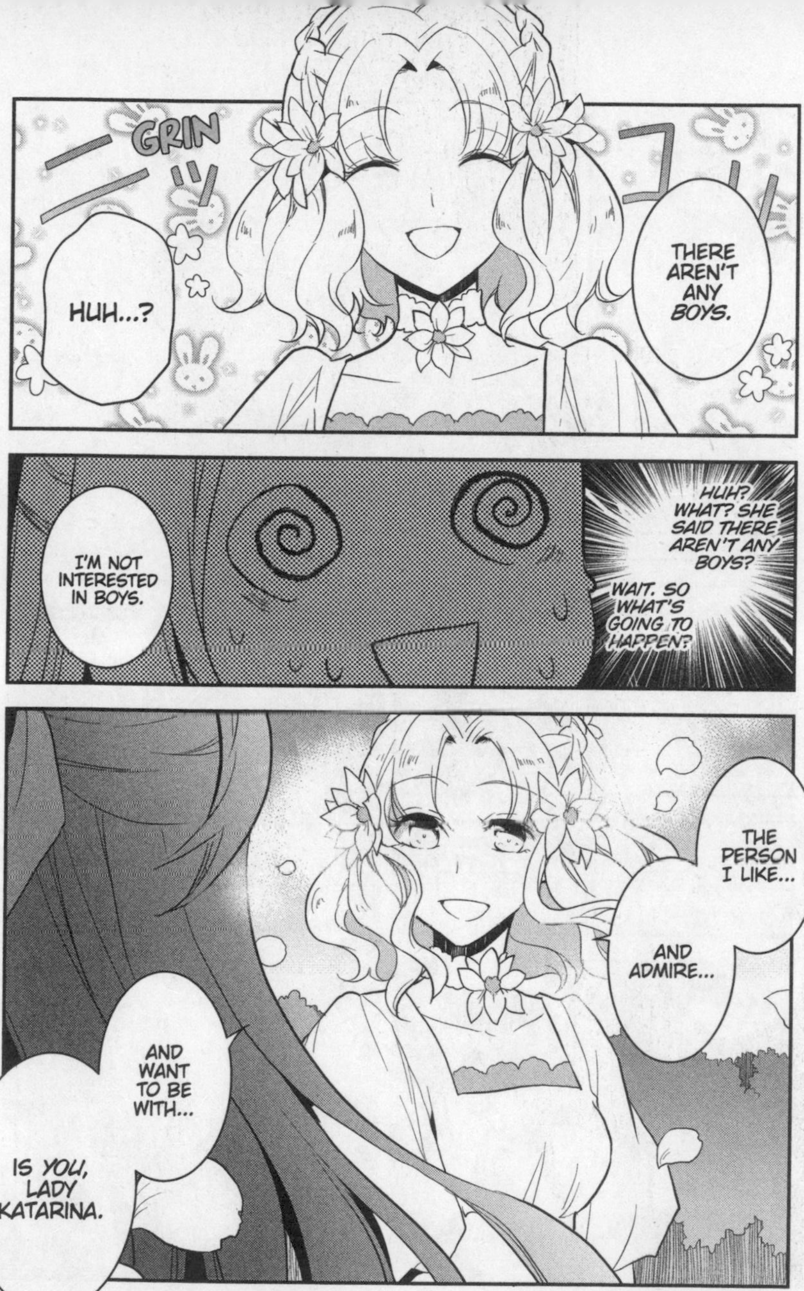
THERE AREN'T ANY BOYS.
GRIN
HUH...?
HUH? WHAT? SHE SAID THERE AREN'T ANY BOYS?
WAIT. SO WHAT'S GOING TO HAPPEN?
I'M NOT INTERESTED IN BOYS.
THE PERSON I LIKE...
AND ADMIRE...
AND WANT TO BE WITH...
IS YOU, LADY KATARINA.

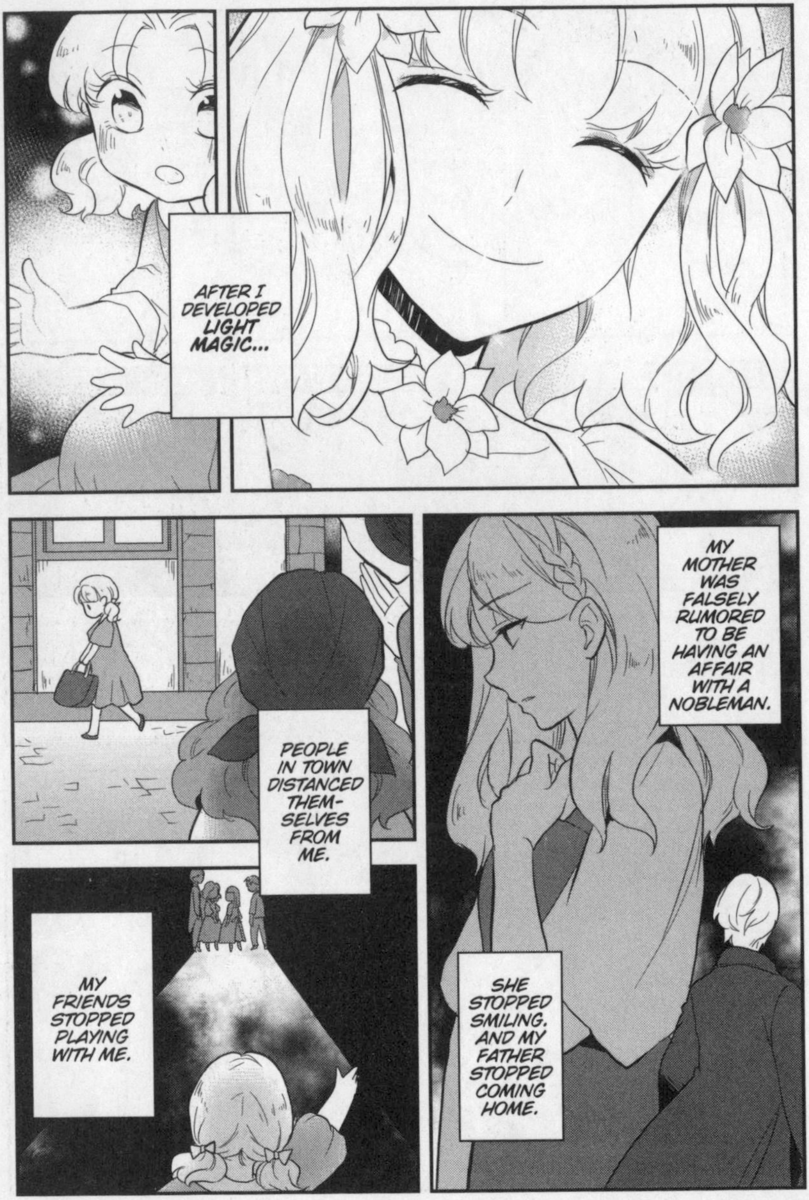
AFTER I DEVELOPED LIGHT MAGIC...
MY MOTHER WAS FALSELY RUMORED TO BE HAVING AN AFFAIR WITH A NOBLEMAN.
SHE STOPPED SMILING, AND MY FATHER STOPPED COMING HOME.
PEOPLE IN TOWN DISTANCED THEM-SELVES FROM ME.
MY FRIENDS STOPPED PLAYING WITH ME.

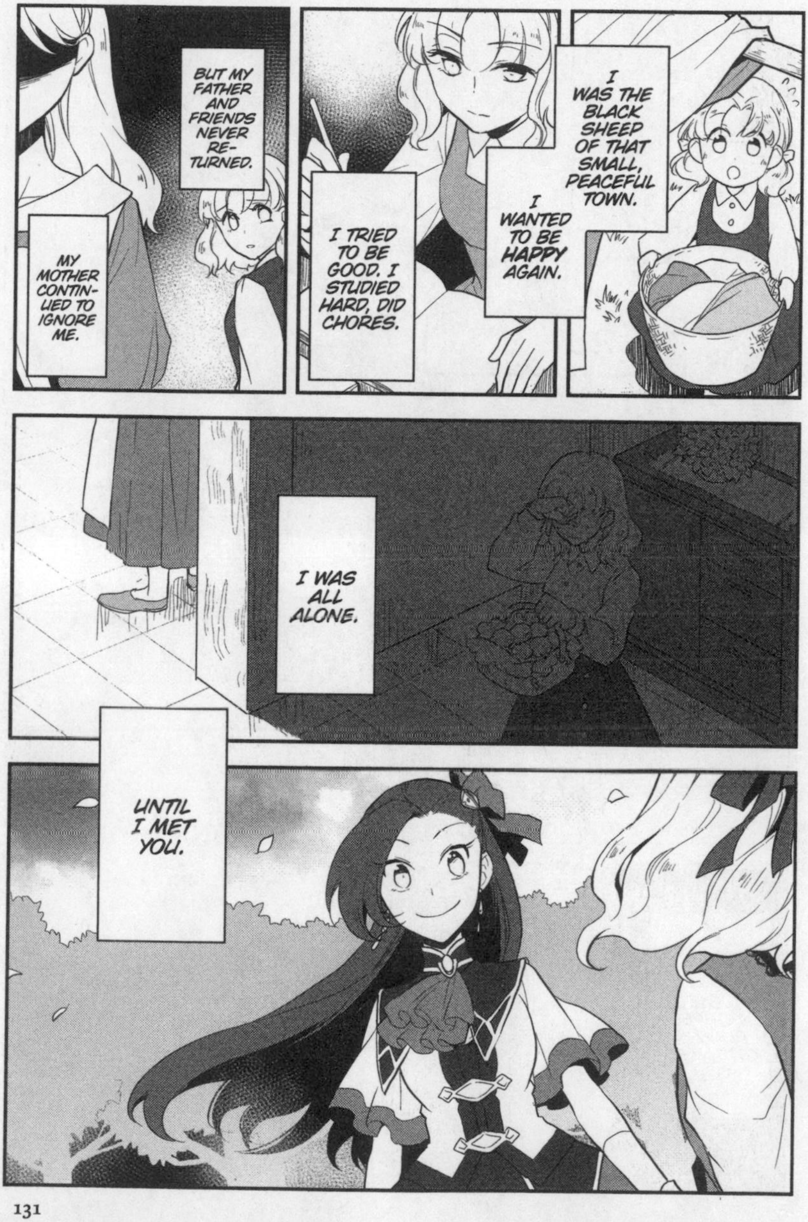
I WAS THE BLACK SHEEP OF THAT SMALL, PEACEFUL TOWN.
I WANTED TO BE HAPPY AGAIN.
I TRIED TO BE GOOD. I STUDIED HARD, DID CHORES.
BUT MY FATHER AND FRIENDS NEVER RE-TURNED.
MY MOTHER CONTIN-UED TO IGNORE ME.
I WAS ALL ALONE.
UNTIL I MET YOU.

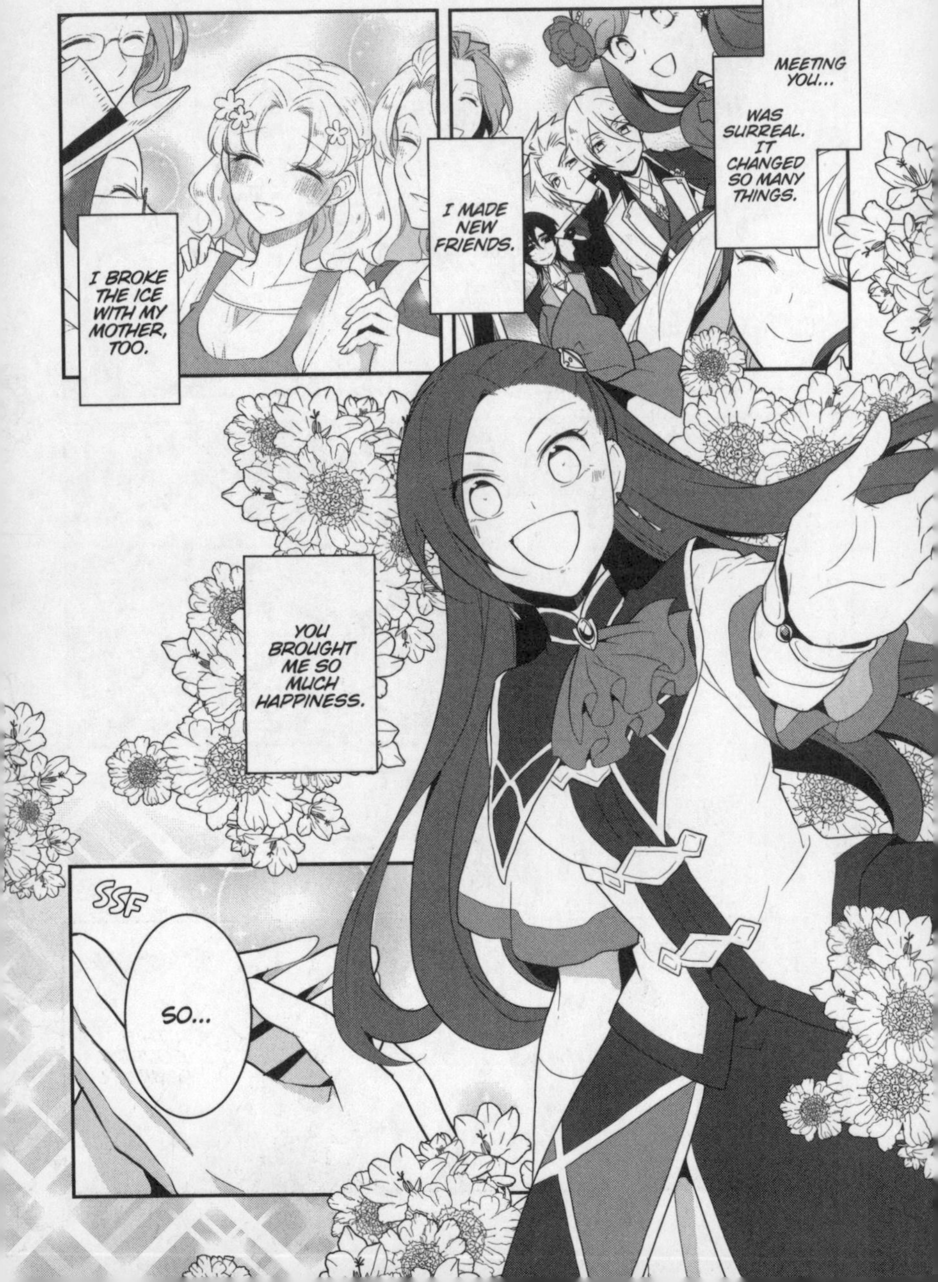
MEETING YOU...
WAS SURREAL. IT CHANGED SO MANY THINGS.
I MADE NEW FRIENDS.
I BROKE THE ICE WITH MY MOTHER, TOO.
YOU BROUGHT ME SO MUCH HAPPINESS.
SSF
SO...

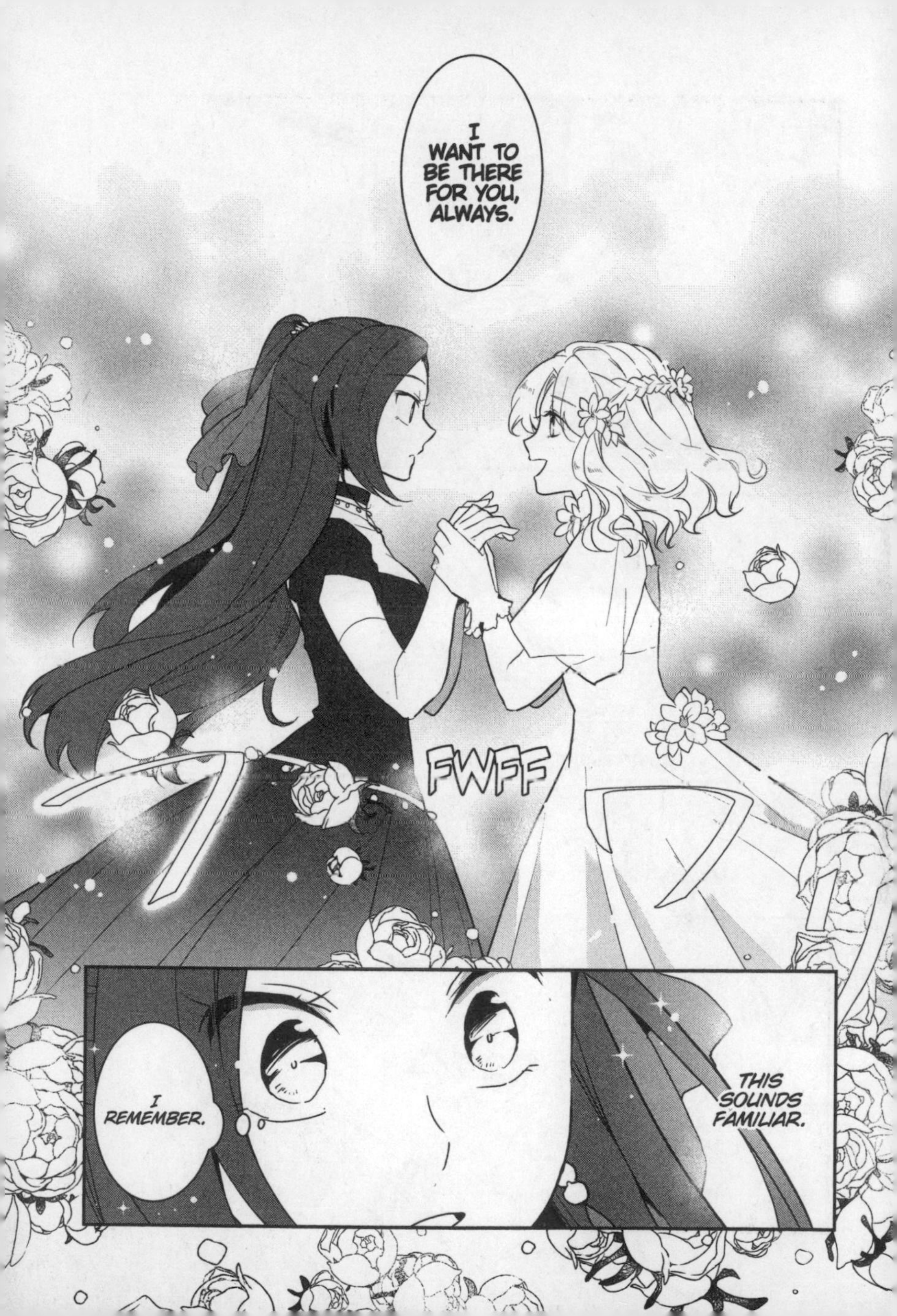
I WANT TO BE THERE FOR YOU, ALWAYS.
FWFF
THIS SOUNDS FAMILIAR.
I REMEMBER.

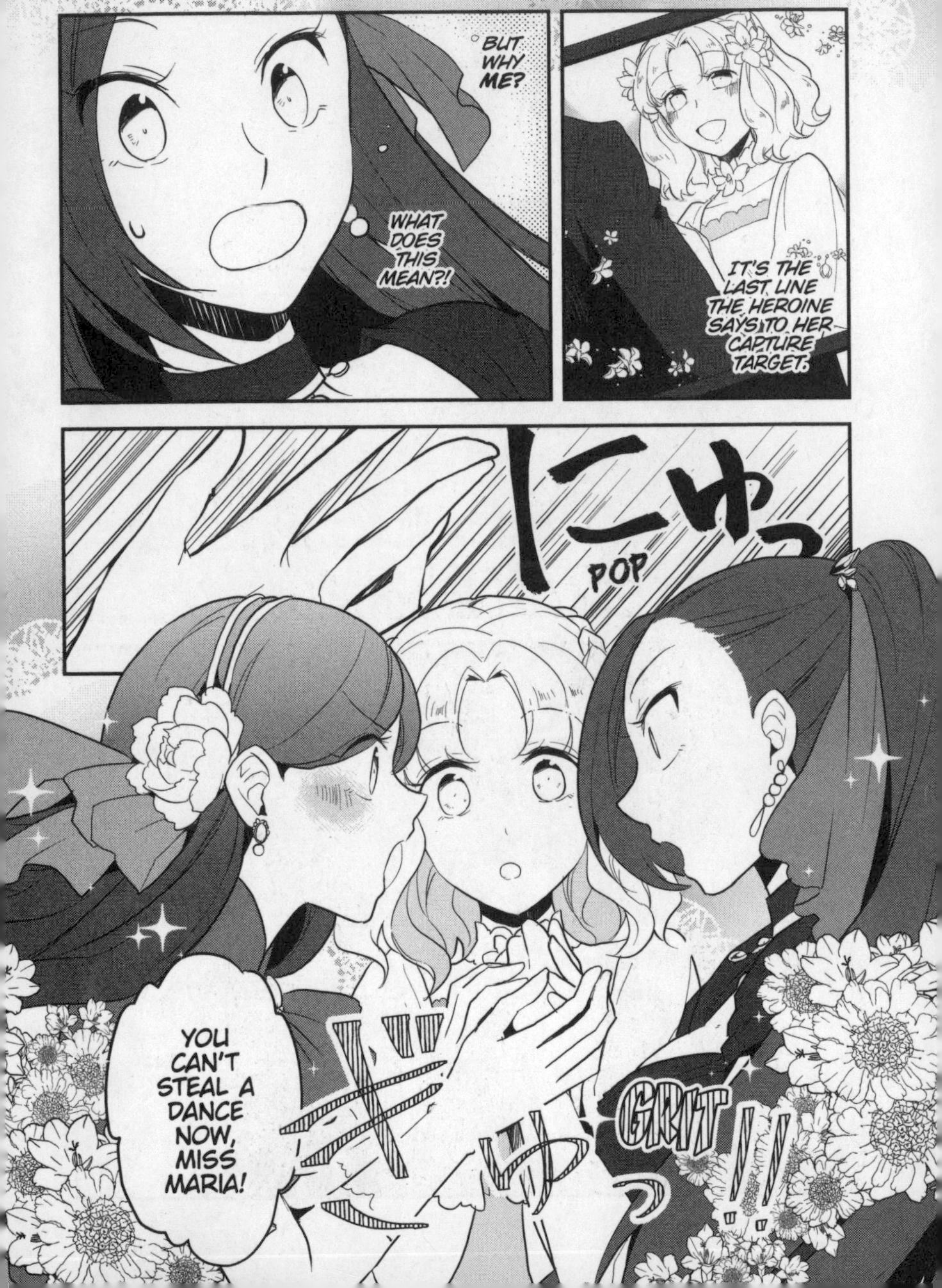
IT'S THE LAST LINE THE HEROINE SAYS TO HER CAPTURE TARGET.
BUT WHY ME?
WHAT DOES THIS MEAN?!
にゅっ
POP
GRIT!!
YOU CAN'T STEAL A DANCE NOW, MISS MARIA!

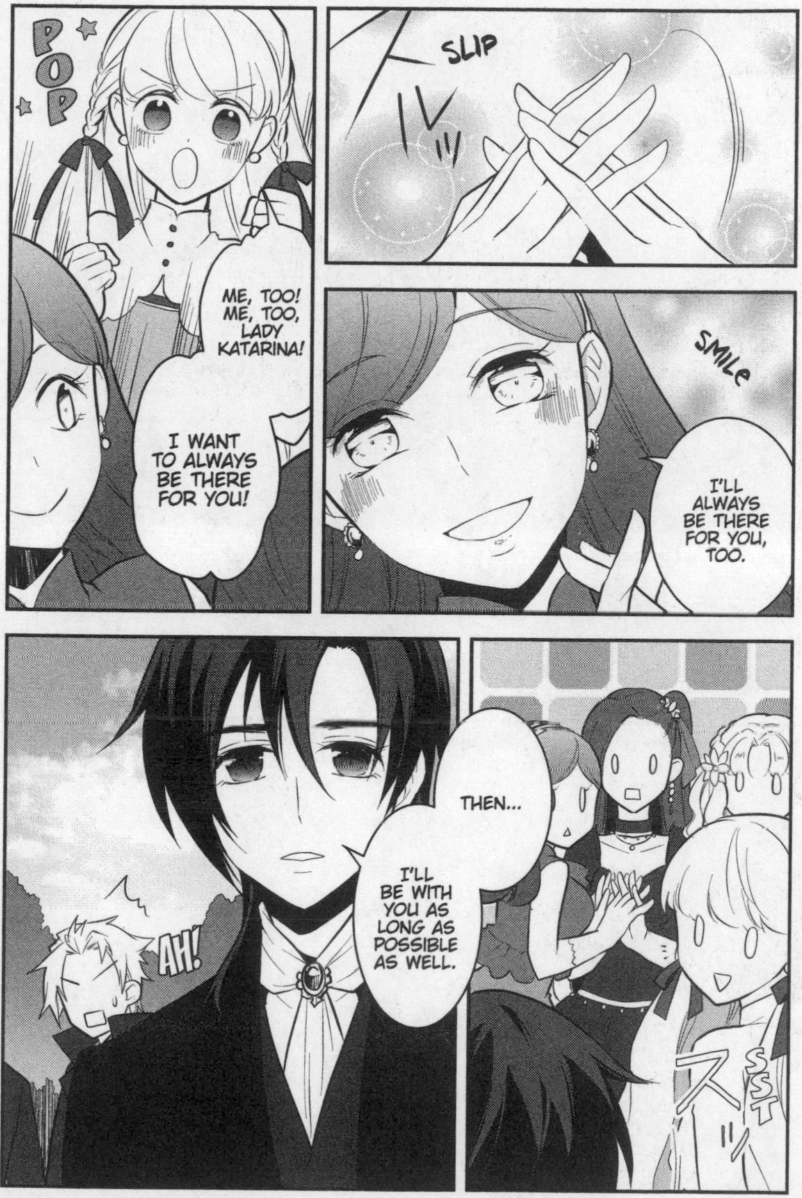
SLIP
SMILE
I'LL ALWAYS BE THERE FOR YOU, TOO.
POP
ME, TOO! ME, TOO, LADY KATARINA!
I WANT TO ALWAYS BE THERE FOR YOU!
SST
THEN...
I'LL BE WITH YOU AS LONG AS POSSIBLE AS WELL.
AH!

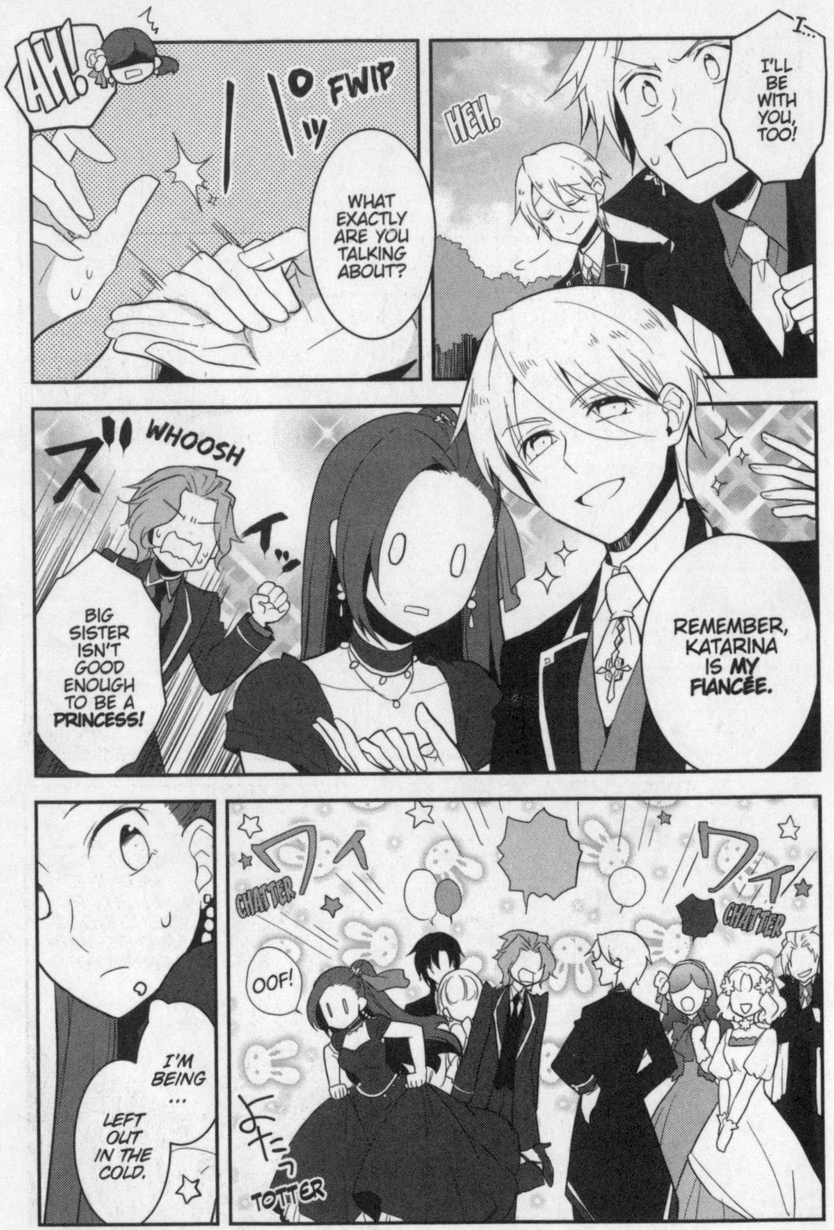
I...
I'LL BE WITH YOU, TOO!
HEH.
AH!
FWIP
WHAT EXACTLY ARE YOU TALKING ABOUT?
REMEMBER, KATARINA IS MY FIANCÉE.
WHOOSH
BIG SISTER ISN'T GOOD ENOUGH TO BE A PRINCESS!
CHATTER
CHATTER
OOF!
TOTTER
I'M BEING ... LEFT OUT IN THE COLD.

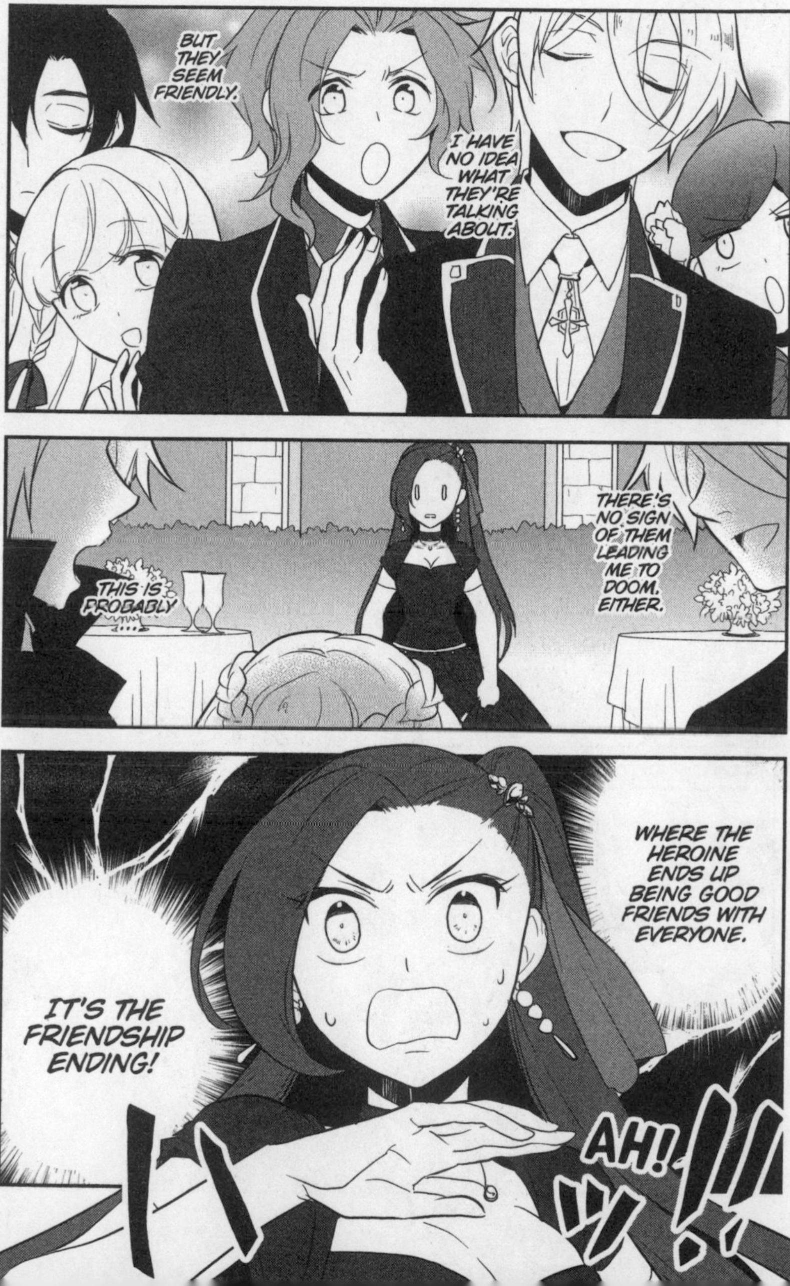
I HAVE NO IDEA WHAT THEY'RE TALKING ABOUT.
BUT THEY SEEM FRIENDLY.
THERE'S NO SIGN OF THEM LEADING ME TO DOOM, EITHER.
THIS IS PROBABLY
...
WHERE THE HEROINE ENDS UP BEING GOOD FRIENDS WITH EVERYONE.
IT'S THE FRIENDSHIP ENDING!
AH!
ッ!!

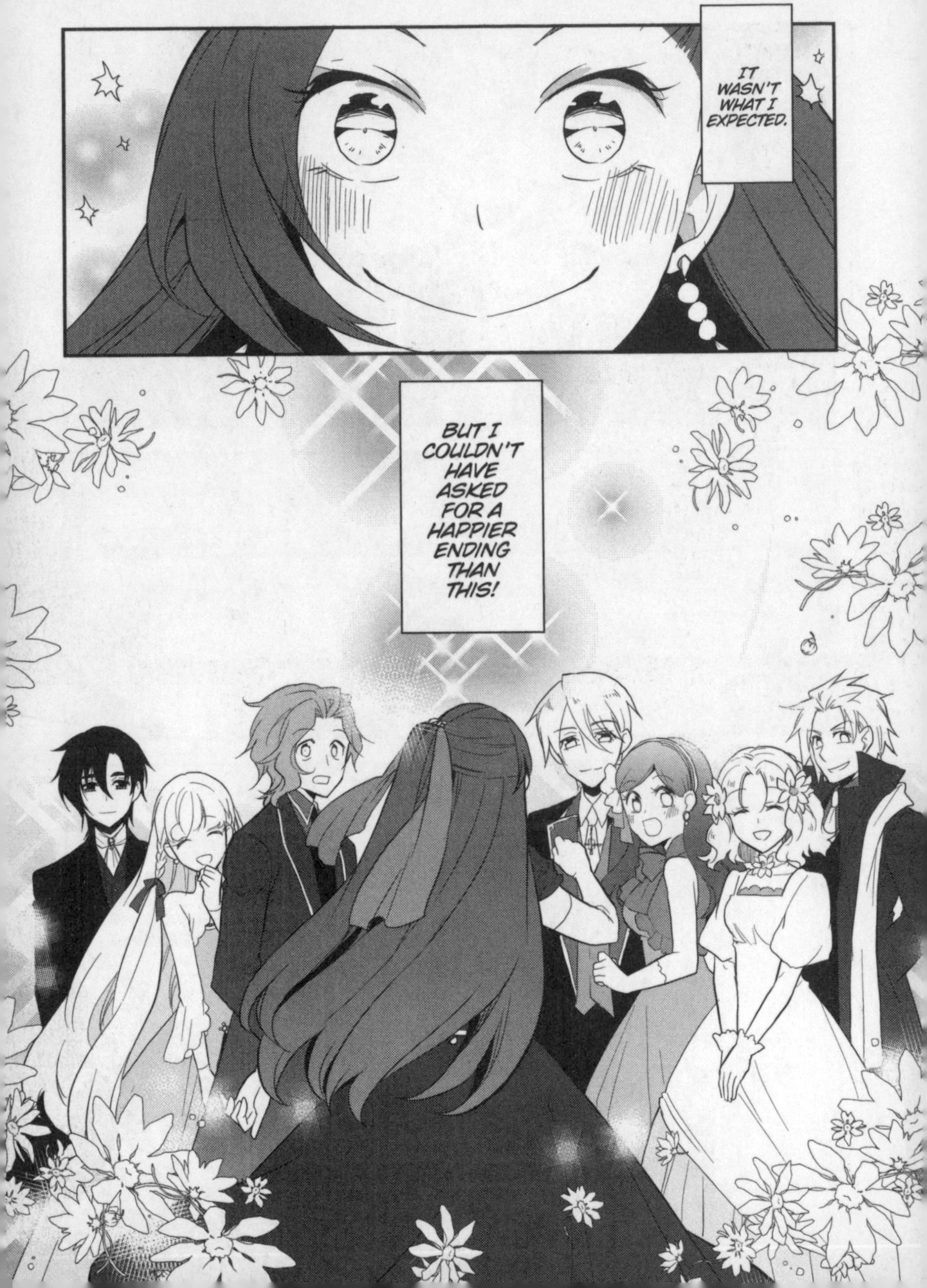
IT WASN'T WHAT I EXPECTED.
BUT I COULDN'T HAVE ASKED FOR A HAPPIER ENDING THAN THIS!

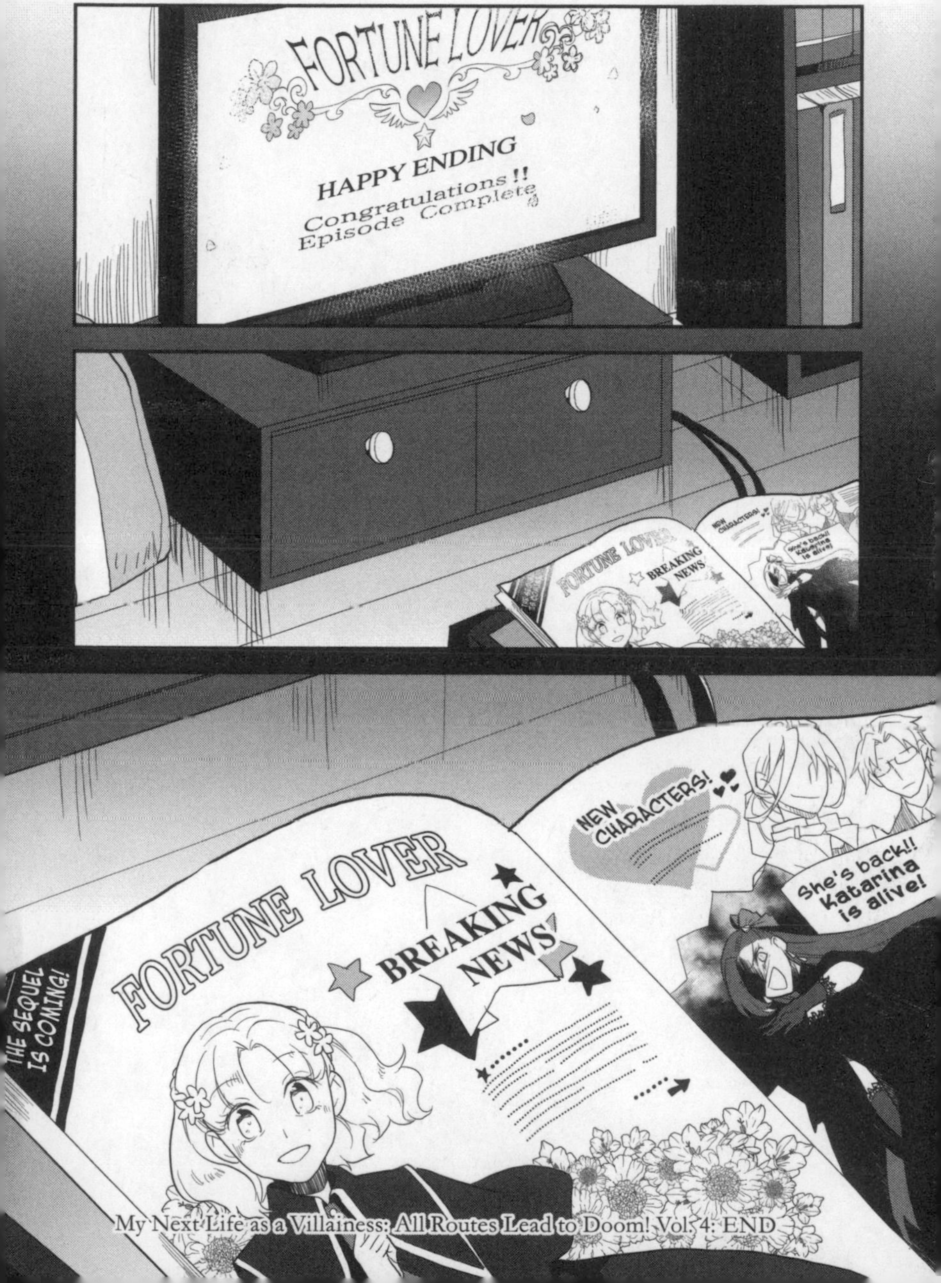
FORTUNE LOVER
HAPPY ENDING
Congratulations!!
Episode Complete
NEW CHARACTERS!
She's back!! Katarina is alive!
FORTUNE LOVER
BREAKING NEWS
NEW CHARACTERS!
She's back!! Katarina is alive!
FORTUNE LOVER
BREAKING NEWS
THE SEQUEL IS COMING!

My Next Life as a Villainess: All Routes Lead to Doom! Vol. 4: END

My Next Life
as a VILLAINESS:
ALL ROUTES
LEAD TO DOOM!

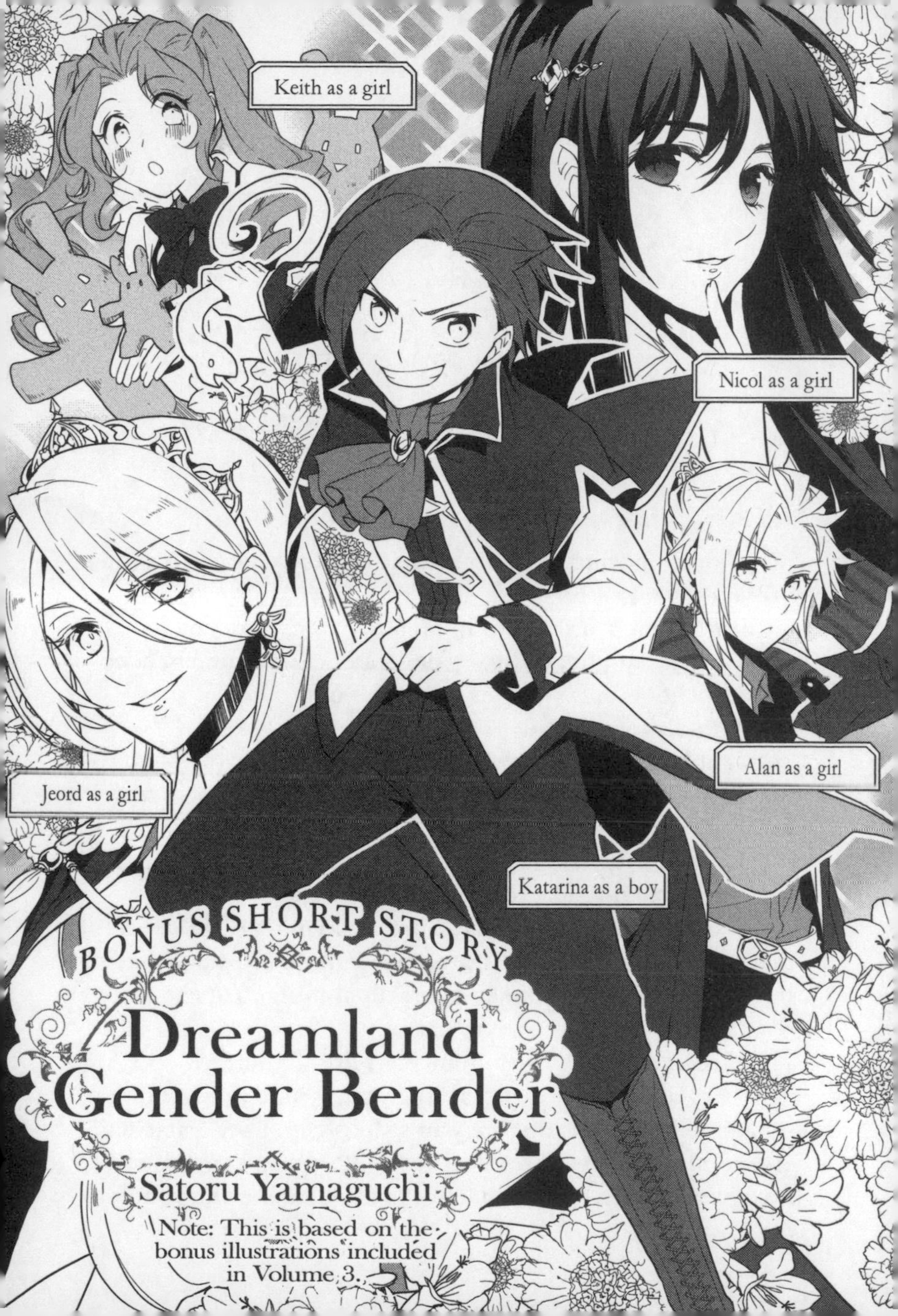
Keith as a girl
Nicol as a girl
Alan as a girl
Jeord as a girl
Katarina as a boy

BONUS SHORT STORY

Dreamland Gender Bender

Satoru Yamaguchi

Note: This is based on the bonus illustrations included in Volume 3.

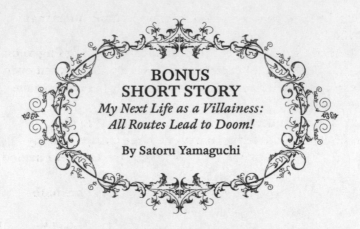

**BONUS
SHORT STORY**
*My Next Life as a Villainess:
All Routes Lead to Doom!*

By Satoru Yamaguchi

"Lord Katarina! Lord Katarina! Please wake up. It's time for you to go to school."

With these words from my maid, Anne, I opened my sleepy eyes. Another ordinary day had begun. Anne handed me my school uniform after I crawled out of bed.

"Thank you," I said.

I rubbed my eyes and looked at Anne.

"What?!" I exclaimed in shock as I stared at the person in front of me.

There was a young man dressed neatly in a suit, with his hair parted to the side, looking like a butler.

"Is something the matter, Lord Katarina?" I had never met this young man, who stared back at me as I stood frozen in place. However, he looked awfully familiar. He had to be...

"Are you Anne by any chance?" I asked timidly.

"You don't need to guess," the young man in front of me responded. "It's me. But are you still asleep, Lord Katarina?" He worriedly lowered his eyebrows. It was an expression I recognized. He might have had the appearance of a young man, but this person in front of me was none other than Anne.

"Now, you must get dressed quickly. You're going to be late." Anne went to place his hands on my clothes, but even a careless girl like me felt awkward having a man help me get dressed.

"U-um, Anne. I know you're Anne, but I'm not comfortable with letting a man help me change into my clothes." When I stated this, Anne gave me another puzzled look.

"What do you mean by 'a man'? You and I are both men."

"That's right. We're both... We are?!" Dismayed by Anne's remark, I looked down at my body. My chest—which was normally moderately sized, though not as large as my friend Mary's—was flat. In fact, I reached down farther and found...something that shouldn't have been there!

"You gotta be kidding meee!" It was such a shock that I screamed.

"Lord Katarina, you need to wake up and get ready. You're really going to be late!" said Anne.

He quickly prepared me for school. Before I knew it, I was all set to go.

I checked my outfit. It didn't look out of the ordinary, but I was wearing pants instead of a skirt.

This seems comfortable to move around in... No, that's not important! What in the world is going on? How did Anne and I become men?

As the confusion set in, someone spoke to me from behind.

"Good morning, Big Brother."

"Huh?" When I turned to look, there was a lovely girl with pigtails smiling at me. Who was she?

"Good morning, Lady Keith." Anne bowed for the girl.

143

"K-Keith!" I shouted.

"Yes?" the girl replied, tilting her head.

She's way too cute.

It seemed the girl in front of me was Keith. If I looked closely, the color of her hair and eyes and even her facial features kind of reminded me of him.

I was starting to get the hang of this world. It seemed everyone's gender had been swapped.

"Let's go, Big Brother! We're going to be late!"

And so we headed to school, with Keith urging me along.

When we arrived at the entrance to the school, a stunningly beautiful blue-eyed girl with blonde hair greeted me. "Good morning, Katarina."

Behind her stood a snobby-looking girl with silver hair in a ponytail. The schoolboys around them were blushing at the sight of them. I put two and two together and figured out who they were.

"Good morning, Lady Jeord, Lady Alan," I responded. My guess was right. The blonde-haired Jeord smiled at me sweetly. Ponytailed Alan looked away as she pursed her lips. It appeared she was something of a stuck-up girl.

Now that I understand how things were, I wasn't as shocked at my new body. I'd regained some composure. I noticed that a lot of things were off, such as having the same names even though we'd swapped genders. This was most likely a dream. As such, I wasn't as bothered by the new appendage on my lower half. I was sure it'd be gone by the time I woke up.

"Good morning, Lord Katarina." The next person to speak to me was a handsome young man with auburn hair and auburn eyes.

I know who this is, too.

"Good morning, Mary," I said.

Mary, the young man, beamed at me. This time, the girls around us squealed and flushed. Oh, yes. My friends were as popular as ever, regardless of gender. Awestruck, I heard sighing from the boys behind me. I turned to find a bewitchingly beautiful girl with black hair and black eyes walking toward me. Her sensuality made the male and female students alike flush.

There was no doubt as to who this alluring girl was.

"Good morning, Lady Nicol." I greeted the girl as she approached.

She responded in a throaty voice. "Good morning."

Her shy smile made the students around us blush. I felt my face flush, too. Earl Nicol the Heartbreaker wasn't that different as a girl. If anything, she'd become even more enticing.

"Good morning, Lord Katarina," said a quiet, handsome boy with snowy white hair and ruby eyes. He appeared from behind Nicol.

"Good morning, Sophia," I replied.

Sophia smiled gently. While Mary had become a gorgeous, capable young man, Sophia was the kind of attractive boy whose appearance just screams at you to protect them. Their new genders had revealed new sides to their personalities.

Just then, I noticed my reflection in a window. I didn't see anything different other than my taller height and shorter hair. I had the same stern, villainous face as before. Honestly, I didn't look that great compared to everyone else. If I was going to swap genders, I would've liked to become a strikingly handsome man.

"We should head to our classrooms," said Jeord, grabbing my arm to wrap it around hers. Her voluptuous chest pressed hard against me.

Wow, Jeord's boobs are huge. They're definitely bigger than mine when I'm a girl. Are they even bigger than Mary's?

Wait a minute. It wasn't a good idea for a boy and a girl to be in this kind of situation. I should probably have chided Jeord for it. But I'd never done anything like that before. As I was trying to figure out what to do, someone pulled my other arm.

"Lady Jeord, it's not appropriate to cling to him like that in public." Keith puffed her cheeks out in an angry manner as she pried me away from Jeord.

This Keith was too adorable. Her shorter height forced her to look up at me, and her pigtails framed a pretty face.

"Keith, you're so cute." I just had to embrace her.

She turned beet red. "B-Big Brother!"

I released her. "I'm sorry! I couldn't resist...because you were so cute."

This only made Keith's face flush more. "Oh, no. I'm not that cute. But I don't mind you hugging me at all." She said this with her usual charming demeanor.

"You're so sweet." This time, I resisted the urge to hug her, instead reaching out to pat her head.

Jeord grabbed my hand. "Just because Keith is your stepsister doesn't mean you have to give her all your attention. *I'm* your fiancée! *I* want your affection! Don't you think I'm more attractive than her?" She pulled my hand to rest against her voluptuous bosom.

Hmm. It seemed as if Jeord and I were still engaged to each other. And Jeord was probably a princess in this world. Was I going to marry into Jeord's family? Or was Jeord going to marry into mine?

"Excuse me, Lady Jeord. You shouldn't be doing that in public! And are you talking about your chest size when you say that you're more attractive than *me*?"

"You and Katarina were holding each other. You call *my* behavior inappropriate? That's a joke."

"W-we weren't holding each other."

"Ha ha ha! A girl's allure isn't all about her chest size. It's about having a nice body, *Little Keith*."

"L-Little? People say large chests aren't everything. Isn't that right, Lady Alan?"

"Eh? Leave me out of this. I don't exactly have a large chest, either."

While I was busy thinking about my engagement to Jeord, our conversation had taken a strange turn. How was I supposed to approach this subject as a boy?

"Jeord, Keith, Alan, that's enough. Look around you. You're bothering everyone with your weird debate about chest sizes." Nicol, the bewitchingly beautiful girl, interrupted our conversation. She'd maintained her maturity, despite the gender swap. However, her loud tone announcing the subject of our discussion made everyone even more uncomfortable. "It's almost time for class. We should be heading to our rooms." She walked away.

I headed to my own classroom with pouty Keith, grumpy Jeord, and Alan, who was displeased at being scolded for no particular reason.

"Good morning!" A boy greeted us—a handsome, blonde-haired, blue-eyed boy with a tidy appearance, whose gentle expression held a clear resemblance to a girl I knew.

"Good morning, Maria!" I greeted him, and Maria smiled. I wanted to chat more with him and the others, but we barely made it to our class in time.

As I half-listened to the lecture, I began to think about this gender-swapped world. This was most likely a dream, but what would happen if it continued? Jeord would have to decide whether I married into her family or she married into mine. I was probably a rival to the heroine—er, hero—in this world, too. But could this still be considered an otome game? All of the capture targets were girls, and the rival and the heroine were both boys, which would make this a bishoujo game.

I had never played a bishoujo game in my previous life, but it made sense to have characters like these—a stepsister with pigtails, a gorgeous girl with a nice body, a stuck-up beauty, and an alluring temptress—as capture targets. But when it came to competing for their affections, I didn't feel like I stood a chance against Maria. Either way, I was probably doomed if everything remained the same as the otome game. If the only difference was our genders, then the bishoujo setting wouldn't affect my fate.

Wait a minute. Boys were usually stronger than girls. That might help me become a farmer if I were defeated and exiled. Working on my muscles might even allow me to become a bodyguard. Awesome! This would broaden my horizons as well. Now that I thought about it, that was even cooler than being the daughter of a duke.

"Katarina, class is over."

"What?!"

Jeord's words made me look around. It seemed that time had flown while I was lost in thought.

"We should head to our next class. Let's go together." Jeord placed her hand on my arm, implying that I should escort her. This was new to me, since I was always the one being escorted. Being a boy was a constant barrage of new experiences. As I tried to properly escort Jeord while thinking about this...

"Big Brother," said Keith, "you're not at a social function. It isn't necessary to escort Lady Jeord."

She was right. Come to think of it, I'd never asked anyone to escort me.

"You're wrong, Keith," said Jeord. "Katarina is my fiancé. I have a right to be escorted by him at any time. See, Alan? Why don't you ask Mary to escort you, too?"

"May I escort you?" Mary flashed a handsome smile, but Alan turned away, ponytail swaying.

"I'm good," she replied flatly. However, her face looked a little red.

Could this be what people called "running hot and cold"? I didn't know why, but it made my heart flutter.

"Um, excuse me. The student council president wants to see Lady Jeord," our classmate announced. I followed his line of sight and saw a pretty girl with soft red hair standing at the classroom door.

As expected, the student council president had also swapped genders. She was tiny and cute. Jeord walked gracefully over to her, and they exchanged some words. Because of her height, Jeord made the president look markedly smaller.

"President, you're so pretty," I said. "You remind me of a fairy with your hair."

Keith's eyes widened. "D-do you like girls like President, Big Brother?!"

"Oh, no. I just thought she was tiny and cute..."

"You prefer petite girls?" Keith was relentless.

"I-Is that true?" Alan took a strong interest in this, too.

"Eh?" I panicked.

"I heard most boys prefer large breasts." Jeord had reappeared out of nowhere.

What on earth is going on here? How do I respond to this?

In that moment, I didn't know the proper response for a boy in my position. I looked to Mary, as if to plead for his help, but he threw up his hands. Then I glanced at Maria, but he shook his head, his face bright red. I shifted my focus to Sophia, but he hid behind a book. Now that the other boys had abandoned me, the girls relentlessly sought my response.

"Tell me, Big Brother. Do you prefer large breasts?"

"Is that true?"

"It's true. You like large breasts, don't you?"

Under assault by Keith, Alan, *and* Jeord, I took a step backward.

I'd never given this much thought to being a girl. Do boys generally prefer large breasts? *No, I've heard that they like small breasts, too.* My mind went in circles, and I didn't know what to say. Did chest size really matter?

"Everyone has a preference for chest size! I don't mind one way or the other!"

I shouted and jumped out of bed to find myself in my usual room. I'd woken up. Anne was next to me, looking perplexed. She was once again a woman dressed in a maid uniform.

"L-Lady Katarina, what in the world were you talking about?"

I laughed off Anne's question and took a peek at my body. My breasts weren't that big, but they were there. And I was relieved to find that that the thing on my lower half was gone. I'd had some fun in my dream, but being a boy was too much of a pain.

"Anne, can you help me get dressed?"

She continued to give me baffled looks as I changed into my usual dress. It wasn't as comfortable to wear as a pair of pants, but I could still climb trees without a problem. I was no longer a boy, but that shouldn't stop me from becoming an expert at farming. And with that, I began preparing myself for another ordinary day in real—otome—life.

AFTERWORD

Nami Hidaka here!
I hope all is well. Thank you for
being there for me! I live each
day with your support.

We're already at Volume 4!
Katarina finally reaches the final
event of the otome game.
What kind of ending is waiting for her?
And what will happen after that?

The game will end when Katarina clears
the final level, but her world won't be
ending any time soon. I have many plans
in the works for this series. I hope you'll
look forward to them.

I can't wait to see
you all next time!

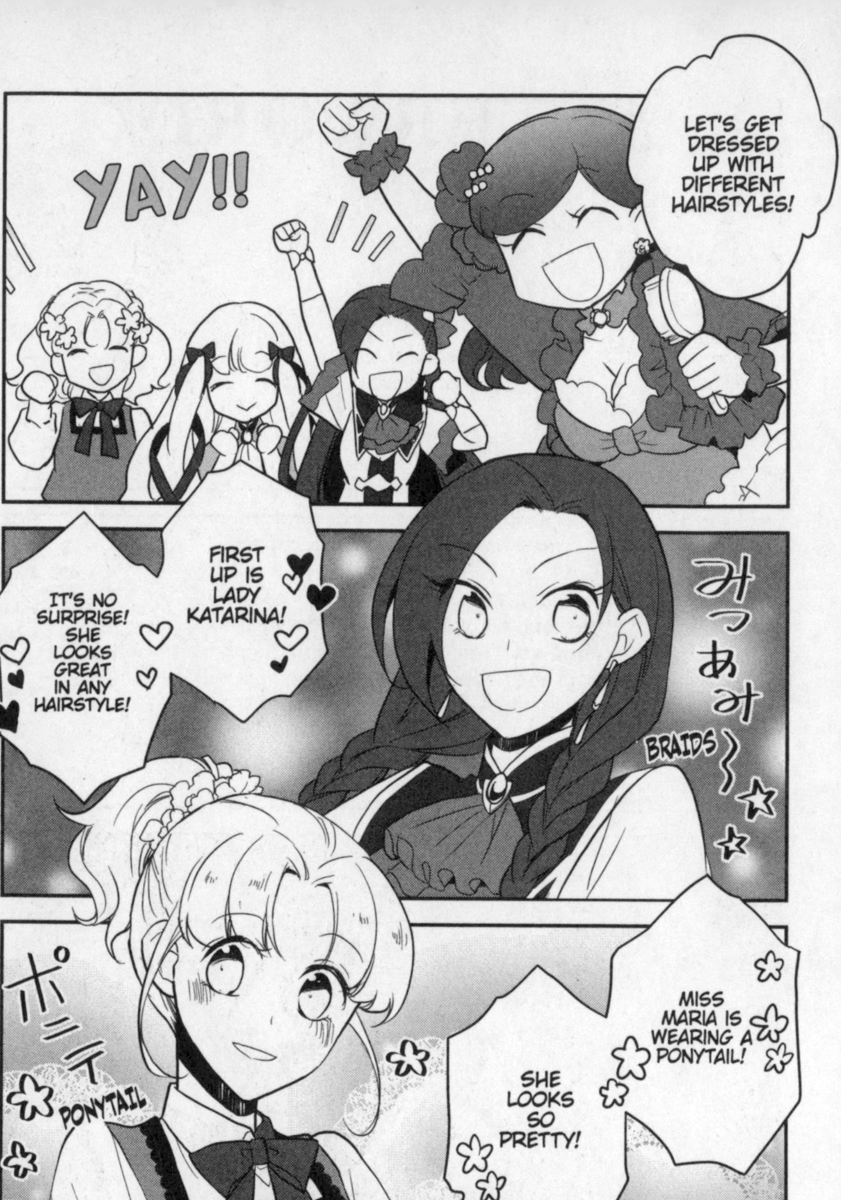
LET'S GET DRESSED UP WITH DIFFERENT HAIRSTYLES!
YAY!!
みつあみ
BRAIDS~☆
FIRST UP IS LADY KATARINA!
IT'S NO SURPRISE! SHE LOOKS GREAT IN ANY HAIRSTYLE!
MISS MARIA IS WEARING A PONYTAIL!
SHE LOOKS SO PRETTY!
ポニテ
PONYTAIL

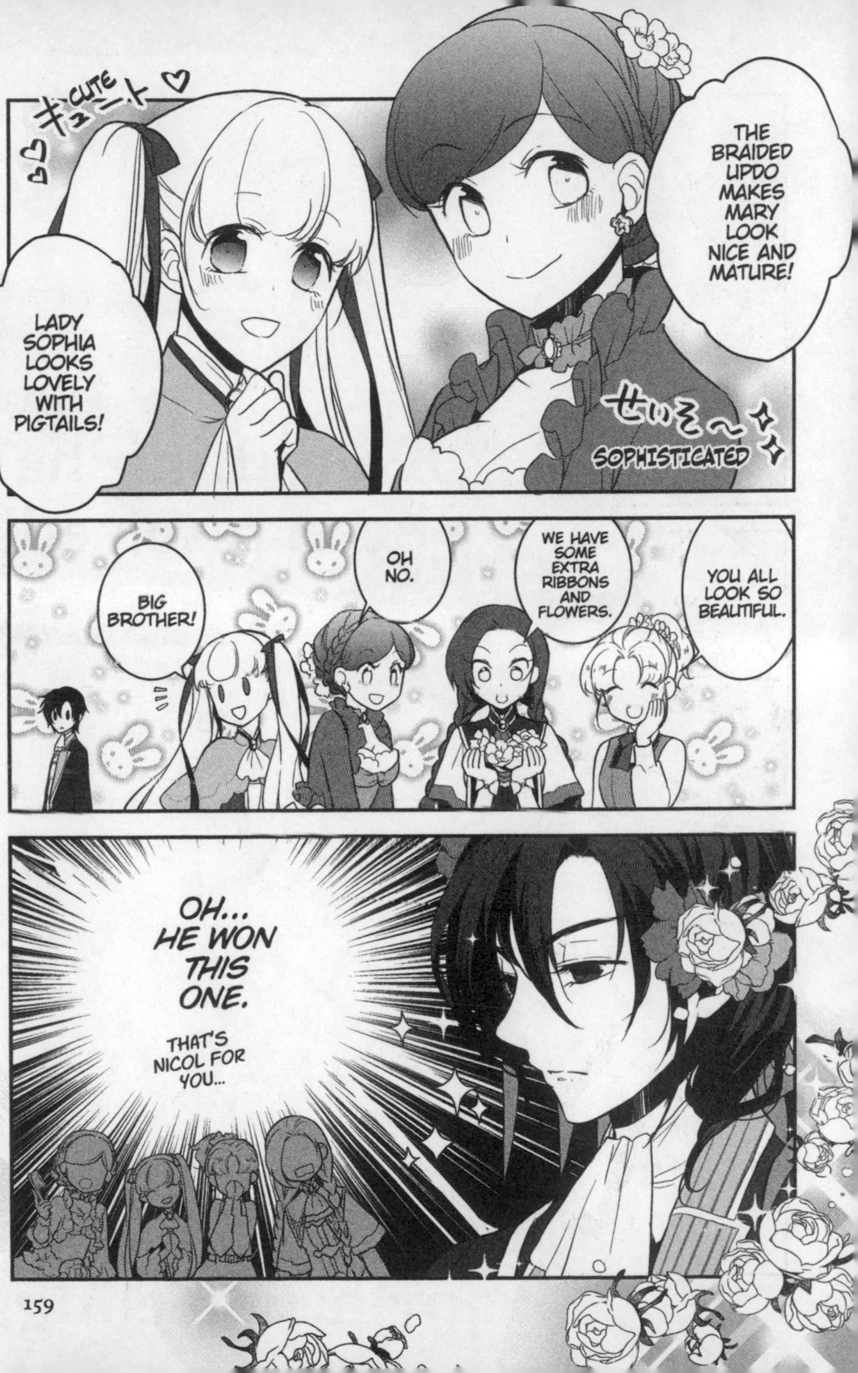
THE BRAIDED UPDO MAKES MARY LOOK NICE AND MATURE!
せいそ～
SOPHISTICATED
CUTE
LADY SOPHIA LOOKS LOVELY WITH PIGTAILS!
YOU ALL LOOK SO BEAUTIFUL.
WE HAVE SOME EXTRA RIBBONS AND FLOWERS.
OH NO.
BIG BROTHER!
OH... HE WON THIS ONE.
THAT'S NICOL FOR YOU...

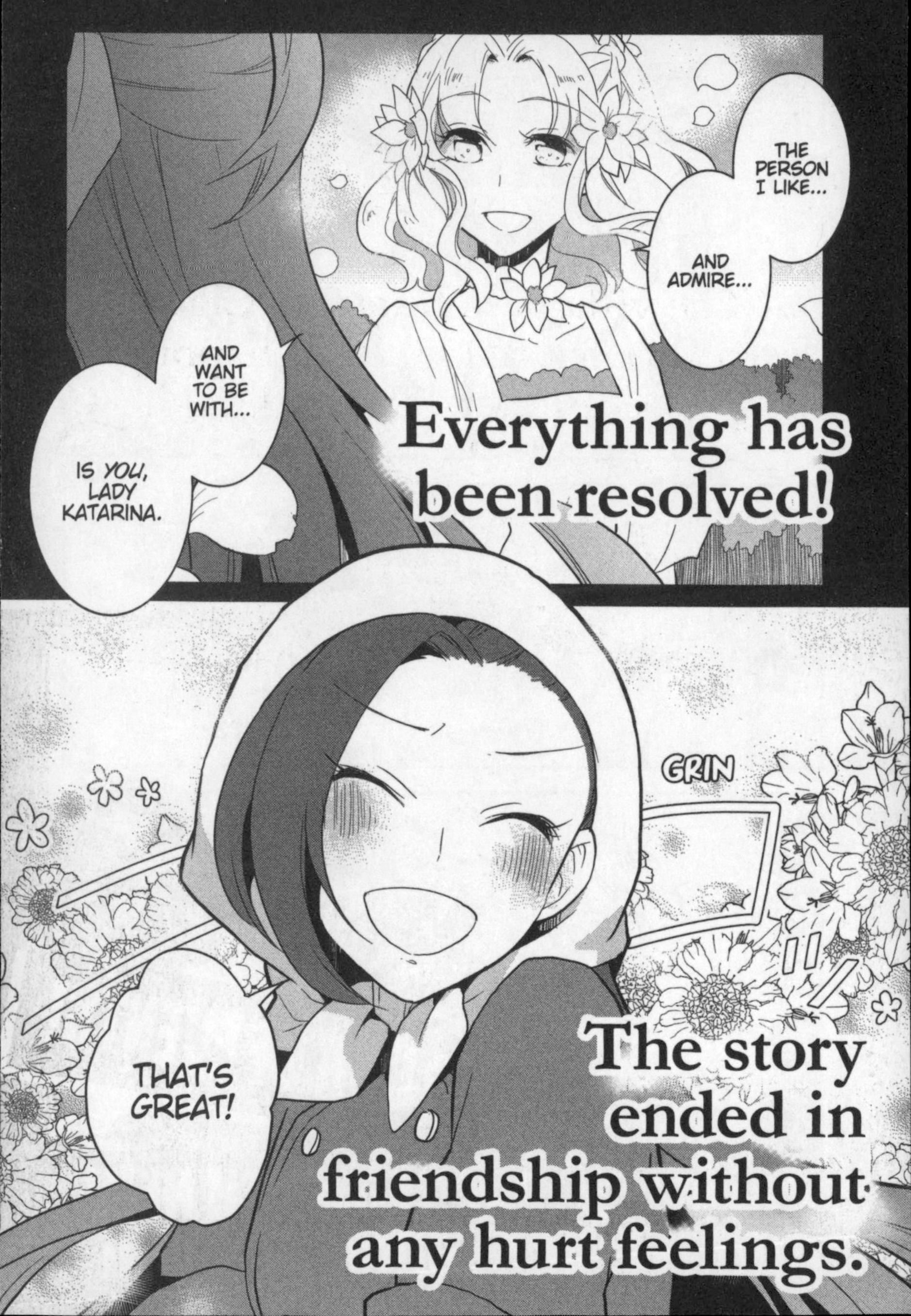
THE PERSON I LIKE...
AND ADMIRE...
AND WANT TO BE WITH...
IS *YOU*, LADY KATARINA.
Everything has been resolved!
GRIN
THAT'S GREAT!
The story ended in friendship without any hurt feelings.

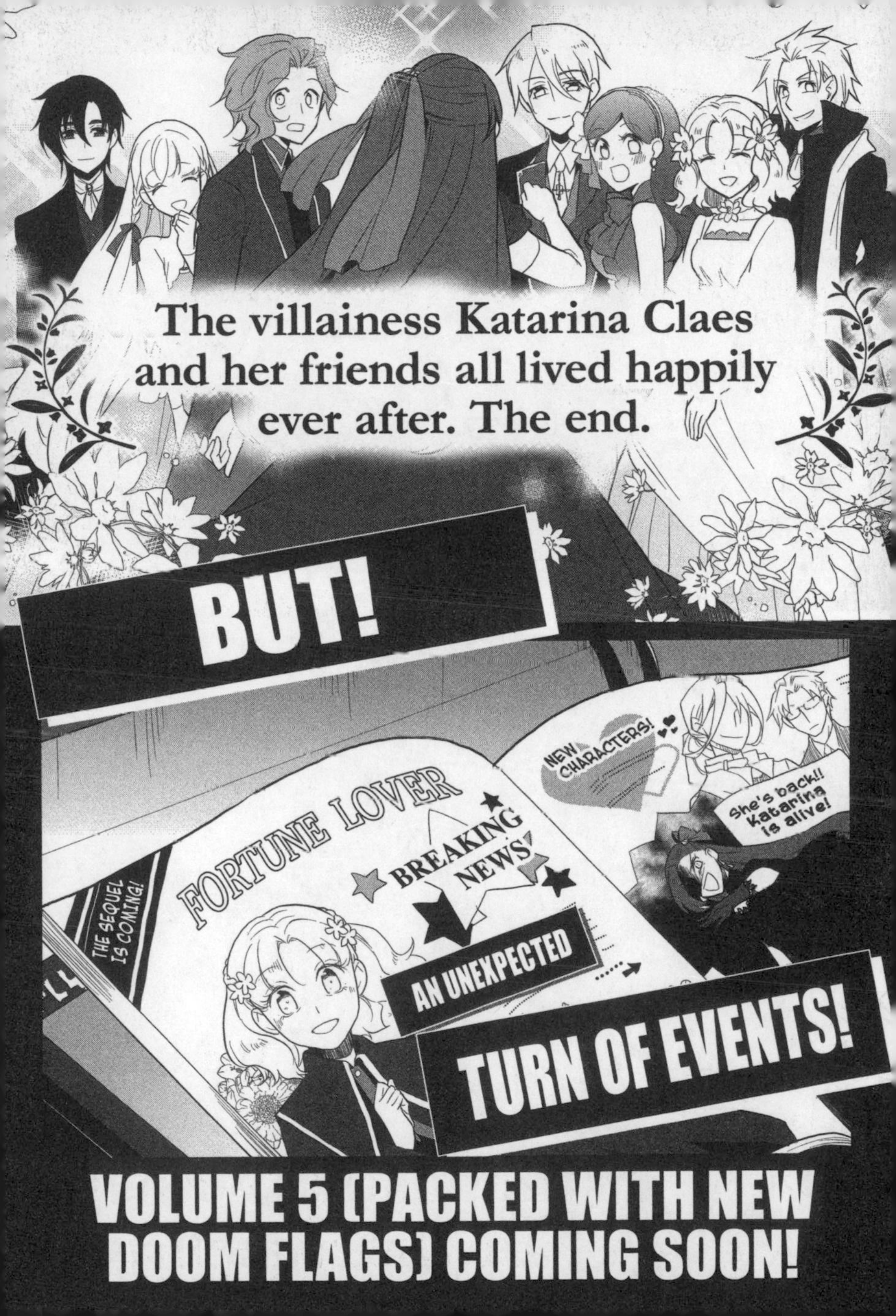
The villainess Katarina Claes and her friends all lived happily ever after. The end.
BUT!
NEW CHARACTERS!
She's back!! Katarina is alive!
FORTUNE LOVER
BREAKING NEWS
THE SEQUEL IS COMING!
AN UNEXPECTED
TURN OF EVENTS!
VOLUME 5 (PACKED WITH NEW DOOM FLAGS) COMING SOON!

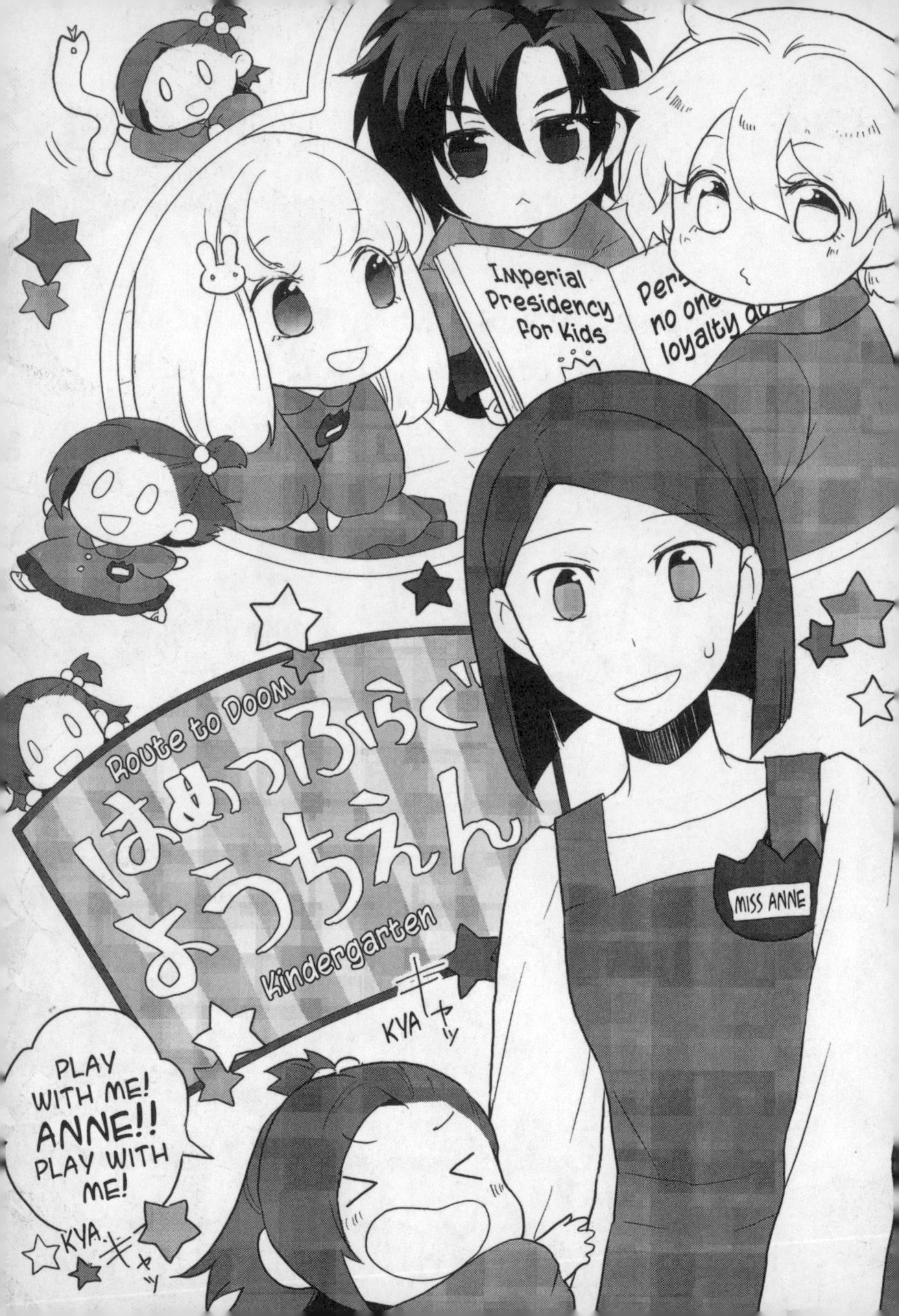
Imperial Presidency for Kids
no one
Route to DOOM
はめつふらぐ
ようちえん
Kindergarten
KYA キャッ
MISS ANNE
PLAY WITH ME! ANNE!! PLAY WITH ME!
KYA. キャッ

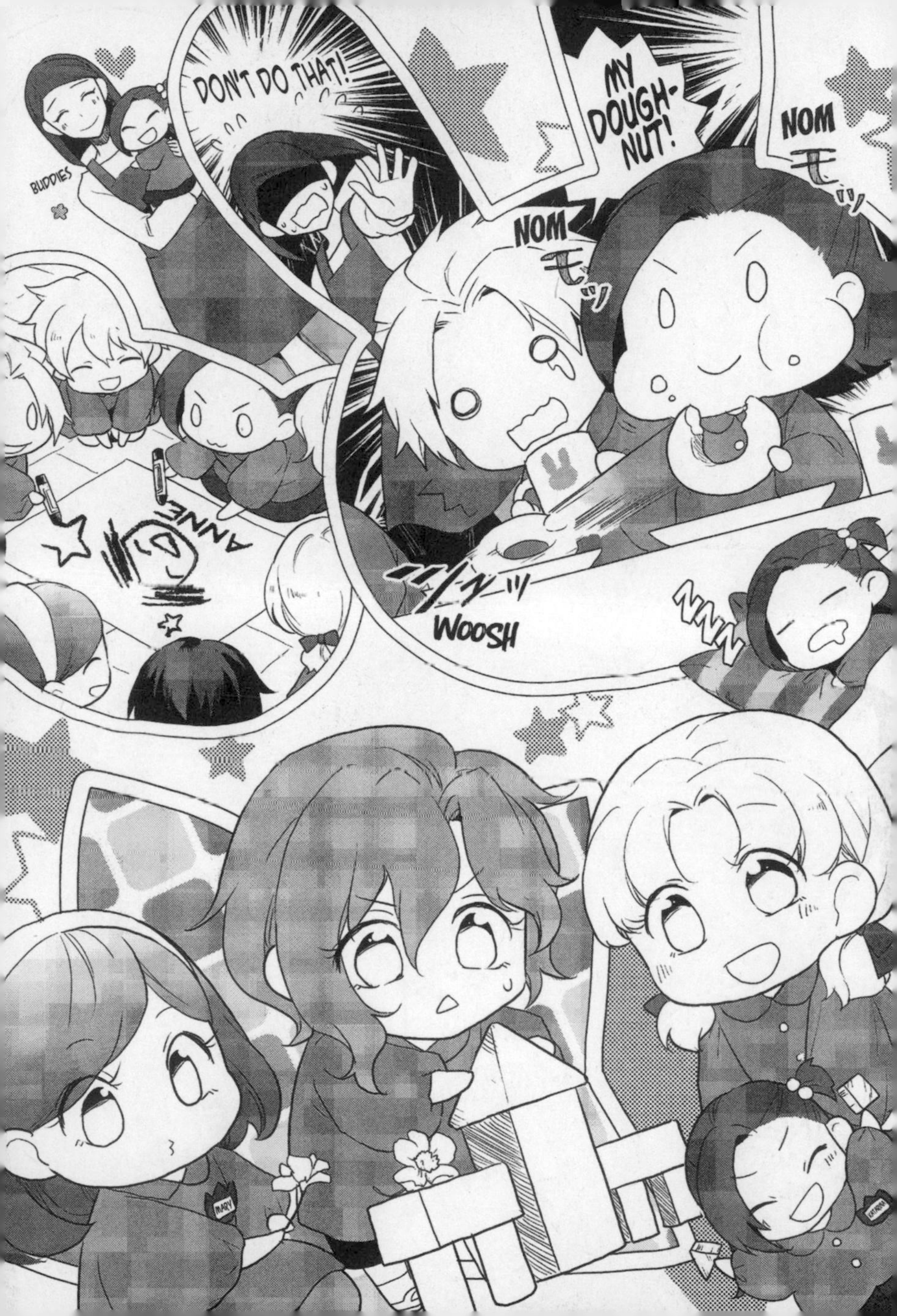
NOM
NOM
MY DOUGH-NUT!
DON'T DO THAT!
BUDDIES
WOOSH
NNN
ANNE

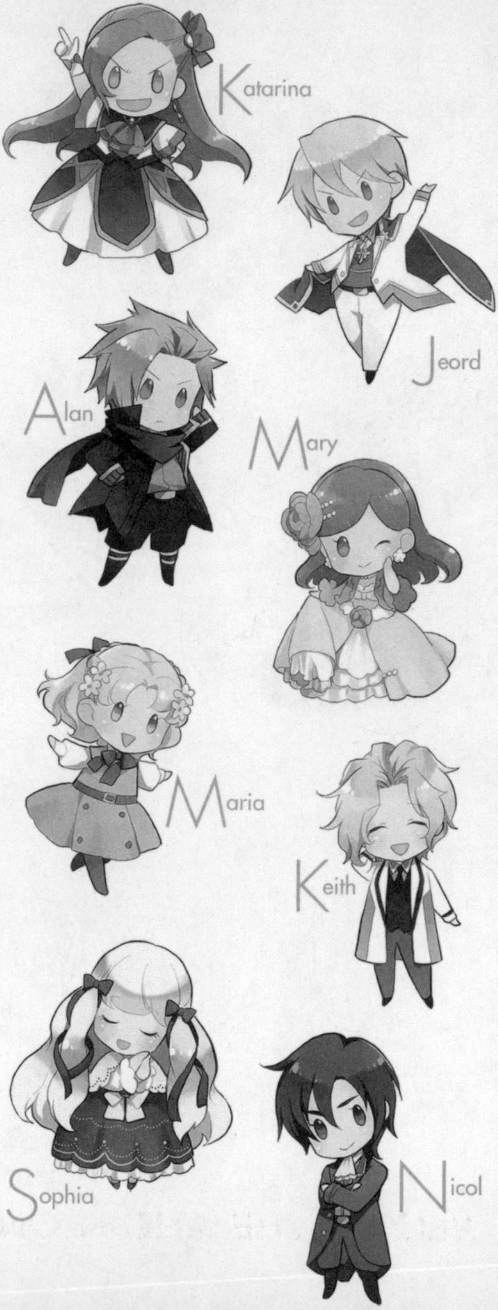
Katarina
Jeord
Alan
Mary
Maria
Keith
Sophia
Nicol

MY NEXT LIFE AS A VILLAINESS
All Routes Lead to Doom!

My Next Life as a VILLAINESS: ALL ROUTES LEAD TO DOOM!